BY IRVING WALLACE

Fiction

The Plot
The Man
The Three Sirens
The Prize
The Chapman Report
The Sins of Philip Fleming

Nonfiction

The Writing of One Novel
The Sunday Gentleman
The Twenty-Seventh Wife
The Fabulous Showman
The Square Pegs
The Fabulous Originals

THE
WRITING OF
ONE NOVEL

by

Irving Wallace

SIMON AND SCHUSTER · NEW YORK

For

ELIZEBETHE KEMPTHORNE

Contents

Among the many characters Balzac invented for his *Comédie humaine,* there was one named Horace Bianchon, a physician of wondrous skills. When Balzac lay dying, it is said that he cried out, "Send for Bianchon! Only Bianchon will save me!"

PART
I

CONCEPTION

It is not always possible to travel backward through the blur of years and remember the exact moment when a work of fiction was conceived. But in the case of my novel *The Prize,* I can even now, although nearly twenty-two years have passed, remember vividly the moment, or several separate moments, of the book's beginning.

It began in 1946.

I had recently been discharged from the United States Army Signal Corps, demoted from sergeant to free-lance writer, and my wife Sylvia had resigned from her editorial job on a national magazine and was reduced once more from editor to helpmate. Together, we had taken a Swedish liner from New York to Göteborg, and then a train to Stockholm, to begin the research for the first of a series of articles I was to do for *Reader's Digest, The Saturday Evening Post,* and *Collier's* magazine. We had a regal corner suite in the Grand Hotel of Stockholm, utterly beyond our means, but worth it for the view from the sitting room overlooking the Strömmen canal and the Royal Palace.

It was the month of September in 1946, and I was constantly out in the chilly, wet northern city, trying to fulfill speculative magazine assignments and possibly find ideas for further assignments. I went everywhere in Stockholm, doing interviews and gathering information on stories that I had planned, yet always questioning, listening, observing, in quest of subjects for additional stories I might write.

One name kept recurring in my numerous conversations. That was the name of Dr. Sven Hedin, who was listed in a government publication as one of Sweden's twenty great scientists of the preceding three hundred years. Dr. Sven Hedin had, in fact, explored Inner Mongolia and Tibet, and had gained an international reputation as hydrographer, cartographer, and author of widely read travel books like *A Conquest of Tibet* and *Across the Gobi Desert*. But the reason Dr. Hedin's name kept coming up was largely a political one. The Second World War had just ended. During that war, Dr. Hedin had been an aggressively unneutral Swede and had given his passionate support to an unpopular cause. Dr. Hedin had backed Nazi Germany and had counted Göring, Himmler, and Hitler among his intimate friends. Dr. Hedin had publicly characterized Hitler as "one of the greatest men in world history."

Now, in 1946, I learned that while Nazi Germany had surrendered, Dr. Hedin had not. He was still, at the age of eighty-one, openly loyal to Hitler's memory. At the same time, he was continuing with his work, writing steadily, adding to the thirty-one volumes he had already published on his explorations.

Among the Swedes I encountered, I noted a curious ambivalence of feeling toward Dr. Sven Hedin. In this small nation, with its shortage of world-renowned figures and celebrities, Dr. Hedin was one of the few remaining international Big Names. There were those who took pride in Dr. Hedin's fame. On the other hand, the fact remained that Dr. Hedin had been the one prominent Swedish citizen to support Nazi Germany—whose atrocities and horrors had recently been revealed—and Germany had lost, and now Dr. Hedin was not only a Swedish hero but a Swedish scandal and embarrassment.

I was fascinated. Here was a possible magazine article. Perhaps I would write about the one notorious unneutral Swede. Or, if he wouldn't talk about that, perhaps I would write about him as a

Swedish scientist who had survived his affiliations and who, despite his advanced years, was going ahead with his work. Or, at least, I might include him as part of a story I had in mind about Swedish scientists in general, and the progress they had made during the years that much of the rest of the world had been at war.

I wrote Dr. Sven Hedin a note. He responded with an invitation to tea. And so one dark afternoon, I found myself in a taxi, riding up the left side of the impressive Norr Mälarstrand through the moody, rain-swept city, to the address that Dr. Hedin had given me. As I noted that night in my Journal:

"September 8, 1946. Arrived at number 66, had trouble getting in until I found buzzer. Hedin's name after apartment 6. Took two-person triangular elevator to sixth floor. Buzzed. Girl in twenties, Hedin's niece, print dress, British accent, burst out, greeted me. Walked me up inner flight of circular stairs. Opened door. Alma Hedin, sister, tall with gray sensitive face, halting English, blue dress, in late sixties no doubt, welcomed me warmly. Sven Hedin leaped up from massive desk at far end of room, came to me, took my hand in both of his."

Presently, after a tour of his two joined apartments, we sat in an old-fashioned parlor (lace doilies everywhere) which contrasted with the modern apartment building in which it was located. I was seated next to Dr. Hedin, a gnome of a man with quick eyes behind thick spectacles, a scrub mustache, a starched wing collar securing, I would note, a "cravatish tie," and a blue pin-striped suit.

From the moment that our conversation began, Dr. Hedin was entirely himself. He spoke with affection of Adolf Hitler, of Goebbels, Himmler, Göring, Doenitz. "Whenever I wanted to see Hitler," Dr. Hedin explained, "I would call Prince Wissen of the German Embassy here, a fine fellow, on Monday. He would call Berlin the same day, phone me back several hours later, and say Hitler would lunch with me on Friday. I would leave Thursday so as not to be late, and then see Hitler. He was a hypnotic talker, a fascinating man."

Dr. Hedin spoke of the inhumanity of the conquering Allies toward defeated Germany. He spoke, with hope, of the probability that America would join a resurrected Germany in a third World

War against Russia. I listened more with wonder than dismay. And when, eventually, I questioned Dr. Hedin about science, since he was a scientist, and about literature, since he was a writer, he seemed not only ill-informed but uninterested.

As our interview continued through the waning afternoon, my host, I perceived, was becoming more and more eager, eager and anxious, to impress me with his importance. He wanted the publicity of my article, and he wanted it to be favorable. Suddenly, during some reply of his, he halted abruptly, and then he said to me, "You know I am a Nobel Prize judge, do you not?"

I had *not* known that, and I was quite astonished and, indeed, impressed. I was impressed because, to me, to most persons I am sure, the Nobel Prize is the world's foremost accolade given by man to man. And here was I, informally chatting with one of the august Nobel judges. And, I repeat, I was also astonished. What astonished me was the fact that this person I was interviewing was a cobweb of prejudices and misinformation and intolerance on many, many subjects, from the sciences to the arts, all of which came within the sphere of Nobel Prize considerations. To picture Dr. Hedin—someone altogether mortal—as a Nobel judge, one who played a decisive role in the annual crowning of gods, was astounding.

I had always believed, without ever having thought about it much, that if there were Nobel judges, they would be the wisest elders of our age. Actually, I suspected, most people did not believe that the Nobel Prizes were decided upon by human judges at all, but rather were selected at a meeting of deities on high Olympus or selected by some massive, invisible computing machine that could X-ray the earth's talented, its geniuses, and appoint the most deserving as winners.

Intrigued by the contrast between what I had expected and what I unexpectedly found before me, I came to life, and began to pepper Dr. Sven Hedin, Nobel judge, with questions about his functions on his committee, about how winners were nominated, sorted out, narrowed down, secretly discussed and debated over, voted upon, and about his own role. Dr. Hedin, sensing my excitement, was pleased and expansive, and he rattled on for another hour or more.

What I learned was incredible. My mind reeled. Dr. Hedin was not a Nobel judge on just one committee. He was a Nobel judge on three committees, the only Nobel Prize judge who voted annually on three of the four categories that Sweden controlled. He had been a member of the Royal Swedish Academy of Science since 1905, and every year since that time he had cast a vote for the laureate in physics and a vote for the laureate in chemistry. In 1913, he had been elected to the Swedish Academy, and ever since then he had been one of the eighteen judges to vote on the yearly Nobel Prize for literature.

Dr. Hedin was full of confidences. Did I know that when Pearl Buck's name had been proposed for the Nobel Prize in literature in 1938, ten of the eighteen Swedish judges present at the secret-vote meeting were against her? Well, continued Dr. Hedin, he and Selma Lagerlöf had been the leaders of the minority who wanted the award to go to Pearl Buck. Dr. Hedin had been the most vociferous in favor of Pearl Buck. He admired her work, her knowledge of China (which almost equaled his own), and he and Selma Lagerlöf had fought and finally overcome the resistance of the majority of their fellow judges. "Pearl Buck and her husband published my last book, a biography of Chiang Kai-shek. They gave me too little money for it, and to think how I got her the Nobel Prize!"

Once, when I interrupted to ask Dr. Hedin why some prominent authors had never won the Nobel Prize, he asked me what authors I had in mind. Well, I said, Maxim Gorki for one. "Ah, he died too soon. His name came in several times; he would have got the prize eventually." What about H. G. Wells? "Too minor and journalistic." What about W. Somerset Maugham? "Too popular and undistinguished." And James Joyce. What about James Joyce? Dr. Hedin seemed puzzled. "Who is he?"

It was difficult to suspend disbelief, but these were the words, and this was a Nobel Prize judge. I wanted more of his behind-the-scenes anecdotes, but I realized that the afternoon had worn away. Yet I hated to leave. I knew that this was a real story—the truth about the Nobel Prize awards, the truth about those who gave and those who took—but I did not know what kind of story it was or could be, or in what form this story might take final shape. I knew only that I wanted more of it. Immediately, I requested a second appointment, to discuss only the Nobel Prizes, and Dr. Hedin' was delighted to grant me another interview.

Two weeks later we met again. By then, I had done my homework, done extensive reading on the Nobel Prizes, and had made notes, got up a list of blunt questions. And this second time we were together, Dr. Hedin's answers were even more stimulating. For three hours he discussed specific ballotings that had taken place behind closed doors over many years within the three science committees, and the literary and peace committees. Without inhibition he named names, he discussed the human frailty of the judges and the judged, he revealed stupidity and brilliance in the voting, and he exposed politics and prejudices and petty vanities as well as honesty and wisdom and courage.

Some of my penciled jottings of the interview were explosive. The bitter personal prejudices of a single judge, Dr. Carl David af Wirsen, a poet and critic, prevented the Nobel Prize from going to Tolstoi, Ibsen, Strindberg. Wirsen resented Tolstoi for advocating anarchism and for denouncing all money prizes as harmful to artists, and Wirsen's colleagues resented Tolstoi for being a Russian. Wirsen, a poet and critic, prevented the Nobel Prize from going to had not written anything worthwhile in eleven years. And Wirsen led the opposition against Strindberg, insisting that the great playwright's dramas were "old-fashioned" and reminding his fellow judges that Strindberg had once announced, "The anti-Nobel Prize is the only one I would accept!" . . . The personal behavior of authors sometimes kept them from receiving deserved awards. Flagrant immorality barred D'Annunzio, and homosexuality delayed Gide's receipt of the award for many years. . . . The anti-Semitism of one prominent Nobel Prize winner, the German scientist Philipp Lenard, may have been the major factor in keeping the award from Albert Einstein at a time when Einstein was expected to win it. Lenard, who had great influence among the Nobel Prize judges, told the judges that the theory of relativity was not actually a discovery, had never been proved, and was valueless. Accordingly, the Nobel judges refused to honor Einstein for his early theory of relativity, and continued to pass him by for seven years. By then Lenard's influence had weakened, and the Swedish judges relented and elected Einstein the physics laureate in 1921 for his lesser work on the photoelectric effect. . . . The selection of Gabriela Mistral for the literary award in 1945, over Hesse, Romains, Croce, Sandburg, and others, was made "because one of our judges, Hjalmar Gullberg, a poet, fell in love with her verse, and translated all of it into Swedish to convince us, and single-handed he swayed our entire vote."

Dazed, I left Dr. Hedin and, so that I could think, I walked the long distance back to the hotel.

I had a treasure, I knew—provided it was not fool's gold. But perhaps Dr. Hedin had become merely a malicious gossip, was even sliding into senility at his great age, or perhaps he felt embittered toward his fellow judges, and his memory was faulty, colored by paranoia. On the other hand, if his mind was clear, if he had presented me with facts, I was possessed of material that few other writers were lucky enough to own. Everyone knew the bright side of the moon; I alone knew exactly what lay on the dark side. Only one thing remained to be done. Somehow, I must confirm the accuracy of my interviews with Dr. Hedin.

Immediately, with the help of Dr. Hedin, of the Nobel Foundation, of several other organizations, as well as of some friends that I had made in Stockholm, I arranged to interview six more Nobel Prize judges who officiated in four fields. According to my Journal entries:

"Mr. Dahlman, spokesman for the Foreign Office, suggested The. Svedberg, Nobel Prize-winning scientist at Uppsala. . . . Went to see Dr. Nicholas Norlen, assistant to Dr. Herbert Olivecrona. Dr. Olivecrona, at 55, is one of the world's leading brain specialists and a Nobel judge for the medical awards. . . . Went to Sturegatan 14 to see Sven L. Hammarskjold, new Secretary of the Nobel Foundation . . . September 23, at 3, took cab to the Swedish Academy, through narrow streets behind National Palace in Old Town. Met a Dr. Lamm, giant, white-haired professor of literature who refused to talk but who took me through auditorium, past book-lined walls to meet a dignified, graying poet of fair reputation in Sweden named Dr. Anders Österling. . . ."

One of my key interviews proved to be the one with the formidable Dr. Österling, Secretary of the Swedish Academy, who had voted on the literary awards for over two decades. Dr. Österling was as candid as Dr. Hedin had been. At the time of my interview with Dr. Österling, no Russian writer living inside Russia had ever won a Nobel Prize. Because of the historic Swedish fear and hatred of its big neighbor, the Nobel committees had ignored Russian genius, and the Swedish Academy had voted down Chekhov, Tolstoi, Andreyev, Gorki. Only one Russian author had ever been awarded the prize. In 1933, a minor writer, an expatriate who lived in Paris and had translated Longfellow's "The Song of Hiawatha" into Russian, Ivan Bunin by name, had been voted the Nobel Prize in literature. When I asked Dr. Österling why Bunin got the prize, he replied, "To pay off our bad consciences on passing over Chekhov and Tolstoi."

Dr. Österling told me that he had fought hard against Pearl Buck's receiving the award. And while Robert Frost, Theodore Dreiser, Upton Sinclair had all been up for consideration and had been decisively voted down, neither Thomas Wolfe nor James Joyce had ever been voted upon, because neither had ever been nominated. He said that often authors' wives tried to nominate their husbands officially. Furthermore, the language in which an author published was sometimes a factor in his winning an award. Anyone writing in Hindi, for instance, would have a difficult time winning the award, since the Nobel committee had no personal knowledge of the language and no experts upon whom they could rely. Dr. Österling frankly admitted that some of the Swedish literary judges, himself included, were prejudiced against certain American novelists. "I am against Americans getting it because they do not need our check and they receive more money from Hollywood than our Nobel Prize is worth." Unfair or not, such were the facts.

The facts. Dr. Hedin had been a fountain of truth. The moon was bright, but indeed, indeed, a dark side existed, and I had been there. Yes, I had a treasure, a true one, I knew at last. There remained only one problem. I had not the faintest idea what to do with it.

My Nobel judge interviews were behind me. Another day or two passed, and I did other work, but always bothered and nagged by this new material, this revelation, and suddenly it was Sunday.

I have already recorded a part of what happened next in my book *The Sunday Gentleman,* where I wrote a reminiscence about my meeting with Dr. Sven Hedin.

It was, as I have said, Sunday. My wife and I slept most of the morning, and after we awakened, we had breakfast in our suite. Outside, the sun was shining. It was noon. I moved to the sitting-room window and looked down upon the Strömmen canal and idly watched and listened as the King's band played before his enormous Royal Palace across the way. The postcard grandeur of the scene, the outer unreality of it, struck me, and then I remembered my interviews and I was again reminded that all that lay before my eyes was a façade, and that plainer, cruder human events happened behind palace walls, behind academy walls, behind institute walls, behind any walls where mere mortals dwelt. And that was the moment of conception. At once, I knew what must be done.

I turned from the window to my wife, who was still having coffee. "Sylvia," I said, "has anyone ever written a novel about the Nobel Prizes?"

From that moment, I was possessed of a brainchild, faceless, almost shapeless, that I would not be delivered of for a decade and a half.

What followed I shall recount as candidly as possible, for those who are writers and readers like myself. I speak of this creative experience with no pretense that it was unique or in any way different from what has been endured by other authors whose books have been as painfully and joyously conceived, but simply to reveal to those whose interest in books is merely the pleasure of reading a story—as well as to those who are writers or who wish to be writers and who may one day write a similar book—something of the starts and stops, twistings and turnings, delights and tortures that go into the making of one novel. I know that, in the long run, I have learned less about writing and received less encouragement from English instructors than I have from reading or listening to a working artist relate how a single creation—poem, play, short story, novel—was brought to life and to maturity and to its public place.

Following the meetings with the Nobel judges and my realization that this material could be utilized in a novel, I spent my remaining weeks in Stockholm visiting the various voting Academies, the Caroline Hospital, the Nobel Foundation, meeting still other judges and officials in the five award fields, and meeting also the administrators of the awards and veteran Swedish newspapermen who had covered previous ceremonies. My notebooks were soon filled, and the information in them continued to be extraordinary.

Finally I left Stockholm and, after spending nearly a year in France, Spain, Italy, I returned to California with my voluminous Nobel Prize notes. Once settled at home in Los Angeles, I put the Nobel material in my file cabinet. This was 1947, and in the two years that followed I devoted myself primarily to making a livelihood as a free-lance magazine writer. But I also persisted, in my limited spare time, in doing research on the Nobel Prize, in building up my file, and I spent countless hours trying to find a fictional approach to my material.

At last, in the spring of 1949, I found my first approach through a character I had devised. My earliest notes began: "A young, mature American scientist, who lives in a rut, does research at a Midwest university. His bachelor life is placid and tweedy. He has an elderly housekeeper, a dog, poker companions, and he is absorbed in investigations of the neutron. One day a cable comes . . . he has just been voted the Nobel Prize in physics. . . . A recluse who has become a nine-day wonder, he learns a physicist can be as popular as a movie star or baseball player. He is happy to escape to Sweden to be free of the turmoil."

In this development, I had the scientist fall in love with a healthy Swedish girl, who was a Foreign Office attaché. The pair had a disagreement, and my physicist rebounded into the arms of a Swedish actress, who represented an enemy power desiring nuclear secrets. Thereafter, the hero was in constant jeopardy, longing for the hermit life he had once led. In the end, calling upon resources that he did not know he possessed, he saved himself and his nuclear secrets, and was able to appear at the Nobel Ceremony in Concert Hall.

I brooded about this approach for two months, with the dark suspicion that it was dreadful. Finally, I wrote it off as a false start. The hero was empty; his women were unreal. The story line was contrived, lacked depth, said nothing, and, worst of all, was not gripping. The approach was too trivial for the serious subject I had in mind.

Impatient to do something with my Nobel obsession and material, I suggested to my New York literary agent, Paul R. Reynolds, that it might make a good factual article or series of articles. A new managing editor had come to *Collier's* magazine, and he was seeking controversial coverline pieces, stories sensational enough to be featured on the magazine's front cover. Reynolds got in touch with this editor, and he was enthusiastic. I was given the assignment to develop my material into a two-part article, presenting both sides of the Nobel Prize medallion.

With a great spurt of energy, I resumed my research. I hired veteran correspondents in Sweden to send me more behind-the-scenes copy. Personally, I interviewed or corresponded with a host of former Nobel Prize winners, and among the many who graciously cooperated with me were Professor Albert Einstein, Dr. Robert A. Millikan, Dr. Herman J. Muller, Mrs. Pearl Buck, and Miss Sigrid Undset.

I still treasure my reply from Professor Einstein. I had asked him, among other questions, how he had learned that he had won the Nobel Prize, the circumstances surrounding his acceptance of it, and if he had any criticisms of the Nobel Foundation's procedures and of the judges' choices. Writing me from the Institute for Advanced Study at Princeton University, on April 25, 1949, Professor Einstein replied to my questions, in part, as follows:

"I was informed that I had received the Nobel Prize by a telegram which I got while on board ship on my way back from a visit to Japan. . . . The prize was not personally handed to me. I was invited, instead, to attend a Swedish scientific congress at Goeteborg [*sic*] where I delivered an address. . . . I find that the procedure of selection of the prize-winners—at least in my field—is fair and conscientious."

However, it was Mrs. Pearl Buck who provided me with some of the best material on the personal adventures of a Nobel Prize laureate. On April 22, 1949, she wrote me:

"I happened to be in New York on the day when the news of the award was cabled from Stockholm. The Associated Press called my secretary and she called me. Simultaneously my husband got the news and telephoned to say that I must come to the John Day office as soon as possible because reporters and photographers wanted to see me. I really could not believe the news and it is considered rather a joke on me that I would not talk with the reporters until my husband had called my Swedish publisher by trans-Atlantic telephone to get confirmation. It was my feeling then and still is that that award should have gone to Theodore Dreiser. But I was told that it was the intent to give the Nobel Prize whenever possible to writers who had not yet reached their fullest development, so that it would be an encouragement and help to them, as indeed it has been to me."

Shortly afterwards, Mrs. Buck's husband, the late Richard Walsh, a prominent publisher, sent me notes describing everything that he and his wife could recall of what had happened to Mrs. Buck from the moment that she arrived in Stockholm until the moment that she left.

As Mrs. Buck revealed it, on the night of the award ceremony she found herself seated next to Dr. Enrico Fermi, winner of the physics prize for his nuclear researches. Presently, as I would soon report in my article—

"She was introduced and asked to rise and go down the steps to the floor of the hall.

"In a moment she was curtsying to King Gustaf. The monarch shook her hand, then gave her a gold medal in a leather box, a portfolio containing the Nobel citation, and an envelope with the document which was to be exchanged for the prize money.

"Then came the ordeal of walking backward. Handicapped both by high-heeled shoes that almost gave way on the deep Oriental rug and by the long train on her gold lamé dress, Mrs. Buck retreated slowly amid almost unendurable suspense. Sensing her difficulty, the audience applauded her every step on the successful journey back up the stairs and into her seat. The next morning a Stockholm paper ran an eight-column banner headline proclaiming PEARL BUCK GOES GRACEFULLY BACKWARDS!

"Later Mrs. Buck confided to a friend, 'I was so afraid that I would land in Professor Fermi's lap that, while the speeches were being made, I memorized the pattern of the rug. Then I followed it right straight back into my chair!' "

This was human, and therefore valuable to me for the article.

My wife and I conducted a number of additional personal interviews with Nobel laureates in our area. Among the most rewarding was an interview that Sylvia had with Dr. Robert Millikan, the 1923 Nobel laureate in physics. Sylvia met with Dr. Millikan in his large office at Caltech's Bridge Laboratory, in Pasadena, California. According to her original notes:

"Two sculptured heads on pedestals in office—one Einstein, one Ben Franklin. . . . He said, 'It is amazing how few mistakes the judges make. In my opinion they have made only one. But what is one mistake in almost fifty years? Besides, that mistake is only in my opinion.' . . . A member of the Swedish Academy of Science told Millikan confidentially (and he told me confidentially) that the committee wanted to give the prize to Einstein. The Academy man said he spent all his time studying Einstein's theory of relativity. He couldn't understand it. Didn't dare give the prize and run risk of learning later that the theory of relativity is invalid."

My wife's interview also provided me with one more tidbit of new information. Dr. Millikan said that the Swedes had given him two medals. "One was solid gold, to put in the vault for safekeeping. The other was a brass replica, just to keep around the house to show people."

But the very best material in my 1949 researches came from professional newspapermen in Sweden, who had covered many Nobel Prize seasons, and who were filled with information they had never been able to use in their routine covering of the Nobel ceremonies. One correspondent—who also held a government post, and whom I paid for replies to a series of questions—sent me a

marvelous anecdote. I had wanted to know what the prize money
had done for each of a number of winners. In response, he told me
what the money had done for Knut Hamsun, a recipient of the
Nobel Prize in literature, so that I was able to write in my article
the following:

"It saved Knut Hamsun from near poverty and afforded him a
historic two-week toot which began the very night of the award
ceremony.

"Tying one on, Hamsun pulled the whiskers of an elderly Nobel
committeeman and then wove his way over to Selma Lagerlöf, who
was also on the Nobel jury. Snapping his fingers against her new
corset Hamsun cried, 'Y'know? Sounds like a bell buoy!' "

When I combined this mass of new material with my three-year-
old notes from Nobel judge interviews, and with all of the reading I
had done since, I was almost overwhelmed by my research riches.
But I managed to condense the material for the two-part article,
and then I undertook the writing of the story. The writing went
smoothly, and on May 25, 1949, I was able to inform my literary
agent:

"Well, here it is. The completed job has turned out very much as
I planned. . . . I have never, in 20 years, undertaken anything
with as much scope. I found myself dealing with big and with
unusual names in medicine, chemistry, physics, literature, and pac-
ifism. It was tough, but honestly fun. When I completed my first
draft it ran 120 pages—exactly. About ten pages or so proved to be
repetitions, and after I got rid of those, I found myself with 110
pages of solid facts, anecdotes, stories. . . .

"I would be most interested in elaborating the Nobel material
into a full-length book. Next year will be the 50th anniversary, the
golden anniversary, of the Nobel Prizes. There have been a number
of books on Nobel, on the Prizes and the winners, but most are
either dull or way out of date. I think there is a place for such a
book. . . ."

On May 31, 1949, my literary agent replied as follows:

"I read your piece Friday and got it over to *Collier's*. You have
certainly done a very exhaustive job on the subject. The piece is
very well written. . . . Frankly I can't see a book on the Nobel

Prizes. I don't see who would buy the book. There is awfully little in books unless you can get an idea that will sell to the public and this wouldn't seem to me one."

In my eagerness to use all of the Nobel Prize material, and since I had no satisfactory approach for a novel, I had been willing to settle for an informal nonfiction history of the Prizes, but the moment that my agent threw cold water on the idea, I abandoned it, and perhaps for the best. Meanwhile, the editors of *Collier's* had accepted the article, had praised it, had agreed to give me four more assignments if I went to Europe, and I was feeling better.

But three months later, as the magazine was preparing the two-part article for the press, and just as I arrived in Paris to undertake the four new *Collier's* assignments, there occurred what today seems an amusing—but at the time was a most serious and upsetting—intervention and censorship. A member of the Crowell-Collier board of directors had routinely scanned the pieces—and suddenly he had seen red.

A letter, dated September 2, 1949, written by my literary agent, had been awaiting my arrival in Paris. It informed me that my four new assignments in Europe had been canceled out of hand. "The whole trouble is the Nobel Prize piece," my agent had written. "The director of the firm thought the Nobel piece was very pro-Russian and I think he got the idea from it that you were a Communist or a fellow traveler trying to sneak stuff in."

This explanation seemed insane, and I tried hard to understand what had happened.

Based on factual evidence, I had shown that the Nobel Prize judges were—up to that time—not only anti-American but also anti-Russian. I accused the Nobel committees of having an unfair bias because they had no respect for American achievements and had hatred for their powerful neighbor Russia. The Crowell-Collier director had said that this was dangerous fellow-traveler propaganda, and so I replied that I was referring not only to prejudice against Communist Russia but against Czarist Russia, and I cited the deliberate boycottings of all great Russian authors under Nicholas I—Tolstoi, Chekhov, Andreyev—and all the great Russian scientists save Pavlov (who won the Nobel Prize only because Alfred Nobel, before his death, had admired and aided him). The Crowell-Collier director remained adamant, and I made one last desperate effort to protect the integrity of the article. On September 5, 1949, I wrote my agent:

"After giving them *exactly* what they asked for at *Collier's,* what is the result? The result is, I arrive in Paris to find four major assignments canceled and myself suspended from the magazine for an utterly mad personal prejudice on the part of one of their directors.

"I resent that pro-Russian crap of his. I don't care if the man is one of your friends, or whatever he is. He may be brilliant, bright, nice to children and agents. But if, in reading my Nobel pieces, he can conceive that I am 'very pro-Russian,' then I say flatly that man is an idiot. . . . Why don't you reread Nobel and tell me how pro-Russian it is. My God, aren't those people interested in facts? Out of my final draft of 90-odd pages, a half-dozen, less, dealt with a simple true fact—that with one exception, no Russian, *under the Czar, or under Stalin,* ever got a Nobel Prize, though several probably deserved it. And because I try to write interestingly and tell all the facts, I repeated instances and anecdotes. What in the devil is Communist about that? I despise working in movie studios, and I always think of the magazine field as fresh air and decent—but this is the first time in 20 years of magazine work I am seriously beginning to wonder."

This outburst availed me nothing. On October 6, 1949, my agent wrote me:

"I lunched yesterday with the managing editor of *Collier's.* . . . Practically all of the Russian material is out, which you won't like. Actually, most of the Russian material should have and certainly could have stayed in except for two or three rather unfortunate sentences. For example, you open a paragraph with the statement that the Swedes showed their anti-Russian prejudice at the time of the Finnish-Russian war by giving a prize to a Finn. Factually this was, of course, true, but to the average American, Russia's attack on Finland before the Second World War is just indefensible and, while that probably shouldn't influence the Nobel Prize Committee, I am afraid the average American would feel sympathetic to the fact that it did. This would be just a matter of changing a couple of words in a sentence. However, now *Collier's* seems to have decided they have a swell feature . . ."

Well, there it was. I was left stranded in Paris with all of my assignments canceled, and with a wife and infant son to be supported back home. Eventually, by redoubling my efforts, I was able to get a few other magazine assignments and salvage something from the trip. But financially, it was a trying period, a period of considerable hardship. And what made it worse was that in the battle over censorship I had lost, and I had no power to prevent the periodical from deleting valuable information and distorting history because of executive idiocy.

This kind of restriction made me more determined than ever to work on this subject in a field where I might be free to write as I pleased—the field of the novel. Another incentive was the response to my two-part article, which appeared in the *Collier's* magazines of November 5 and 12 of 1949, as "Those Explosive Nobel Prizes." The blurb over Part One read: "The inventor created another form of dynamite when he left his fortune to establish the world's biggest giveaway for men of real distinction." The blurb over Part Two read: "The distinguished juries that grant the world's most important awards are prey to their own foibles and obscure terms in the inventor's will." The response to this article, both in the press and in my mail, was so electric that I was encouraged to think further about the subject.

Once more I returned to the idea of a novel. In the next five years I outlined two more versions, and made numerous notes on both. One of these was called "Journey to Malmö." While en route to Stockholm, six Nobel Prize winners—a disillusioned American author, a French woman scientist, a Scandinavian, an Indian, two Russians sharing one science award—were stranded by a snowslide in the Swedish port of Malmö. The plot centered on the two Russians: one did not want to return to Moscow after the awards, for fear that his bacterial discovery would be adapted to warfare; the other, his Russian co-winner, was not a scientist but was posing as one to keep an eye on the real scientist. Apparently I had a novel of regeneration in mind. I had the group of Nobel laureates cooperate to save the Russian who wanted to be free, and my last note on this approach read: "End book with giving of awards in Stockholm, now that winners are genuinely deserving at last."

Examining this, I felt that for a second time I was wrong. What I had was a confined situation for a melodrama reflecting the formula of *The Petrified Forest*. It was interesting but too shallow and familiar. Moreover, it merely skirted the Nobel Prize awards, and failed to penetrate the heart of my basic idea.

Doggedly, while making my livelihood writing for magazines and films, I persisted in trying to find a satisfying approach to the novel, and by 1956 I had written my third version, a sketchy outline which, for the first time, I entitled "The Prize." I will quote directly from my preliminary notes:

"Open book in plane from Paris to Stockholm. Passengers are three Nobel Prize winners going to get awards. One is German refugee, physicist, who fled Communism, faced with moral dilemma (whether to reveal a destructive discovery to his new homeland, America); another is a Frenchman (like Malraux) who has won literary prize and flirted with Communism; third is youngish English doctor under fire from older colleagues. Hero is American pilot of plane."

My notes went on to develop the characters, and then worked into the story:

"Plane blown off course, has engine trouble, makes forced landing in wheat field in East Zone of Germany. Passengers and crew taken to hospital, cleared. All released, except German refugee physicist. Others realize Communists know who he is, want to hold him, make use of his mind or keep him from working for America. Others decide to save him. They rescue him and are on the run, through Germany, hunted the entire week before the Nobel ceremony."

From that point on I developed mounting tensions, growing inner conflicts and outer obstacles, and described the character changes in the Nobel Prize winners who were forced to convert their theoretical knowledge into the practical skills needed for survival and flight. In the end, they survived and reached their objective, the Copenhagen ferry to Malmö, Sweden.

I seriously considered this approach to the novel for many

months. Yet the whole time I was troubled by some vague negative feeling—that this was not the book I really wanted to create about a subject so powerful. It was as if I were still circling the main subject, somehow incapable of meeting it head-on. Gradually, any enthusiasm that I had had for this development of the story withered and died, and I put the outline away and went on with the writing of magazine stories that were shorter and easier, work that fed my family if not my soul.

Suddenly, there occurred a series of events that changed my life and directly affected my attitude toward "The Prize"—this title and a few wisps of characters being almost all that I had salvaged from my last discarded outline. Up to 1958, I had published only two books. These were collective biographies brought out under the Alfred A. Knopf imprint, and both had been affectionately received by critics and reviewers but both had sold only moderately well. Now, while the creation of books was my great love and passion, I found that I could afford to give the writing of books only the smallest portion of my time. For most authors, a career devoted full-time to books can rarely support a family even poorly. As I had more or less given up magazine writing out of weariness with formula and lack of freedom to write as I pleased, I now obtained my main income from writing screenplays in motion-picture studios. But screen writing proved just as tiresome and restrictive as magazine work. And by 1958 I had become so frustrated by and bored with this communal writing, a form giving me little opportunity for self-expression and no sense of fulfillment, that I determined to break away from it at any cost.

I had an idea for a short novel—I had never yet written a complete novel—and in the summer of 1958, going hard, I wrote that first novel. It was a failure financially and artistically (although, years later, it would have a curious success with the public and critics in Great Britain and Italy), but it proved to me that I could write a publishable novel and write it as I pleased. Meanwhile, that same year, I finished a biography of Phineas T. Barnum, which provided me with a welcome share of Literary Guild book club money. Encouraged, and with rising confidence, I began to write my fifth book and second novel, and this was *The Chapman Report.*

I had no idea of what I had in this novel, knew only that I was fascinated by it, especially by the women in it, who represented part of my immediate social circle. I wrote my pages, I hoarded them, and when the book was finally done, I showed it to my wife, agents, and publisher for the first time. I was emotionally overwhelmed by the ensuing reception given the book—the high percentage of favorable notices and comments it gained, the vast international readership it achieved, the controversy it brought on—and thereafter I was more often infuriated than amused to read that I had contrived or manufactured a prefabricated best seller. In the years to follow—even with my most recent novels, *The Man* and *The Plot*—every novel I would publish was to be greeted by the more naïve members of the press as the product of some secret commercial prescription. Often, I wished to write these literary gentlemen and tell them that if any best-selling author possessed such a mathematical formula to use in the place of the inevitable brain-racking agony and back-breaking effort and lonely, lonely days and nights that go into the creation of any book, he would immediately patent it and lease it out to would-be writers turned critics (who might thus write best sellers of their own), and he himself would retire to the Riviera or Majorca, permanently free of the hell that all writing writers know.

At any rate, it was the confidence gained from having written *The Chapman Report,* even though it was not yet published, the joy of at last being independent and a full-time writer in the field of creativity that I loved the most, that inspired me to find the exact Nobel award story that I had so long sought.

I had been thinking about the Nobel novel off and on, as always, and then late in 1959 I saw fully, all at once, what I had refused to see before but what I must finally come to grips with and overcome. I realized that until then I had always been afraid of doing the big central story. While I had promising fictional characters in mind, I had avoided the real challenge of the subject itself. I had walked around and around it, which was safer. For only when you are fully engaged can you fail—in your own eyes or the world's eyes—as often as succeed. I had not wanted to chance the failure apparently. Or perhaps I had been fearful of pitting my untried resources against so monstrously frightening a test. In my earlier outlines I had been ready to undertake only small hells, never the big one.

I have since found that this fear is common among writers not only when attacking an overall subject but when facing up to a single scene inside a novel. Too many authors will avoid what threatens to be an impossibly difficult scene, although an obligatory scene, and instead will write around it rather than into it, simply from fear that they do not possess the perception or skill to master it. This detour into exposition or past tense or summary, as a substitute for daring to dramatize or play out a crucial confrontation, may be entirely unconscious. But once the fear is understood, and once the work in progress dominates the writer and drives him into the big Hell, the author has a chance to live up to his potential. He may be bad before he is good, but one day he will be good, or as good as he can ever be.

Thus, ultimately, I understood how I had been keeping my fictional characters out of the natural arena where they belonged, and how I had been avoiding the real story of "The Prize." Once I admitted this, supported as I was by my newly won confidence, the real and honest story for the novel, the one that I could live with, came to me all in one piece.

My very first jottings were dated only "late 1959." On a sheet of scratch paper I typed the following notes to myself:

"Entire novel takes place in Stockholm during forty-eight hours or twenty-four preceding Nobel Prize awards. . . . See whole machinery I exposed in *Collier's* . . . politics, shenanigans, prejudices and favoritism, as well as honesty, nobility, in each Prize group—literature, physics, medicine—told through drunken American novelist, who desperately needs money. . . . German professor stolen or saved from Russians by West, getting physics honor . . . three others getting awards. . . . Rep of royal family . . . Swedish girl escort in charge. . . . Russians and Germans and Norwegians and Finns. . . . World press corps, publishers, science politicians. . . . Drama of someone trying to get ex-German physicist to Russia or Finland. . . . Maturing and growth of the embittered American novelist. . . . Climax is award, American's speech, his preventing defection."

More notes from the next day or two, dated "later 1959," still rough but enlarging upon the first set, and some would be useful and some would not. I jotted the following:

"The hero, old-young novelist who dwells in Wisconsin, became famous young, then married, and wife (fearing to lose him) encouraged his drinking so that he became dependent upon her. She's a real bitch; he has power in moments of sobriety, but drunk, he is a fool and miserable and craven. . . . Or, better: in first flush of fame was able to propose to girl he truly loved, and she accidentally was killed, and he drank, and her sister encouraged it to bind him close so he would not leave. Wrote little afterwards, but one book remains unfinished for past five or seven years. . . . He is out of touch with real world, a recluse who won't face life or self, a subject and ward of this woman and the bottle, knowing the true situation and yet not able to overcome it. Too, a person with no real identity except in dreams on paper. . . .

"When the story opens he is almost unknown, and revered only by a loyal cult. Then, by accident, chain of events, he's translated into Swedish, acclaimed in Europe for what he has had to say that is now suddenly important, wins Nobel Prize. In Sweden this happens— becomes involved with an obscure, unlettered, beautiful Swedish girl who doesn't even know who he really is—only sees him as a funny, older, helpless American whom she is sorry for and then loves. . . . At first aloof from fellow winners, he is forced into their company—especially the old German—and in the end, when above the battle, he descends into it to save German.

"Also, old Nobel character who knew Alfred Nobel and is writing definitive history of the awards. Perhaps déclassé nobleman. . . . The three other winners. . . . Head of literary committee . . . Swedish hostess . . . Tass man . . . German girl. . . . Make secondary stories of other winners almost as important as hero's. Restrict story to boundaries of week before award."

But even as I imagined my characters and story in brief notes, my mind teemed with what else I might write about the hero's background and thoughts and current problems and the places he had lived. I was writing thousands of words, single-spaced on the type-writer, without thought of style, grammar, spelling, or even any certainty that they would fit into the projected book. I had no name for my hero or his wife or any of the other characters, and no place names for the settings, so I invented proper names as I went along, using any proper names that came to me. In these earliest writings of *The Prize,* for my eyes only, I called my main character "the hero" or "Doak" or one of a half-dozen other names, and I called his wife "Doris" or "Liz" or "Agnes," and I called their town in Wisconsin by the name of "Marvale." Before long the hero would have his final book identity as Andrew Craig and his wife would become Harriet and their town would become Miller's Dam.

I began these earliest writings by feeling out a familiar setting, the land and place where I had been raised and had attended school until I was nineteen years old.

"Marvale was located fifty miles northwest of Kenosha and Racine," I wrote. "From Lake Michigan the land rose and fell gracefully like long, lazy ocean swells, what they call a full sea, and this was full earth, rural earth, the landscape bright and unvaried except for occasional billboards, road signs pointing to a gasoline station or hamburger joint, windmills, haystacks, great fields of wheat and corn, and cows grazing on slight yellow slopes. And then you were in Marvale, which was bisected by the little-traveled gray cement highway. . . . No one really lived in the town, except salesmen at the hotel and some women and a few who lived behind the stores. Everyone else lived at the edge of town in two-story flats or on pieces of farmland, and Doak and Agnes lived at the edge of the town, too."

Then there were other patches of writing I was trying, partial probings into my main character, efforts to appraise him, know him, know the very work that had unexpectedly vaulted him to the Nobel Prize heights and Stockholm.

"The genre in which he wrote was also a subtle avoidance of life," I noted on paper for myself. "As the compromise of a fright-ened yet vital mind, he hid his concern for pressing problems of to-day in resurrections of the past. Somewhere he had read that Plato, having advanced his ideas for a utopian state in the suburban grove known as the Academy, became eager to practice what he had preached in his thirty-six Dialogues. It is said that Plato journeyed to Syracuse to teach the new twenty-five-year-old dictator, Dionysius II, his philosophies of government, help him establish a constitutional monarchy, and create a perfect socialist state. But Dionysius, drinker and lecher, ever fearful of Greek ideas, rebelled, and Plato fled back to Athens and his Academy. The perfect state with its etc. and etc. would have to wait.

"Hero seized upon this historical episode as an ideal transmitting agent for his ideas about growing state socialism and communism. Hero's novel took Plato and fictional character from Academy to Syracuse and showed what happened when their philosophic ideas were put into actual use and the gradual downfall of this utopia through corruption. Though the action was set in 100 B.C., the book's barbs were aimed at twentieth-century communism. . . . Book made hero great intellectual reputation, but only moderate money. Pressed by wife, hero set to work on modern book for first time. Then she was killed and his disintegration.

"His earlier book picked up in Scandinavia five years later, translated, so apt and timely, discussed in all papers and on all tongues, for in small country like Sweden you can chance only indirection when taunting and hating a neighboring enemy who is a giant. This brought hero's other books into translation within a year—gained repute he'd never had in America—and because this advocated Nobel's ideals, hero nominated for the prize.

"Reflecting on it in his euphoric states, hero saw these historical books not as a small triumph but as an act of creative cowardice, another kind of frightened hiding like living in Marvale."

Countless other notes, one-line, one-paragraph, ten narrative pages, toying with, testing, invented people, their stories, an overall story, and with the coming of a new year the novel began to take form in a way that excited and pleased me. I had found the way I wanted to write *The Prize*. Please God, it was the right way, the best way. Regardless, for me, it was the only way, and now I was ready to go ahead. One more act was necessary: to commit myself to the book publicly. Perhaps a childish game, but one necessary to a person with my psychological makeup. When you are a free and independent writer, without employer, without hours or deadlines, you have to play little games to force yourself into the actual writing. For me, one game is to announce to my family, my literary representatives, sometimes my publisher, that I have finally decided on my next book, that I am ready to write it. I won't tell anyone much—I cannot endure any reaction to or comment on a book still in the formative stage and as yet unwritten, I find any response too unsettling—I prefer to keep the writing in progress a secret, as a youngster may prepare and hide a secret gift for the holiday. Yet, when my final idea has solidified, when I am sure of it, I let it out to a few persons who are close to me—to put my pride on the line, a promissory note that must be paid one future day.

On February 3, 1960, I sent my literary agent in New York, Paul R. Reynolds, a 900-word general outline of what I had in mind.

"I think this will be a very big book about a subject which, to my knowledge, has never before been handled in book-length fiction," I wrote. "The entire story of *The Prize,* except for the opening, takes place in Stockholm in the seventy-two hours preceding the awarding of the four Swedish Nobel Prizes.

"The book opens on the sending of five cables—one from Oslo, four from Stockholm—to five men or women in different corners of the world who are being notified that they have won Nobel Prizes in peace, physics, chemistry, medicine, and literature. Each will have $50,000—and immortality. We pick up each of the major characters individually in Michigan, Massachusetts, Paris, London, Rome, at the moment each is notified—we learn their immediate situations, something of their unresolved problems, a good deal of their tensions. Several of the problems are not those of the winners alone—the French doctor has a young daughter, etc.

"In the first chapter, we will meet our hero-author, the man through whom the entire novel will be told. He is dead drunk at his moment of immortality. . . . The second chapter opens with the arrival of the hero, the other winners and those close to them, in Stockholm on December seventh—the Prize is given each December tenth, the anniversary of Nobel's death.

"The drama that quickly evolves is three-edged. First, we see the development and growth of the hero, as he finds his identity, frees himself of his guilts. It is also the story of his involvement, in Sweden, with two women. One is an obscure, unlettered young Swedish girl—who doesn't even know who he is—knows him only as a sardonic, too old and helpless American for whom she is sorry and whom later she will probably love. Next, we have our secondary stories of the other winners, notably an elderly German physicist who had fled the Russians in Berlin to find a haven in America. Of course, East Germany and the Communists want him back. Finally, behind the characters, based entirely on researched facts, we will see for the first time the inner workings of the Nobel machinery —the politics, prejudices, deals, courageous moves—humanized and told from the inside.

"I want to take the reader behind locked doors. I want to show how sudden greatness ennobles and corrupts, both giver and taker alike."

At last, after so many false starts, I had overcome the two great barriers—I had found both the way I must do the novel, and the people about whom I wished to write. My agent and my American publishers were as enthusiastic about the preliminary outline as I was at the time. However, my reprint publisher, Victor Weybright, of The New American Library, wondered about my "hero-author" who would be "dead drunk at his moment of immortality." Weybright, apparently, had read Robert Coughlan's *The Private World of William Faulkner,* wherein it was pointed out that Faulkner imbibed steadily after he was notified that he had won the Nobel Prize. Consequently, friends worried about Faulkner's being sober for the Nobel festivities. One close companion warned Faulkner, before he took off for Stockholm, "Now, Bill, you do right." Faulkner snapped back, "I'm so damn sick and tired of hearin' that. Everybody from the Swedish Ambassador to my damn houseboy has been tellin' me to do right." It is a matter of history that William Faulkner did do right. Now my reprint publisher was apprehensive that I might do wrong. I hastened to reassure him in a letter dated February 24, 1960, "Dear Victor, *The Prize* will not have its hero from below the Mason-Dixon. Nor will the hero reflect Faulkner or O'Neill—except in drinking and winning the big prize. Of course, it's too early to tell how he'll really turn out, but I suspect he'll resemble me more than anyone else."

Outside reactions to my idea had bolstered my confidence. But then there was something else that troubled me. This was 1960, and I had not seen Stockholm since the postwar period of 1946. Was it all as I remembered it? Was it drastically different? I knew that I must have a second look. Accompanied by my wife and two children, I sailed for Europe in June of 1960. From Paris I took a train to Copenhagen, then the ferry to Malmö, and finally the overnight train to Stockholm.

"Trip on Nord Express was great," I wrote from the Grand Hotel to my editor, Michael V. Korda, of Simon and Schuster. "Stockholm as divine—and dull—as I knew it fourteen years ago. But am highly stimulated by the daily research I'm doing on my next novel. Material and ideas developing wonderfully."

I found that Stockholm had changed extensively, and for the better. I also realized that the passage of fourteen years had distorted my memory of certain locales in the city, and the plans of certain buildings, and now I was able to straighten this out. At the same time, I was stumbling across new sites, as well as persons and information, that stimulated me with new ideas for the novel. The contrasts between what I had seen in 1946 and what I was seeing in 1960 so intrigued me that I would later give my hero, Andrew Craig, the similar experience of having visited the northern capital twice in a span of fourteen years.

I was full of the novel, and I was on the move. While I was visiting or revisiting sites that I knew I must use in the novel, my Swedish publisher at the time, Sven-Erik Bergh, took me to Riche's restaurant and the Djurgårdsbrunns Wärdshus, two eating places which later became backdrops for major scenes in the novel. And the manager of the Grand Hotel—he had been in its service forty years—escorted me on an exploration of the hotel premises, including the suites occupied by Nobel Prize winners. One day I might be browsing through the Swedish Academy, where the literary laureates were elected, and the next I would be in the Caroline Institute, where the medical laureates were chosen. I was in and out of the Nobel Foundation several times, interviewing, jotting down notes, taking photographs with my miniature Minox camera.

Wherever I went, I scribbled these penciled notes, and nightly, sustained by an excitement that overcame fatigue, I transferred these scrawled notes into a typed record of my research.

On July 20, 1960, I noted: "Across from a large park, in better section of residential Stockholm, stands a narrow six-story building (six stories by American count, but only five stories by Swedish count, since the European first floor is our second floor). This is the Nobelstiftelsen or the Nobel Foundation. . . . Upstairs, from Executive Director's office, enter into the main conference room of the Nobel Institute. Physics and chemistry judges meet and vote here. Once voted in private apartment upstairs. Others—Lit vote in the Swedish Academy in the Old City, and medicine in the Caroline Institute or the Karolinska Institutet, as the Swedes call it. . . . If one enters conference room from reception hall, it looks like this— a long, leather-topped (beaten and worn leather) table in center. Ten chairs, one at head and one at foot, and four and four, covered in old oxhide or similar material and much used. To right on wall is lively portrait of Alfred Nobel's mother by Zorn. At far end are three pictures. Dominating all, in center, an oil portrait of Nobel painted by Österman in 1915. To one side Bertha Suttner. To the other Ragnar Sohlman who died in 1948. . . ."

On July 20, 1960, I noted: "Phone call from Miss Margareta Delin of Nobel Foundation. Answers to questions I left. . . . At Concert Hall ceremony the King gives medallion. Following afternoon at Institute, winners get checks. . . . Most winners arrive a day or two before ceremony. Some known to arrive a week before . . . Nobel Foundation pays for one week at Grand Hotel and breakfasts for winner and family. . . ."

On July 21, 1960, I noted: "Visited with Miss Delin, took pictures, learned . . . Minister of Foreign Affairs assigns an attaché full-time to each winner. Attachés are young diplomats.

. . . During forty-eight hours before award, winners have a press conference, dinner hosted by Swedish colleagues in same field, go sight-seeing, evening of Dec. 9th attend reception at home of Chairman of Nobel Board so that winners may meet one another and other Nobel people involved. . . ."

On July 22, 1960, I noted: "Visited the Swedish Academy across bridge in Old City. Two librarians helped me. Eighteen members on Swedish Academy committee voting literary prize. Most know French, English, German. Big problem is Chinese or any exotic language. About fifty nominees proposed annually. Four of eighteen judges sift nominees with help of linguists who are literary specialists. Everyone reads throughout summer. Middle of September they come here, meet, discuss, and most often in last week in October make final vote."

On July 23, 1960, I noted: "Nobel winners usually stay in one of six major suites of Grand Hotel overlooking canal and Palace. . . . In winter, canal never frozen. Last winter snow and below zero, but rarely snow in December here. . . . Visited suite 525 used by Nobel winners. Small entry, then large hall done in blue with chest of drawers built-in. Off hall large bath, two sinks, bidet. Airy sitting room, desk at left, marble table, sofa, maroon chairs, very modern. Through sliding drapes twin beds and tables revealed. . . ."

On July 24, 1960, I noted: "Spent time last night rereading a diary I kept in Stockholm on first visit. Got fascinated with an entry I made on September 16, 1946, as follows: 'A typist, tall Swedish girl with angular face, came to work for me. Had once wanted to be actress. She told me her two younger sisters each had illegitimate children by longtime boy friends. One sister dated interned American flyer who wanted to marry her, she said No, is now sorry. This sister became pregnant. My typist took her to State hospital, she was given a guardian to look after her and see she got money from boy involved. She had baby at cost of eight kronen (State paying the rest). Illegitimacy in Sweden created partially by excess of women. One friend told my typist she wanted two children before she was thirty, had them, and now at thirty-five calls self Mrs. and is respected and loves kids but has not yet found man she loves enough for husband.' . . . Will look up story Sylvia published on illegitimacy in Sweden. Will check into it further here. Today my driver explained Swedes under eighteen cannot marry without permission of the King in writing. Twenty-one legal age. No pressure to marry young to prevent unwed mothers. Boys and girls encouraged to live together few years first, even to have children before marrying. Have idea I want to give my Swedish girl in book something like this—illegit son, she is matter-of-fact about boy, which may unsettle hero, make him reevaluate some of his own attitudes."

While I knew that I wanted a young, unmarried Swedish girl in my novel, I also knew that I still had much to learn about this character. I had read considerably and heard much about the habits and morals of unmarried Swedish women. I had known some of them personally in Europe and in America. But now I felt that I must be certain that my understanding of their behavior was correct. With the help of Swedish friends—and the tolerance of my wife—I was able to drink and dine with a half-dozen different Swedish girls, and their revelations proved of value to my book. One blond ingenue-type, a white pancake hat tilted on her lovely head, said, "I hate our upper-level cocktail parties. The men talk to the other men about business, and to women only to sleep with them." A girl who had a job on a newspaper told me over cocktails, "We Swedish women are good women. We're aggressive, lively, adaptive to travel. It's our men who are formal, humorless, too demanding of respect, and generally are bores. I'd guess one out of every four Swedish girls marries a foreigner."

One important bit of research came about unexpectedly. Because *The Chapman Report* was a best seller in the United States at that time, and was soon to be published in Sweden, I was invited to give a mass press conference in a large room on the first floor of the Swedish Press Club. Later I made notes on what I remembered of the one-and-a-half-hour inquisition:

"I sat behind small corner table on settee. Two dozen reporters and five photographers. Reporters pulled up chairs directly around me. Questioning began gradually. What are you doing in Sweden? Who you with? How long staying? How Swedish women different from American women? What other aspects of Sweden will you include in your novel? What do you think of Henry Miller and Tennessee Williams? . . . Grueling. Would not reveal why in Sweden, except to use it as background for novel I could not discuss. . . . During interview sherry and Scotch-on-the-rocks served and cigarettes offered around. Everything consumed."

This experience, I would realize months later, had been invaluable. When I came to write *The Prize,* my memories of my press conference enabled me to create realistically the four abrasive press conferences that my fictional laureates were to undergo.

I had finished my firsthand fact-hunting in Stockholm, and now I had no patience for anything but the fictional aspects of my novel. My imagination was stimulated by all I had seen and heard and felt. The creative process—first unconscious and leading me with its fancies, then more conscious and led by me into the realm of possibilities and probabilities of make-believe—had begun to engage all of my senses. I was nearly ready to go ahead, give my characters and their stories and the central story more exact form.

But first, after leaving Stockholm, I took a breather in Copenhagen, and from the Hotel Tre Falke, on July 25, 1960, I summed up the Swedish visit for my editor:

"I think I wrote you that Sweden proved more enchanting than I had previously remembered it to be. I did some marvelous research on the new novel. The visit was a complete success. We took the overnight train from Stockholm to Malmö, with the ferry crossing to Copenhagen. I'm a romantic about European trains; I find the passengers intriguing. I remember the one year when my friend Joe Wechsberg and I both undertook to write factual articles on the Orient Express, he for *The New Yorker,* I for *The Saturday Evening Post.* He saw it as a fraud; I saw it as pure Hitchcock. And we were both telling the truth. Anyway, today Sylvia and I are in Copenhagen and footsore and agreeing this is the liveliest city up in these northern parts. Tonight—Tivoli. Will be in Paris again Friday."

When I returned to Paris, my mind wasn't yet entirely on my new project. On August 1, 1960, I was writing my editor:

"One interesting experience the other eve. Ann and Art Buchwald threw an impressive party which we attended—the Josh Logans, Roz Russell, Bill Saroyan, Pat Suzuki, Carmel Snow, Emlyn Williams, Nancy Spain and such—and one part of the fun, from my point of view, was that nearly everyone present either had read, was reading, or at least knew about *The Chapman Report,* and they discussed it pro and con heatedly. An English actress, Margalo Gilmore, said she had just crossed on the *Queen Elizabeth* and the book was all over the Prom Deck. If this is a reflection of what may be happening elsewhere, in other communities, and with as much controversial talk, the book may still be just on its way. Who knows? Future reorders, I suppose, spell the future's verdict."

But before long, in Paris, my every thought was directed to the work in progress. In my hotel room in the rue de Berri, I wrote about two thousand words of rough character notes for *The Prize,* attempting to clarify the main players and their lives and their problems, and I developed sketches of promising peripheral characters. These spontaneous notes reflect the early creative process. A few brief excerpts will show the growing development of the novel:

"Paris, August 4, 1960. Hero quit living after life wronged him once. When he wins prize, he considers it a mockery. What he learns is that other men have suffered even more, yet have greater courage, and the point is you do the best you can, always. The real prize is the inner knowledge that life is worth fighting for, for its gift of existence. . . . Suspense is: will he appear in Stockholm and will he find himself? and will he break away from caretaker who encourages him to drink? . . . He had been there on honeymoon, and this evokes old memories and he drinks again. He antagonizes a press conference and one reporter in particular. He becomes involved with three women. . . .

"Old German physicist has had several heart attacks and knows the next one will end him. Trip strenuous but he needs money and publicity to finish his great work—and provide for daughter or niece, who has become center of his life aside from his work. . . . Russians want to use him or stop him. Seek to reach him first through getting him award, second (after initial failure to persuade him) through his daughter or niece.

"The award in chemistry goes to a French team, man and wife, who worked jointly on project, but once goal achieved they have nothing in common—on verge of split-up—he has broken off with her and gone to his mistress. Now they are thrown together by the award. . . . Story is from Frenchwoman's point of view, I think. Perhaps there is a truce to get award. She finds self disinterested in award because is discovering she is a woman not just a scientist. . . . In Stockholm, they become absorbed in research done by colleague in related field—he is stuck with an investigation in chemistry—meeting with colleague engineered by Kruger-like character—and the couple sees a new line for collaborative inquiry, what can be done. . . .

"The medical award goes to two rivals from different countries who despise each other, and after each plots to destroy the other, or discredit the other, they come to realize that their work is bigger than their petty differences. . . . Possibly American or Englishman and Italian winners. . . . Dramatized by case where one of them, or rather someone important in Stockholm, becomes ill, and doctor laureates forced to work together.

"Definitely drop peace award. Would make number of leading characters top-heavy. More important, since given out in Oslo, it would harm unity of keeping entire central action in Stockholm. (Besides, never believed in it. Too inexact, erratic, confusing.)

"Two Swedes of major story importance. . . . One a judge who tries to manipulate Nobel Prizes to suit his prejudices. In case of physics award, wants to satisfy East Germans and that way win a coveted university chair, so works with East Germans and Russians. Always bitter that not fully recognized in own country. . . . Other Swedish judge had known Nobel. He tries to carry on in true tradition of Nobel. Is also historian of awards. Becomes mouthpiece for history and machinery of awards. . . . U.S. girl reporter who has no morality, only survival instinct. Arrives to do a series exposing awards. Antagonized by hero, sets out to prove that his was phony award, too. . . . A soldier-of-fortune spy who worked both World Wars, but time has passed him by, now ludicrous figure always writing memoirs. Could read lips from distance in Turkey. Gets job from Russians, then killed. . . . On an isle lives an international businessman like Ivar Kruger or Zaharoff, cold, tough, the opposite of Nobel. Perhaps he is the one who has young chemist work for him, gets him together with French winners. . . . Instead of Italian actress might it not be better to get legendary Swedish actress who collects writers who win literature prize, always looking for perfect man and vehicle for her comeback. Possibly thirty-eight. This is a good character."

Traveling from Paris to Venice to Rome, I wrote steadily, in great rough bursts, all unpolished but useful. Often, I wrote out of sequence. I wrote a draft of the last major scene in the novel—a confession made by the enigmatic heroine, Emily Stratman, to Craig, the literature laureate—almost a half year before I would come to it in the actual writing of the novel.

In Rome, I thought that I would have a vacation at last. As a lover of Shelley's work and life—I had been collecting books about him, and owned a holograph check he made out to Leigh Hunt in 1817—I was eager to visit Shelley's grave, and so my wife and I made the romantic excursion to the poet's last resting place. But it was no vacation. Nothing, no day, could be anymore. I was enslaved by *The Prize*. That evening, on the stationery of the Hotel Excelsior in Rome, I typed four pages of narrative about my hero. One paragraph began:

"He remembered that week in Rome with her, just after the war. They had taken a taxi to the Protestant Cemetery, where a little boy had opened the gate, and they went up the gravel walk, climbing, and then to the left, to the highest portion near the old Roman Wall, and there they had found the white slab pressed in the earth —Shelley—or what had been left of Shelley, saved from the pyre on the beach . . ."

A year or more later, that vacation day, those notes made in my hotel turned up in the published edition of *The Prize* as follows:

"In Rome, the first afternoon, they had a pilgrimage to make. From the starkly modern Mediterraneo Hotel, they took a battered taxi to the Protestant Cemetery, and then dismissed the driver. At the gate they waited, until a little black-eyed boy opened it, and then they went up the gravel walk, climbing, and then turned to the left and continued to the highest rise near the ancient Roman wall, and there they found the white slab pressed in the earth—Percy Bysshe Shelley—or what had been left of Shelley saved from the pyre on the beach at Viareggio—and beside him, so eager to be beside him, the one who had buried him here, the old pirate, Edward John Trelawny.

"As Harriet and Andrew Craig stood in mourning, the sun came through the great quiet trees and touched each grave, and the gentle silence that day made death seem lovely and possible, the peaceful resting after the long travail. Later, they had walked hand in hand downward, beyond the Pyramid of Cestius, and arrived below, at the far corner of the cemetery, where stood the majestic shaft without a name—writ on water—and beside it, vigilant, faithful, the resting place of Joseph Severn.

"Shelley and Keats. That day, Craig felt an affinity for them, felt a sense of history as had they, felt that he was not one of the faceless of the world, the nonentities of time who come, stay briefly, and are blown away into nothingness, forgotten and unremembered as the flying sands on a windswept beach. He, too, would leave a shaft on earth that would stand as long as men stood or could incline their heads before it. That day, in Rome, he knew strength and purpose, and he was filled with his uniqueness and his mission."

That day in Rome. "How is a novel written?" students often write me. "What writing hours do you keep?" interviewers sometimes ask me. "What do you do when you're not working?" reviewers frequently inquire of me. Trying to answer, I remember that vacation day in Rome, and I know there are no absolute answers.

Then, on to Florence. There were bad moments during the writing, and there was a bad one here.

One night, at the Hotel Excelsior-Italie in Florence, it suddenly came to me that while I had my fictional Nobel winners, I had absolutely no notion of what concrete individual achievements had won them their Nobel Prizes. For the literature laureate this was not difficult. I had already sketched out a several-thousand-word biography of him for my own private reference. Now, to this, I added a detailed bibliography of the titles and contents of the novels I supposed he had written, as well as a rundown on how they had sold and been reviewed. However, the fictional achievements of my scientists provided a real impediment. This omission meant that I had to undertake a series of new researches in the fields of physics, chemistry, and medicine. I had to learn about scientific experiments and advances occurring throughout the world, the ones that were important, dramatic, uncompleted yet probable, and that might one year in the near future lead to Nobel medallions.

From Italy, I wrote to my research assistant of many years, Elizebethe Kempthorne, in Riverside, California, and I laid out the problem and the kind of material I was looking for and asked her to start searching popular magazines, scientific periodicals and papers, as well as books, for current experiments that might logically succeed in years to come and could honestly be deemed worthy of Nobel Prizes.

From abroad, later from my home, and even after I had begun writing *The Prize,* I continued to bombard Kempthorne with questions, as I proceeded with research reading on my own. Gradually I began to focus on certain subjects. A typical note from myself to Kempthorne:

"Dear E, I've become wildly fascinated by the following—

"Geneticists working at 'keeping human male sperms alive'— i.e., a great man could deliver sperms to be used for children by artificial insemination decades after his death! Men doing early work on male sperms are on enclosed slip. Look them up for me soonest.

"Thinking of sperm deal for my chemistry team. What think you?"

Weary months later, after studying and finally rejecting several dozen of the more promising experiments in the three scientific fields, I settled upon a chemistry prize for discoveries in sperm structure (leading to a practicable sperm bank), a physics prize for conversion and storage of solar energy, and a medicine prize for introduction of a surgical technique for cardiac transplants.

I might add that such prognostications in fiction can leave an author on thin ice. If they were to be ridiculed by eminent scientists after they appeared in print, they might negate the impact of an otherwise realistic novel. But I was very lucky. After *The Prize* appeared, not one scientist faulted the achievements I had projected from experiments still in their early stages. In fact, a number of scientists wrote me that my fictional discoveries might one day become real discoveries. Therefore, it was with satisfaction that I read, recently, that two of my three fictional achievements had become very real indeed.

In my novel, I had Drs. Denise and Claude Marceau win the Nobel Prize for freezing male sperms and implanting them by artificial means in women years later. In my book, I had one of my prize winners tell the press: "If our [discovery] had existed in the sixteenth century . . . today Shakespeare's actual sperms might be taken out of storage, thawed, and a dozen of your English ladies impregnated with them and in nine months these would bear his children. If our [discovery] had existed in the last five hundred years, we would today have a storage bank containing the living reproductive sperms of Galileo, Pasteur, Newton, Darwin—Voltaire, Milton, Goethe . . . Casanova, Napoleon Bonaparte, Nietzsche, Benjamin Franklin. . . . Had we made our discovery earlier in our own lifetime, we might have in the storage bank the living sperms of Luther Burbank or Professor Einstein. . . ."

That I had written in 1960. Six years later, on April 7, 1966, I read a headline: 29 MADE PREGNANT BY SPERM FROZEN 2 YEARS. According to a wire-service story, Dr. S. J. Behrman, a University of Michigan biologist, had announced that "29 women had been made pregnant by male sperm which had been frozen up to 2½ years." Dr. Behrman went on to speak of a future when "we can freeze the male cell through which life has been passed on over the centuries . . . we will be able to take the sperm of an Einstein or a Beethoven and preserve it for reproduction centuries later."

Also, for *The Prize,* I created two fictional doctors, Dr. John Garrett, of Pasadena, California, and Dr. Carlo Farelli, of Rome, Italy, who were to win the Nobel Prize for "the discovery of antireactive substances to overcome the immunological barrier to cardiac transplantation" and for "introduction of surgical technique to perform successfully a heterograft of the heart organ into the human body." In other words, Garrett and Farelli found a serum that neutralized "the human body's rejection or immunity mechanism" after living calves' hearts had been transplanted into human chest cavities.

That was in 1960. In 1966, I was not surprised to read that Dr. Michael D. DeBakey had implanted "a half heart" in a rheumatic-heart victim, and the so-called artificial heart kept a dying man alive four days. In recent years I learned that surgeons at the University of Indiana "have developed a complete mechanical heart that might work in a human patient for a short period of time," and that the National Heart Institute is now on a crash program "to develop a substitute for the human heart." Meanwhile, in Capetown, South Africa, during December of 1967, Dr. Christiaan Barnard dramatized the possibility that the best substitute for a failing human heart might be the transplantation of a healthy human heart. Making medical history, Dr. Barnard succeeded in a human heart transplant when he removed the pulsating heart of a young woman who died after an automobile accident, and grafted it inside the chest of a fifty-five-year-old man who was dying of a heart ailment.

However, when I decided to develop and use these discoveries in 1960, I had no inkling of how soon it would be that science would catch up with achievements that grew largely out of my imagination. I knew only that I was working in a dangerous area, that any discoveries I projected from tentative theories and seminal experiments could as easily damage my book as enhance it. As a consequence, after doing my homework, I proceeded with caution; then trusting instinct, I gambled on what I should use—and hoped for the best.

So that bad night in Florence, in 1960, when I realized that I must do more research, proved to be only a temporary setback. For a short time, it hampered my progress. Still, once this research was initiated, I found that the very problem stimulated me in an odd way. Since it promised to give more body to the backgrounds of my characters, I was able to return to my characters and the story. And by then, I knew that the time had come to leave Europe and go back to my desk to begin formally outlining and writing *The Prize.*

I returned to Los Angeles, and shortly after unpacking I went into my isolated study, eager to resume work on the novel. It wasn't easy to resume. "I'm wearing three heads and am a little top-heavy," I wrote my editor on September 29, 1960. "One head watches *The Chapman Report* and tries to help out. The second is busy bending over revisions on *The Twenty-Seventh Wife.* The third, usually at night, works slowly away at laying out my next novel, *The Prize,* which you know a little about and which has me increasingly absorbed."

A week and a half later I was wearing one head again. I was able to inform my editor, "I've been busy with *The Twenty-Seventh Wife* rewrite. Now that's done—and I'm several days on *The Prize* full-time, trying to coordinate my notes and thinking of the entire past summer, trying to lay out the vast, complex novel. I had a wondrous day yesterday: licked two of the characters completely and projected some scenes I can't wait to write."

By now I had assembled my research and spread out on my desk the seemingly countless pages and fragments of pages of preliminary notes. Slowly I began to organize the scattered notes that belonged to each character.

There was Max Stratman, who still had no name.

A typical background sketch on him, which I studied, read as follows:

"Make German physicist Russian-born who, like my parents, leaves home in teens and goes to Poland and then Berlin. War comes and he escapes Russians and goes to American Army. Use my parents' background for his earliest memories. . . . Possibly Russian-born physicist went to Berlin for education, then England where he spent most of his life, and finally USA for sinecure at Advance School."

A typical dramatic note for a scene, the one introducing the German physicist in the book, seemed worth retaining. It read:

"For Schmidt, at sixty-seven, it was always pleasant to lie on the doctor's hard table in the examination room while the comely nurse applied electrodes to his chest and legs. It was soothing, quiet, and he could think.

"But today, lying bare-chested, with trousers rolled up, it was less relaxing than ever before because today it was important. Something vital, besides his future life, hung on the cardiograph result, and this had never been quite true before."

Having absorbed these notes on the German physicist, I set to work expanding his story and the story of his niece. On October 8, 1960, I wrote 1,400 words of rough notes under the heading The German Physicist's Story. These notes began:

"Open with German taking cardiogram. This is regular thing, but today more significance. Offered new contract to head crash program in his field or develop new idea that he has. Much more money and now realizes how little he has and wants money for niece.

"(His brother had saved him, got him out of Germany, brother killed by Nazis. Later inherited brother's little girl. Now she wants to be a painter, go to school, needs money to study—he wants that for her instead of being clerk or secretary.)

"Learns he has not passed cardio and cannot undertake big traveling job for more money. . . . Troubled, wanders over to faculty club as does every day and watches poker game or bridge, and thinks. Has beer. Chats. Goes home. Niece is waiting with news of Nobel Prize.

"Revise above to read: German has been offered big supervisory job on solar power system he invented. Would take his time from theoretical work, but move program ahead. Means more money, much travel. After heart test, learns no added exertion, travel permitted. Returns and learns won Nobel Prize. Despite heart, decides to accept it in person—this will get him money, can refuse traveling job, devote self to basic research. Calculated risk, but solves everything.

"(The niece, a lovely and lush German Jewess, had been fifteen when sent to concentration camp with father. To save father, had been forced to accommodate head of camp and his aides—called upon almost daily to perform intercourse. When camp abandoned, had told U.S. army psychiatrist, who helped but too busy—she sent for by famous uncle. Never gone out socially except with uncle. Froze when man touched her, as many wished to. Uncle realizing after his death no one left to care for her—no husband or man possible—was concerned to provide for her. Now was lovely, with-drawn, shy, rather well-read and thoughtful woman—whose lush-ness belied what was eroded beneath.)

"On doctor's advice, German and niece take Swedish boat to Göteborg. The last night on boat, she is misunderstood and has bad experience with steward or passenger or someone. Uncle finds her sobbing, not at man whom she does not blame, but at self. Uncle gets ship's doctor for sedative, then explains whole thing to him. Doesn't explain own heart condition now. . . ."

I wondered where, in the United States, the German physicist and his niece should be living. I wanted a city I had visited, and one which provided the right background. I remembered that my last assignment as an enlisted man in the United States Army Signal Corps had been to Lawson General Hospital in Atlanta, where I had stayed at the Briarcliff Hotel for fourteen days late in 1945. Very well. I would have the German and his niece living in Atlanta, and have the niece doing part-time volunteer work at Lawson Hospital. I consulted a Journal I had kept in Atlanta, as well as letters written to my wife. From these I compiled a page of factual notes, which went as follows:

"Peachtree Street, main thoroughfare with no peach trees, turned into Decatur Street, Negro quarter . . . Henry Grady Hotel on Peachtree. . . . At Five Points turned into Decatur . . . Briarcliff Hotel on Ponce de Leon Avenue . . . Lawson Hospital fourteen miles out . . . Lawson Hospital low-slung dull wooden buildings along cement highway . . ."

To these notes, I added more up-to-date jottings from recently published books about Atlanta:

"Atlanta loves tradition . . . 302,000 people . . . 2,500 factories . . . mercantile center . . . Coca-Cola millionaires, therefore 'architecture rococola' . . . Druid Hills section, the rich . . ."

Of course, the German and his niece were traveling to Göteborg on a ship rather than by airplane because my fictional character had a weak heart, and it would definitely be a Swedish ship because my wife and I had taken one, the S.S. *Drottningholm,* on our first visit to Sweden in 1946. From my Journal notes and letters I had

written my parents about the sea voyage, I wrote these background
travel-notes for the German and his niece:

"Rooms 3 and 4 on B Deck . . . sail at 12:30 afternoon. . . .
Captain's table seats twelve . . . waiter carried portable smorg-
asbord . . . sat in wicker chair on Upper A deck within glass en-
closure . . . Swedes toast after every drink, everyone but host—
schnapps, pure alcohol flavored with caraway, held rigidly before
chest, swallowed while looking into another's eyes, then glass back
to chest and set on table. . . . Deck steward blows bugle for
lunch and dinner . . . 8th day see Orkney Islands and Scotland,
walked open B Deck. . . . Arrive Göteborg 5 afternoon 9th
day. . . ."

With the German and his niece coming under control, I moved
on to the pile of notes I had gathered on the chemistry winners, the
Frenchman, his wife—and on his mistress. I examined these earlier
notes, and then I wrote about 1,200 words for myself on the possible line of their story. I had not settled on names for these characters, so I simply headed my notes The Jacques, Simone and Denise
Story. Then I began as follows:

"Jacques Jordan and Denise finish eating near the Halle aux
Vins, walk to river, past Tour d'Argent, watching couples, talking.
. . . Had been seeing each other like this, but it could not go on.
Night is seductive, and this, more than he, seduces her. . . . They
go back to her apartment. Never speak a word. He sleeps with
her. . . . Later he speaks of how and why he needs her, and she
him, and they speak of future. . . . Simone Jordan phones, stunning them. Orders him home—the press is coming—they have won
Nobel Prize.

"Second chapter picks Jordans up on plane, hour from Stockholm. Not speaking. . . . She has not spoken to him much since
evening of award announcement. Retrace that evening. He had
come home, press already there. Questions. All night visited by
colleagues. She'd gone to sleep alone. Once he tried to explain, she
would not listen. . . . Exposition about their work, and how it is
finished, success after so many years; the good times. Then restless,
nothing new to do but rehash old. How she learned of mistress, and
about her, and how wife had seen her. Hadn't planned what to do,

except Nobel thing opened it up. On impulse had let him know she knew truth. . . . Now speaks. Going to divorce him after. Keep truce because he wants special chair, prestige, or some Académie. But after—no more. . . . Land in Stockholm. Greeted. Reporter asks ironic question: 'Do you recommend all married couples have a work in common?' "

My notes went on to show the French wife in Stockholm, how a Nobel judge introduces her to a "Kruger-type" industrialist, who in turn "introduces her to shy young Swede who has wanted to meet her, is doing work in synthetic food that may interest her." The "Kruger type" needs the French pair to help the young Swede solve a chemistry problem "to keep alive factories that would otherwise collapse." The Frenchwoman, in turn, sees how she can use the young Swede to revenge herself upon her husband, even make her husband jealous. "Coldly, now, she sets out to seduce timorous Swede. . . . Husband goes to Kruger-type lab to beat up Swede, becomes entranced by work problem."

I was ready to christen my characters.

Back on August 4, 1960, I had made a list of likely characters, among them the following:

Hero-author
Sister-in-law
Young Swedish girl
American or Italian actress
Old German physicist
Daughter or niece
French chemist
French chemist's wife
Israel-Hungarian doctor
German doctor
Ambitious Swedish judge
Swedish prince-historian
U.S. or English girl reporter
Wenner Gren-Kruger-Zaharoff type who is Swiss
Selma Lagerlöf-type ex-winner
Russian auto agent

By October 11, 1960, each of these characters had a name or the last in a series of names. The hero-author had become Andrew Craig. His sister-in-law had become Leah Decker. The young Swedish girl, after I had gone through a Stockholm telephone directory, was Lilly Hedqvist. The American or Italian actress had been transformed into a Swedish actress, Märta Norberg. The Wenner Gren-Kruger-Zaharoff type was Ragnar Hammarlund. All of these names were retained when, a few days later, I typed my final list of characters. But now there were many other changes. The French chemist had evolved from Jacques Jordan through Julian Marceau to his final name, which was Claude Marceau. The "Jordan" I transferred to his mistress, who became Gisèle Jordan. The wife was definitely Denise. The old German physicist had evolved from Schmidt through Schimmer and Dr. Hans Haber to, finally, Dr. Max Stratman. His daughter or niece had a list of ten names, including Arilda and Eva, before I settled upon Emily. The Israel-Hungarian doctor was now an American doctor who would be Magill or Bassett or Garrett, and at last was Dr. John Garrett. His co-winner of the Nobel Prize was no longer a German doctor but an Italian doctor, Dr. Carlo Bertini, whose name I quickly changed to Farinelli and finally to Dr. Carlo Farelli. The Russian auto agent had been abandoned for an East German scientist, Stratman's ex-friend, who was first named Mueller and Ernst, and then Dr. Hans Eckart.

I was nearing the end of my preparatory work.

Every author prepares for a book in the way that best suits his psyche. Apparently, something in my writing system requires that I do an enormous amount of foundation-laying on paper before I can undertake the actual writing of a book.

While most novelists do some preparatory work on paper before starting a new novel, and while a few do a great amount of this work, for years I did not know of any writer who had laid the groundwork for a nonhistorical novel as exhaustively and obsessively as I did. Nor could I say whether such groundwork was a virtue or a fault. It has made me feel easier to discover recently one modern author who approached a novel, in the pre-writing stage, with even more thoroughness than I do. I refer to Sinclair Lewis.

CALIFORNIA HOTEL
16, RUE DE BERRI
CHAMPS-ÉLYSÉES
PARIS
TÉLÉPHONE: ÉLYSÉES 93-00 (7 LIGNES)
TÉLÉGR.: CALIFOROTEL-PARIS

Gisele Jordan background, description —

born — Rouen, France
age – 27
Ash Blonde bouffant   make her
5'7"   Balenciaga
112 lbs   mannequin —
32 bust
20 ~~hip~~ waist
34 hips
flat bust, moon breasts — pale blue eyes
high cheekbones
mask of beauty, emotionless
lips generous, full soft
eyebrows penciled dark & high
knees too spare, bony,
skeletal

Every novelist, sooner or later, finds himself compared, to his advantage or detriment, to some one or to several of his literary predecessors. I have found myself compared to a vast mélange of different writers. One day, Robert Saffron was to write about *The Prize* in the New York *World-Telegram,* saying, "It would seem, actually, that Wallace has created . . . a novel in the tradition of the good, old American muckrakers: a mass of exhaustive details revealing the 'inside story' of an important but little explored milieu, all festooned on a fast-moving plot line and energized by a dose of indignation." It was, Mr. Saffron would contend, "the technique" of Harriet Beecher Stowe in *Uncle Tom's Cabin* and of Upton Sinclair in *The Jungle.*

Because I write multi-charactered novels of great breadth, I have found myself compared to Honoré de Balzac—and Kathleen Winsor. And because I am devoted to storytelling, I have been compared to Charles Dickens, W. Somerset Maugham—and Gene Stratton Porter. But most often, in reviews, my name has been coupled with that of Sinclair Lewis, basically because my novels are frequently concerned with contemporary sociological themes and because my novels are "popular." In an essay in the *Los Angeles Times,* August 9, 1964, Robert Kirsch generously wrote, "Irving Wallace is, in my opinion, a better writer than, say, Sinclair Lewis, and may in time emerge as a writer of real importance on the American scene. . . . In order to understand why these writers have found and kept a large audience, one has to examine what people want from a novel and what they have always wanted. It is, basically, entertainment."

While I had read all of Sinclair Lewis, I had never read in depth about him. Now I was provoked to learn more of his methods. To my amazement, I found that the pre-writing preparation I undertake had been an obsession with Sinclair Lewis, also. Mark Schorer, in his definitive biography, *Sinclair Lewis,* explained the preparations for *Arrowsmith*:

"Thus the work progressed: maps of towns and cities; floor plans of houses, hospitals, laboratories; time schedules; full biographies of a score of characters; endless notes on yellow sheets—and

then all of it systematically fed into the maw of the growing plan."
And again, when Sinclair Lewis was preparing *Work of Art*:

". . . Lewis would dictate notes at a rate of about two hundred words a minute and Florey [his secretary] would take these words down in something resembling outline form. In those notes, characters were born and named and described, cities and towns named, population figures recorded, homes and rooms and furniture described. . . . Once his plan was set down . . . Lewis himself took over the typewriter and, from the plan, typed out a twenty- or thirty-page summary of the novel, and if it remained too vague to satisfy him, he rewrote it in forty or fifty pages."

Thus, going from the notes that he called his plan, to the outline that he called his summary, Sinclair Lewis approached the writing of a novel.

It was enlightening, this knowledge, and it made me feel more comfortable, less embarrassed, to admit that I had always struggled and fussed so much with preliminary details.

For *The Prize,* I had my voluminous notes. But one more crucial task faced me before I could undertake the actual writing of the first draft. I had small paper mountains of research, character progression, possible scenes, bits and pieces of narrative, and written dialogue. Now I must pull these together into a coherent story, progressing from sequence to sequence. One of my sequence outlines read simply: "1. Notification. 2. Arrival. 3. Press reception. 4. Cocktail party. 5. Tour of city. 6. Hammarlund's banquet. 7. Visit places of prize voting. 8. Private scenes. 9. Kidnaping. 10. Ending. Fifteen to twenty chapters."

For me, that was not enough. Because of the complexity of my story, I needed an outline, still short perhaps but more complete than any preceding one, to use as a sort of word map of where I hoped to go in the writing. With my notes fully absorbed, I quickly settled down to develop the final outline.

I might add that the opinions of writers differ on the subject of outlines. Over many years, I have discussed writing techniques with countless novelists I have known socially or met casually, from the late Raymond Chandler and Horace McCoy to living authors like

Robert Nathan, Irving Stone, James Jones, Ray Bradbury, Leon Uris, Jerome Weidman. From conversations with these writers, and with numerous others, it has become clear to me that there are two contrasting approaches to the writing of a novel. One school believes that you start with no more than a general idea of what you want to do, maybe have a few characters and scenes in mind, or a so-called theme or background, and create everything else as you go along. The second school believes that you work out your idea, characters, story as much as possible in advance, so that you know fairly well who is in the story, what it is about, where it is going, and only then do you actually begin to write.

There is something to be said for and against each approach. In favor of the let's-sit-down-and-see-what-happens school is the spontaneity that inevitably results. The writer is not restricted by a plan. He invents as he goes along. He has more scope for invention. He is less apt to become tired of his work while it is in progress, since he does not know what will happen in it from day to day. Everything is a surprise to him. What may be said against this approach is that an unplanned novel, not having been thought out with care, can go off in the wrong direction, with minor characters and subplots being overemphasized, thereby making the finished book unbalanced and uneven. This approach can, and often does, lead to wasted effort and time, and inevitable discouragement.

The planned or outlined novel has in its favor the virtue of being creatively thought out, worked out, disciplined in the author's mind and on paper, with the major characters getting their due, with the main stories and subplots being told in proper perspective and balance, and with the novel getting done fairly close to the way it was envisioned. What operates against this method is that the novelist who plans too carefully in advance may cast his book into such a rigid mold that he leaves no room for his imagination to soar freely or for new ideas to take root and grow, which would expand his narrative more widely.

As I have said, I am strictly an outline man, but with certain personal modifications. On each new novel, I have always written many outlines for myself, developing scenes and characters, underlining story problems that need further thought. I work a novel out, in chronological sequence, over many weeks, in my head and then roughly on paper before beginning it. I want to know that it is right for me. I want to know that it will progress. I do not want to take a wrong turning. And this is doubly necessary in my case, because my novels usually contain large casts of characters, and these characters have interwoven problems, and my books have plots and subplots, so that without some kind of literary Baedeker of my own, I would soon be hopelessly lost. But at the same time, I try to leave a broad area for spontaneity in my outlines. I leave so many holes, so many points undeveloped, so many characters or possible scenes touched on in merely a line or two, that there is always room for considerable creative invention as I go along.

This was exactly the way I approached *The Prize*. I tried to organize my notes, to set them down briefly in some kind of dramatic sequence, and I constantly turned these sequences inside out until I was more or less satisfied with them. The outline was never quite completed. Frequently, a single sentence in the outline became a scene that ran ten to twenty typewritten pages in the first draft. Also, so many new characters or situations came to me as I wrote —people or scenes or conflicts not in my outlines—that I was constantly revising and replotting what lay ahead.

My final outline, the one that would be adequate to start with, was written during two days. On the first day, October 18, 1960, I wrote the terse sequence and content outline for six of the chapters, and the second day, October 19, I wrote the outline for the last ten chapters. This added up to seven pages single-spaced, or about 2,000 words. When I was almost done, I combined the last two chapters, which then gave me an outline for fifteen chapters in all. Later, while writing the book, cutting and switching and changing material, I condensed this outline sequence into only twelve chapters.

Since the final outline is too long to reproduce here in full, I will confine myself to showing the chapters I started and closed with on each of those two difficult days.

On October 18, I began my final outline with the following:

"CHAP. I: Open with Count Bertil Jacobsson in Stockholm sending congratulatory wires late at night from Nobel Foundation.

. . . In Paris, Claude Marceau is enjoying affair with Gisèle Jordan, until interrupted by wife Denise's call about cable. In Atlanta, Professor Max Stratman is having a cardiograph test, when learns news from niece Emily. In Los Angeles, Dr. John Garrett is in group-therapy session, learns news through call from wife in Pasadena. In Miller's Dam, Wisconsin, Andrew Craig is passed out, drunk, when sister-in-law Leah awakens him with news. (Work in Garrett's co-winner Dr. Farelli of Rome somehow.)"

I closed this first day's work with the following:

"CHAP. VI: In morning, Craig gets hell from Leah over his behavior at Royal Banquet and his staying out all night. For first time he revolts a little. They have tour coming up. . . . Count and Craig's publisher take Emily and Max Stratman and Craig and Leah on tour. Churches, Old City, City Hall, Skansen. Visit place of literary awards in Old City. (During tour pass villa, find Hammarlund and Lindblad playing boule. Hammarlund asks about his dinner, and finds out they have already accepted.) . . . Craig tries to talk to Emily, get her alone so he can apologize, but each time Leah breaks it up. Toward end of tour, Craig conspires with driver to take Max and Leah into a building and then say he and Emily have gone off. . . . Walk on Kungsgatan. . . . Evening eat at Den Gyldene Freden. Mellowed, Craig speaks about Harriet and himself, something he has done with no woman. Tries to explain Leah, also. But can't really get Emily to talk about herself. Almost, but not quite. . . . Leah not angry but coy and provocative when he returns. Tries to hold him by sleeping with him. He refuses. She rails against bitch Emily. He slams door and does what he had not meant to—drinks alone. For moment escapes recent past with its guilts, but it is ever with him. Drinks and drinks."

The following day, October 19, I resumed my final outline with the following:

"CHAP. VII: Activities of three Nobel judges. . . . Jacobsson takes Denise and Claude Marceau on tour, then to Institute to show them how and where they won prize. Conflict between Marceaus . . . Ingrid Påhl replaced Krantz, and takes Garrett to Karolinska, where Dr. Öhman greets him. Garrett learns how won prize, of past medicine prizes, now wants to see transplant patient.

Learns Farelli has already been there with reporter Sue Wiley. Is furious. . . . Krantz is driving from airport where met Berlin plane. Has greeted Dr. Hans Eckart. Tells how he managed to win the prize for Stratman (some judges felt Stratman's find not proved), although other physicists were favorites. . . . Combine part of Chap. VIII here: from Stratman's point of view. Craig finds Emily studying Swedish. Scene where they study together. Stratman dressing to leave. . . . Stratman has had wire from Dr. Eckart who has news on Stratman's brother Walther. Stratman meets Eckart who explains he helped Walther get to Russia, but now dead, gives mementos for Emily, Walther's daughter. Eckart feels Stratman out so far as working in East Berlin, its potential and future. Eckart offers job, which Stratman refuses. . . . Add most of Chap. IX later."

I closed the second day's work, and had a final outline, after I completed the following notes:

"CHAP. XV: Morning of award ceremony. As seen through Sue Wiley's eyes, press taken on tour of Concert Hall and briefed. . . . At Karolinska, transplant of Öhman's threatens to fail for first time. Garrett realizes, à la Koch, he can't take award. Farelli explains his desperate past and clears self of Nazi-collaboration charges. They work together and save transplant case. . . . Craig tells off Leah and moves out, though she threatens him with destruction. He has message from Emily. Tries to call Emily, can't find her. . . . Phone ringing in Emily's room, but she doesn't answer. She has just learned Max Stratman has had heart attack. Rushes to him. At clinic, learns he is not there. She is then abducted . . . Craig goes to Emily's room. . . . (New note on opening of this chapter: Open with Jacobsson's Journal on previous ceremonies—Kipling, Buck, Hamsun, nearsighted King. Then Jacobsson goes down, meets press, briefs them.) . . . Craig finds door to Emily's room open. Receives tape and message. Finds Max napping. Reads note, plays tape ordering Stratman to defect if he wants Emily back intact. Craig keeps kidnaping from Stratman, acts on his own. . . . Remembers something ex-spy Daranyi said. Runs into Gottling who offers to drive him. Goes to Lilly, reveals his love for Emily. She helps him get to Daranyi. . . ."

And I continued the final outline in this manner to the end of the last chapter.

I was now as ready as I would ever be to undertake the writing of the book. But that night—the night before the beginning—I was afraid. I am always frightened when I am on the verge of starting the writing of a new book. To research, to plan, to plot, to dream, those are as nothing. Actually to write, that is everything. And then comes fear, fear of the overwhelming task ahead, the slavish dedication, the inadequacy.

I was up late that night, alone, drinking, reading.

I wondered—not for the first time, but it always seems the first time—why I was undertaking a novel. Why does anyone ever undertake a novel?

Is the challenge undertaken, as so many critics insisted about my previous novel, purely for money? Is it done, as so many professors have said, to find a means of expressing one's self? Is it, as someone has written, an effort to find some degree of immortality? Or is it done, as Dr. Edmund Bergler, the eminent psychoanalyst, stated after treating thirty-six author-patients, to satisfy a neurotic need for "exhibitionism" and "voyeurism" and "masochism"?

That night, late, I reread sections of W. Somerset Maugham's *Great Novelists and Their Novels*:

"Dr. Johnson, who said that: 'No man but a blockhead ever wrote, except for money,' wrote one of the minor masterpieces of English literature to get enough money to pay for his mother's funeral. Balzac and Dickens without shame wrote for money. The critic's business is to judge the book he is concerned with on its merits. The motives for which the author wrote it have nothing to do with him. . . .

"If one may judge by these examples [Stendhal, Flaubert, Dostoevski, etc.], one may safely say that it is not much of a writer who hates writing. That is not to say that they didn't find it difficult. It is not easy to write well. No one writes as well as he would like to; he only writes as well as he can. . . . Tolstoy and Balzac wrote, rewrote and corrected almost endlessly. But still, to write was their passion. It was not only the business of their lives, but a need as exigent as hunger or thirst."

A livelihood, yes. A passion, a need, yes.

That same night, late, I also reread sections of another Maugham book, *The Summing Up*:

"Every production of an artist should be the expression of an adventure of his soul. This is a counsel of perfection and in an imperfect world a certain indulgence should be bestowed on the professional writer; but this surely is the aim he should keep before him. He does well only to write to liberate his spirit of a subject that he has so long meditated that it burdens him and if he is wise he will take care to write only for the sake of his own peace. . . . For the disadvantages and dangers of the author's calling are offset by an advantage so great as to make all its difficulties, disappointments, and maybe hardships, unimportant. It gives him spiritual freedom. To him life is a tragedy and by his gift of creation he enjoys the catharsis, the purging of pity and terror, which Aristotle tells us is the object of art."

For the sake of peace, yes. For a purging, a catharsis, yes.

I remembered something that I had read in another book, and in the silence of the night and the large house I went to find it. I found it in *Arrow in the Blue* by Arthur Koestler, and now, with the night giving way to the first gray of dawn, I read Koestler:

"I have no idea whether fifty years from now anybody will want to read a book of mine, but I have a fairly precise idea of what makes me, as a writer, tick. It is the wish to trade a hundred contemporary readers against ten readers in ten years' time and one reader in a hundred years' time. This has always seemed to me what a writer's ambition should be."

That one reader, yes.

I went to bed, at last, and lay awake for a long time wondering if there were more.

There was much that went through my head, and some of it I later recaptured when Roy Newquist interviewed me for his book, *Conversations*. Thinking back to that night, I was to tell him:

"There exists a stupid literary tradition . . . that a hungry writer is the best writer—an empty stomach and slum dwelling being considered most conducive to good books, honest books, uncorrupted books. Revolting nonsense, I say. Why can a better novel be produced in a grimy attic than in a Riviera villa? Tolstoi and Flaubert did very well without attics or hunger pangs. The really hungry writer, I truly believe, is the one most susceptible to corruption and dishonesty, for he has a problem that must intrude upon his creativity. The problem is: he must eat. And to eat, he must often put aside writing as he pleases, to write potboilers for the marketplace, to write what he is told to write.

"The writer who has money, enough or a lot, has to compromise with no one, do nothing he does not want to do. He can afford to write as he pleases. There are exceptions, of course. Hungry writers can survive on bread and water, by begging and stealing, and never compromise, and produce fine works. And financially secure writers can lose touch with life or repeat themselves because of a neurotic need for more and more wealth. But generally, I suggest, better books are written by men who have survived starvation, have bank accounts, and are beholden to no one. And in the end, I suspect, rich or poor has nothing to do with it; for if hunger is the driving force behind literary honesty, then the real writer is always hungry, a hunger in the mind, the heart, the conscience."

I thought, late in that black-gray night, about something else, which I also told to Newquist later:

"I think there have always been too many young people who look at the Bromfields, Maughams, Fitzgeralds of their time and say, 'That's what I want,' forgetting what comes before. . . . What these aspirants forget is that every creative person who has attained such fame and freedom did so in the historic literary way —by applying the seat of the pants to the chair—by sitting in a little lonely room or a big lonely room for ceaseless lonely hours, and sweating and cursing and writing word after word, sentence after sentence, alone. Nor is there ever an end to it. . . . If there is to be a next book, it has to be written—alone. The most glamorous, brilliant, prestigious authors still sit by themselves with their tortured psyches and numbed fingers and write and labor under conditions resembling solitary confinement. Tell the boys who want to be authors that that's the name of the game—work."

Work, yes. But why?

Because I have something to say.

Because I am committed.

Long after that difficult night, another interviewer—a French novelist—would ask me in Paris, "Do you consider yourself to be a committed author? If that is the case, is it not true that you do not feel concerned by the critics who remark upon your style and your technique if, as of the moment, you estimate that you have convinced your readers and rallied them to your ideas?" And I was to think about it, and my mind would again go back to my thoughts on that dark gray night, and I would reply:

"I don't think that every writer must be committed. Of course, one is always committed—from the social point of view and in one's current life. But as a writer, it is not absolutely necessary. A writer is what he is; and I think he should write what he feels like writing and do it as best he can. I live in the world of ideas, and I want to propagate my ideas.

"However, experience shows that it is not ideas that permit a work to survive but characters. Ideas change, but man remains. I believe that it is possible that the novel of commitment can be literature, but if it is so, the reason is the depth of its characterizations. But one simply can't think of that as he writes. You simply don't think of such things; you simply write."

I was ready to sleep, and ready to wake.

I was ready to write.

PART

II

GESTATION

EARLY IN THE MORNING of October 19, 1960, I walked across the patio to my study, took out my outline and supplementary notes, sat down before my thirty-year-old rebuilt typewriter, rolled a sheet of white bond into it, thought a while, and slowly I began writing *The Prize*. Throughout the day, with increasing intensity, the periods of furious writing alternated with long halts and interminable pacings, during which I lit and relit my pipe—I yanked out pages, discarding them and doing them over again, and then once more over again. By midafternoon I had finished five double-spaced pages. Pulling my swivel chair up to my desk, I reread them:

"Night had come early to Stockholm, and that meant that autumn was almost gone and winter was near. For Count Bertil Jacobsson, as he walked slowly through the lamplit park, his lion-headed straight cane barely touching the hardened turf, it was a happy time, his favorite time of the year. Soon, as this cold night promised, the winds would come, and the mists sweep in, and eventually the snow and ice, and there would be no guilts about locking himself in his apartment, hibernating among his beloved mementos of a half century, and working on his encyclopedic notes."

I read on to the fifth page. From the Nobel Foundation, old

Jacobsson had, that night, sent off five telegrams notifying five persons that each had been voted one of the Nobel Prizes for that year. Within the hour the telegrams would be transmitted to Swedish Embassies in three nations, and then be relayed to the winners themselves.

I read the concluding paragraphs of this opening section of the book:

"The winners themselves, Jacobsson thought. He knew their names well now, since the long months after the nominations, the investigations, debates, haggling, and voting. He knew their public names and records. But who were they really, these men and women he would be meeting in less than four weeks? How would they feel and be affected? What were they doing now, these pregnant hours before the telegrams arrived and before their greatness became public glory and riches? He wished that he could go along with the telegrams, with each and every one, and see what happened when they reached their destinations.

"Ah, the fancies of an old man, he thought at last. Enough. He must join his colleagues in the upstairs apartment for a drink to a good job done. Still, it would be something, something indeed, to go along with those telegrams . . ."

I finished my rereading, and while, in overall feeling, I thought that I had captured the essence of what I wanted to say, had it the way I had visualized that the novel should begin, I was not satisfied with some parts of the first section. For my opening, the style was too tight. It wanted more ease in the writing, sentences more in tempo with Jacobsson's leisurely stroll. Also, it was too general. While I had mentioned Stockholm in my first sentence, I suspected that I had not evoked the mood of a Swedish city on an autumn night nor had I really made it seem Stockholm, nor had I offered a foretaste of the dark and chilly events to come. And somehow, the first paragraph should become two paragraphs.

I returned to my typewriter, and slowly I began to rewrite.

"The northern night had come early to Stockholm this day, and that meant that autumn was almost gone and the dark winter was near at hand.

"For Count Bertil Jacobsson, as he walked slowly through the lamplit Humlegården park, his lion-headed brown cane barely brushing the hardened turf, it was a happy time, his favorite time of the year. He knew the promise of this cold premature night: the winds would come, and the mists sweep in from Lake Mälaren, and eventually, the snow and ice; and there would be no guilts about locking himself in his crowded, comfortable apartment, hibernating among his beloved mementos of a half century, and working on his encyclopedic Notes."

Better.

It was coming closer to what I wanted, and so I wrote on, carefully reworking the five pages of the opening section. Reaching the last page, I considered the two closing paragraphs. Jacobsson was speculating about what would be happening when the notification telegrams reached their destinations and immediately thereafter. "What were they doing now . . . what happened when they reached their destinations?" Jacobsson could not know, of course. Only my readers would soon know. Still, there was an invitation here to bring in new material that might improve the section. After all, Jacobsson had known previous Nobel Prize winners personally, and I had already stated that he was an informal historian of the Nobel Prize awards and that he maintained "encyclopedic Notes." As an old man, a lover and student of the past, would he not at this point remember what had happened on other occasions after he had sent out his telegrams? Certainly he would. Furthermore, the use of such facts at the outset could anticipate and alleviate any disbelief a reader might feel in the dramatic circumstances under which I would have my characters receive their notifications. I thought about it, and then I began to rewrite, expanding my closing two paragraphs into the following three paragraphs:

"The winners themselves, Jacobsson thought. He knew their names well now, because he had heard them repeated regularly in the long months after their nominations, through the investigations, debates, haggling, and voting. But who were they really, these men and women he would be meeting in less than four weeks? How would they feel and be affected? What were they doing now, these pregnant hours before the telegrams arrived and before their greatness became public glory and riches?

THE PRIZE

A Novel

by

Irving Wallace

Night had come early to Stockholm, and that meant ~~that~~
that autumn was almost gone and winter was near. For Count
Bertil Jacobsson, as he walked slowly through the lamp lit
park, his lion-headed straight cane barely touching the
hardened turf, it was a happy time, his favorite time of the
year. Soon, as this cold, early night promised, the winds
would come, and the mists sweep in, and eventually the snow
and ice, and there would be no guilts about locking himself
in his apartment, hibernating among his beloved mementos of
a half century, and working on his encyclopedic notes.

When he emerged from the park, and stood on the sidewalk
of Sturegatan, he knew that his evening's walk was over
and the exciting business of the night - the culmination of
nine months of intensive activity - was about to begin. For
a moment, almost wistfully, he looked back at the park. What
had recently been so lush and green now stood stark and
denuded, the trees stripped of foliage outlined grotesquely
in the artificial light like gnarled human symbols in a
surrealistic oil. Yet, the symbols were the annual warning
that his favorite season had ~~####~~ arrived and that this would
be a memorable night. ~~How, glancing to the left and then~~

THE PRIZE

by

Irving Wallace

The Northern night had come early to Stockholm this
day, and that meant that autumn was almost gone and ~~that~~
the dark winter was near at hand.

For Count Bertil Jacobsson, as he walked slowly through
the lamp lit park (Humlegården), his lion-headed brown cane barely brushing
the hardened turf, it was a happy time, his favorite time
of the year. He knew the promise of this cold premature
night: the winds would come, and the mists sweep in from
Lake Malaren, and eventually, the snow and ice; and there
would be no guilts about locking himself in his crowded,
comfortable apartment, hibernating among his beloved
mementos of a half century, and working on his encyclopedic
Notes.

Emerging from the park, Count Bertil Jacobsson arrived
at last on the sidewalk of Sturegatan. The evening's
constitutional was over, and the final exciting business of
the night - the culmination of ~~nine~~ ten months of intensive
and abrasive activity - would soon take place. For a moment,
almost wistfully, he turned to look back at the park. To
any other man, what had recently been so lush and green ~~and~~
might now seem stark and denuded, the trees stripped of
foliage and outlined grotesquely in the artificial light
like gnarled symbols of life's end in a surrealistic oil.

"His mind went back to his Notes, to what others in past years
had been doing at the moment of notification: Eugene O'Neill had
been sleeping, and been pulled out of bed to hear the news; Jane
Addams had been preparing to go under ether for a major surgery;
Dr. Harold Urey had been lunching with university professors at
his faculty club; Albert Einstein had got the word on board a ship
from Japan. And the new ones? Where and how would the prize
find them? Jacobsson wished that he could go with the telegrams,
with each and every one, and see what happened when they
reached their destinations.

"Ah, the fancies of an old man, he thought at last. *Nog med
detta.* Enough of this. He must join his colleagues in the upstairs
apartment for a drink to a good job done. Still, it would be something, something indeed, to go along with those telegrams . . ."

This was closer to what I wanted.

I pulled the last page from the typewriter. I made a photocopy of
the opening pages, as a security copy to secrete in another room of
the house, lest a fire (there are recurrent brush fires in the hills near
us) destroy my study and my original manuscript.

Dropping the original copy of those first pages into a file cabinet
drawer, I felt no sense of achievement yet. But I felt good. For this
was a beginning, a start. And now *The Prize* was a living thing that
was a part of me. As I left my study and went back to the house for
a drink, I wondered how long it would be before this brainchild
emerged full-born, and I wondered what shape it would have and
whether it would be attractive and interesting to me and to all men.

How can I recount the pain and pleasure of the actual writing of
this book? I can recall the preparations for it in detail. Notes exist.
I can, and shall, tell of what happened after it was completed. Correspondence, rewrite memorandums, clippings exist. But of the
central act of creation, the writing of the book, there is little raw
evidence left afterwards except for the final manuscripts of the
novel and the published novel itself. What is there of the experience
that still remains stored in the bank of memory? Little that is apparent, and what is stored is mixed with memories of books written
before and since. It is as if there were some psychic healing tissue

that grows over the mind and memory of a writer, covering any visible signs of his despair and depression and exhaustion (even his ridiculous and often premature exhilarations), just as nature has a way of making human beings finally forget physical pain or injury or sorrow. If this did not happen to a writer—if, instead, all of the agonizing creative process stayed vivid in memory—it is unlikely that any author would be able to undertake, to face, to endure the thought of a next book.

So, then, what does exist to help me re-create the writing of *The Prize?* There exists a very tiny lighting, on and off, of remembrance. There exist files of disorganized notes about characters or story points made while I was in the process of writing. There exist a few notations kept in a personal Journal in which I wrote at irregular intervals. There exist copies of my letters written to my research assistant, to my publisher, to my editor, to my literary agent, but not many of these for I was too tired writing the book to write letters, and I usually wrote the letters about other pressing matters, making only brief references to my work on the new novel. And finally, I still have my daily work chart.

I kept a work chart when I wrote my first book—which remains unpublished—at the age of nineteen. I maintained work charts while writing my first four published books. These charts showed the date I started each chapter, the date I finished it, and the number of pages written in that period. With my fifth book, I started keeping a more detailed chart which also showed how many pages I had written by the end of every working day. I am not sure why I started keeping such records. I suspect that it was because, as a free-lance writer, entirely on my own, without employer or deadline, I wanted to create disciplines for myself, ones that were guilt-making when ignored. A chart on the wall served as such a discipline, its figures scolding me or encouraging me.

I had never told anyone about these charts, because I always feared that their existence would be considered eccentric and unliterary. But through the years, I have learned that their usage has not been uncommon among well-known novelists of the fairly recent past. Anthony Trollope, author of more than fifty popular novels including *Barchester Towers,* was perhaps the greatest record-keeper known to literature. In his *Autobiography,* published in 1883, Trollope wrote:

"When I have commenced a new book, I have always prepared a diary, divided into weeks, and carried on for the period which I have allowed myself for the completion of the work. In this I have entered, day by day, the number of pages I have written, so that if at any time I have slipped into idleness for a day or two, the record of that idleness has been there, staring me in the face, and demanding of me increased labour, so that the deficiency might be supplied. According to the circumstances of the time,—whether my other business might be then heavy or light, or whether the book which I was writing was or was not wanted with speed,—I have allotted myself so many pages a week. The average number has been about 40. It has been placed as low as 20, and has risen to 112. And as a page is an ambiguous term, my page has been made to contain 250 words; and as words, if not watched, will have a tendency to straggle, I have had every word counted as I went. . . . There has ever been the record before me, and a week passed with an insufficient number of pages has been a blister to my eye, and a month so disgraced would have been a sorrow to my heart.

"I have been told that such appliances are beneath the notice of a man of genius. I have never fancied myself to be a man of genius, but had I been so I think I might well have subjected myself to these trammels. Nothing surely is so potent as a law that may not be disobeyed. It has the force of the water-drop that hollows the stone. A small daily task, if it be really daily, will beat the labours of a spasmodic Hercules."

This revelation, as well as other confessions made by Trollope, indicated that "he treated literature as a trade and wrote by the clock," and this offended literary assessors and damaged his reputation for years after. Yet numerous authors have been just as meticulous about their writing output and about recording it, and they have fared better in the eyes of the literati. Arnold Bennett, for one, devotedly charted in his *Journal* his daily progress, by word count, for each new novel. Here are some entries from Arnold

Bennett's *Journal* at the time he was writing *The Old Wives' Tale:* "Wednesday, October 9th [1907]. Yesterday I began *The Old Wives' Tale.* I wrote 350 words yesterday afternoon and 900 this morning. I felt less self-conscious than I usually do in beginning a novel. . . . Wednesday, October 16th. I have now written 7,000 words of the first chapter of the novel. . . . Monday, October 21st. Today I finished the second chapter of my novel. . . . Wednesday, October 23rd. I have written over 2,000 words of third chapter yesterday and today. . . . Saturday, October 26th. 18,000 words of *Old Wives' Tale* in 2 weeks 4 days. . . . Friday, January 10th [1908]. 5,400 words in 3 days—despite worry. . . . Wednesday, March 18th. In two hours of work this morning (1,600 words) I absolutely exhausted myself. In 3 days 4,000 words of *Old Wives' Tale,* 2 articles, some verse, and general scheme of long article. . . . Thursday, March 19th. I have never been in better creative form than I am today. A complete scene of the novel (1,700 words) this morning in 2½ hours. . . . Monday, May 11th. Since Tuesday last I have written an average of over 2,000 words a day, including 12,500 words of novel. This makes half of the book, exactly 100,000 words done."

Ernest Hemingway is an example of a word or page counter in recent times. According to the *Paris Review:*

"He keeps track of his daily progress—'so as not to kid myself' —on a large chart made out of the side of a cardboard packing case and set up against the wall under the nose of a mounted gazelle head. The numbers on the chart showing the daily output of words differ from 450, 575, 462, 1250, back to 512, the higher figures on days Hemingway puts in extra work so he won't feel guilty spending the following day fishing on the Gulf Stream."

As I have said, from the first day I began writing books, I kept private charts of my work progress. For *The Prize* I kept a chart posted on my study wall upon which I noted in pencil the number of pages I had written each day, and I found this acted as a conscience and a goad.

Let me see if I can revive, even if sketchily, something of the four and a half to five months it took me to write the first draft of *The Prize.*

As on my first writing day on the novel, work began every morning around ten o'clock, and usually ended every afternoon around six, give or take an hour, with a one-hour break somewhere in between for a sandwich lunch and a glance at the day's incoming mail.

How can a writer adhere to such rigid hours? Once, long ago, deceived by the instructors, professors, by an old romantic tradition, I had believed that a writer writes only when he feels like it, only when he is touched by mystic inspiration. But then, after studying the work habits of novelists of the past, I realized that most successful writers invest their work with professionalism. From Balzac, who worked six to twelve hours a day, and Flaubert, seven hours a day, and Conrad, eight hours a day, to Maugham, who worked four hours a day, and Aldous Huxley, five hours a day, and Hemingway, six hours a day, these authors were uniformly industrious, and when they were once launched upon a book they wrote regularly, day in and day out. While the story may be apocryphal—I should like to believe it is not—it is said that Victor Hugo sometimes forced himself to work regularly by confining himself to his study. To do this, he had his valet take away every stitch of his clothing, and ordered this servant not to return his attire until the hour when he expected to be through with his day's writing.

In short, no matter how they effected their routines, the vast majority of published authors have kept, and do keep, some semblance of regular daily hours. Indeed, if they did not, the libraries of the world would stand nearly empty. Occasionally, the hour-keepers were inspired when they went to their desks, but if they were not, they simply wrote as well as they could, as craftsmen, and hoped for the best.

For myself, I have found that the writing of a long work of fiction is so demanding upon my mind and emotions—so much a life lost in the processes of creating fictional people who become more real than the real people around me—that I do not wait for the Muse to lead me to my desk nor, once writing, can I stop. In doing *The Prize,* I kept long hours. On the best days, the inspired days, I knew that I was delivering to the limit of my capabilities, and every page produced was usable. On the worst days, if what I had turned out after seven or eight hours of writing was flat, dull, wrong, undeniably bad, I would discard the pages, and start at the beginning of the same section the following morning. These were the long days I worked. These were six-day weeks, sometimes seven. And most of the evenings, after wife talk and children talk, were devoted to making notes on scenes that lay immediately ahead, thinking them out, developing them, making rough drafts of them in longhand, and then going to books for my ever-continuing research.

There were some terrible, empty, wasted days—horrible days and dreadful nights when, as F. Scott Fitzgerald put it, "in a real dark night of the soul it is always three o'clock in the morning, day after day." Those were the times when I wanted to give up, when I felt that I did not have the gift needed to transfix the brilliant fancies lodged high in my brain upon the blank sheets of paper so far below, that what left my teeming mind became misshapen and ugly in space and thudded down on paper strangled by the limitations of words, cloddish and leaden words, words barely reflecting the marvelous imaginings in my head. I felt the frustration that so many novelists have felt throughout history, the frustration so exactly expressed by Gustave Flaubert in a letter to his off-and-on mistress Louise Colet: "I am irritated by my writing. I am like a violinist whose ear is true, but whose fingers refuse to reproduce precisely the sounds he hears within."

Those were the times, also, when I reached dead ends, when my plans proved faulty and led into black walls, when there was no light, so that the characters could not walk ahead, where nothing could move, where all thought was stifled and I was helpless. Those were the times when the novel was not the novel I had meant to write or hoped to write, when it went its own way, not naturally, not recognizable or right, somebody else's bastard. Those were the times when, late at night and alone with *it,* I wondered if there were not better ways to spend one's time on earth, better livelihoods and careers, better areas for self-expression. Then it seemed to me as if every other man was sensible and normal, since he could shut the ledger on the workday at five o'clock and seek hedonistic rewards, whereas I could not shut anything off for even one of twenty-four hours, because a whole new damn demon planet, inhabited by people that I had created, was orbiting around in my skull and wouldn't let me have peace or pleasure. Those were the worst times. But in the soothing distance of retrospect, they were the exceptional times.

For, as I recall, far more of my working days were difficult but productive days, filled with the exciting new life I was living on paper. The choicest of these were incomparable days sweet in memory. I had fascinating new friends in my head and on paper, friends all my own that no one else knew, friends who were so close as to be part of me, and if they were troubled or in trouble, they would do my bidding so that I could help them. With these friends I enjoyed refreshing new adventures, more exotic and intense than any I had known in my own life, and we were sharing them together, and it was thrilling and each day with them was vitally alive. And sometimes, at the end of a strange absorbed day—where had the swift hours gone?—I would sit back and glance at the small pile of pages I had written, and know that what I had written was the best writing I could do, that the words had come out almost exactly as I had dreamed they would, and the accomplishment of the day was not nebulous, was very real, had substance, could be touched, could be read, might please others as it now pleased me. Not too many of such choice days, but some, enough to sustain me.

The inner creative process, in that period, was of two kinds, assuming that it can be accurately described at all. Sometimes I would consider my characters and a scene I had planned for them, and the end that should grow naturally out of the scene, and I would sit and think rationally, logically, of how these characters would behave in this situation. Or I would rise, and pace my study floor, as I consciously, objectively, considered what should be done, could be done, or what these people of mine might have done.

But more frequently a different kind of creative action took place inside my head. It was a process over which I had little control. In this process, I would study my sketchy outline of what might follow after what I had already written, and gradually the characters and background and situation would drift from outline into my mind, and there the characters would behave on their own, moving as they wished, speaking to one another as they liked, behaving in the manner that best suited each one of them. These mental playlets, staged in my head, seemed not to result from the conscious me, and I would sit in my chair and watch them with my mind's eye as if I were merely a spectator. Then, suddenly realizing that I was more than a mere spectator, realizing that I was the recorder of the emotions and dialogues and activities of these people, I would grab up a pencil and try to capture what I had just witnessed inside my head. And then, from these hastily scrawled transcriptions, I would write, with care, applying as much art as I could to these episodes.

Few authors have been able to explain the miracle of these near-spontaneous, unprompted inner playlets, but most novelists I've asked have confessed that this was the way it happened to them when they wrote their books, too.

Recently, in rereading *The Literary Situation* by Malcolm Cowley, I was pleased to find that he understood this kind of creative process but had explained it in another way: "The writer . . . is a person who talks to himself, or better, who talks in himself. Usually when alone, but sometimes also in company, he conducts a silent conversation that is often described as a solitary monologue; in most cases it is really a dialogue. . . . One of the speakers is the writer himself, and the other is his inner audience. The writer does most of the talking; perhaps he starts by presenting a situation in what he thinks are the right words to impress the audience, which seems to consist of a single person. . . . Often—perhaps in most cases—the finished story is a transcription and revision of what the writer has already told his inner audience."

Or, I might add, at least in my case, the finished story of *The Prize* was a transcription and revision of what I had seen and overheard of my characters as they performed on the stage of my brain for an inner audience consisting of one person—me.

Much of this unconscious, as well as conscious, creating of my novel took place after my daytime working hours. Late at night, perhaps an hour or two before going to bed, I would sit alone at the dining room table with notepaper and pencil, and think of what scenes I wanted to do the following day or in the days thereafter. I would jot down ideas, emotions and behavior of this character or that, fragments of dialogue, notions of how to develop story twists and turnings, all of this forming notes for prose as yet unwritten. Also, more consciously, on those late evenings, I would take up my seven-page single-spaced typed outline, and see what I had planned ahead for the next day. Then I might take three sentences of that basic outline and think about them, and accept what came to me from the inner playlet, and expand the terse three sentences to perhaps three scribbled pages, which enlarged and defined and dramatized what had earlier been only literary shorthand.

These crude nightly notes on *The Prize,* many of which I have saved, are reminders of much that went on inside me, and, indeed, offer some evidence of how the novel developed from one day to the next.

Let me illustrate by showing the actual development of several scenes while I was engaged in writing them.

In Chapter I, I planned a scene where the hero, Andrew Craig, was to be notified that he has won the Nobel Prize in literature:

Character Notes, October 6, 1960: "Telegram comes on wire to Miller's Dam, Wisconsin, but girl busy in back room with a boy. Meantime, comes in on local AP wire, and young reporter sees it, telephones, then queries for interview, and tries to rouse up someone. (No, not this way. Instead, end on telephone call.) . . . Sister-in-law on phone. As she hangs up, Dr. Lucius Mack comes downstairs, says has put Craig to bed. She tells of call. How could this be—not written in years. Mack says could be—GBS got for year didn't write. Suddenly, official wire comes. . . . Upstairs, Craig not asleep. Lying, thinking. Just fragments. Maybe nods off. Someone at door. They wake him now, tell him news. Wants to sleep. Force black coffee. . . . An interview for AP. Then visitor, publisher or head of state library, deal offered—but he has passed out."

Final Outline, October 18, 1960: "In Miller's Dam, Wisconsin, Andrew Craig passes out drunk, then Leah awakens him with the news."

Notes Before Writing Scene, November 2, 1960: "Lucius Mack puts Craig to sleep, goes downstairs. Leah waiting, drink milk, a scene. Phone or visit from Binninger of Mack's paper. News of prize. AP and UPI and others on way. . . . They wake Craig. Tell news. Dress him. Downstairs fill him with black coffee. Leah finds him attractive. . . . Craig has informal interview with Mack. Then AP arrives for formal interview. Finally head of library near Madison comes down. Offers honorary job like Archibald MacLeish had with Lib. of Congress—board meeting Jan. 2. Craig must perform well. No scandal. (Midwestern Historical Society.) $12,000 a year—time to write. . . . When come back Craig has passed out. Leah worried."

Further Notes Before Writing Scene, November 2, 1960: "Binninger in kitchen. Leah kisses Craig. . . . Drinks coffee. Mack starts interview with Craig, oddly never knew many facts on friend. . . . Doorbell. Mack: If it's press, tell them has flu. I'll talk for him. Let them stay over, see him tomorrow or later. . . . Inglis arrives—congrats—lists immortals—has big job offer. . . . Call from NY—lecture agent—Hollywood agent—publisher —everything going for him if prove sobriety by good show in Sweden, appearing sober. . . . Mack resumes interview. . . . Craig feels self slipping away—GBS and life belt and self—then he passes out cold."

The following morning I began writing the end scene of Chapter I, where Andrew Craig is notified that he has been awarded the Nobel Prize in literature. I had my notes, but the scene was difficult because I wanted to show my hero in a drunken state, thus underlining the depths to which he had fallen as contrasted with the high honor that he was about to receive. Because he was drunk, and asleep early in the scene, I could not write it from inside him, from his point of view. So I wrote it from the point of view of his closest friend, Lucius Mack, the editor of the local weekly newspaper. I tried to establish Craig's situation with a further scene between Mack, representing hope for Craig, and Craig's sister-in-law and caretaker, Leah Decker, representing hopelessness for Craig. After the stunning news came that Craig had won the Nobel Prize, I brought Craig, half drunk and sleepy, back into the scene, and tried to show the exciting things that immediately start happening to a laureate. I tried to project the uneasy feeling that each person involved with Craig has about his future performance, to set up a strand of suspense about his visit to Stockholm, and finally I tried to keep Craig in character by showing his defeat and cynicism. This last I dramatized at the close of the scene and of the chapter itself, and this is how it came out in the published draft:

"Leah signaled Inglis, and he quietly rose and tiptoed out of the kitchen after her. Mack followed them.

"Andrew Craig was alone.

"He felt a thousand years tired, and his head felt stuffed and heavy, and his deadened, sodden nerves begged for unconsciousness. He circled his arms on the table, and laid his head in his arms, and tried not to think of the turn of events. But his fatigued brain did not sleep. He thought: I was only trying to die slowly, peacefully, unobtrusively, like a forgotten old plant in the shade. He thought: Why did those Swedes expose and humiliate me by forcing me to die in public? He thought: I'm an immortal now, in the record books, but I'm as sickeningly mortal as I was when I awakened this morning. He remembered George Bernard Shaw's sardonic remark, when he received the Nobel Prize at sixty-nine: 'The money is a life belt thrown to a swimmer who has already reached the shore.' He thought: Only in my case I'd rewrite it . . . a life belt thrown to a man after he's drowned. He thought: Nothing.

"Andrew Craig had passed out."

In Chapter IV, I planned a joint press conference in Stockholm at which Dr. John Garrett was to appear with Dr. Carlo Farelli, who Garrett believed had stolen his medical discovery and whom he hated for sharing half of his Nobel Prize in medicine:

Character Notes, October 11, 1960: "In Stockholm, Magill [as I called Garrett before starting the book] and Italian give joint press conference. Magill speaks over their heads—and Italian interrupts, explains grafts in common terms, and takes over whole conference. In papers next day quotes are from Italian—and Magill feels reduced to status of lab technician."

Final Outline, October 18, 1960: "The Count looks in as Garrett and Farelli being questioned, with Farelli taking over as Garrett steams. Garrett obtuse, Farelli popular, full of analogies."

<u>Notes Before Writing Scene</u>: "Jacobsson sees press concentrating on Farelli—can see why—wonders whether Garrett senses this. . . . Garrett also overwhelmed by Farelli. Expected monster, finds him charming and friendly, is speechless—Farelli gives him credit, like tolerant parent. . . . Farelli tells—History of transplants and grafts, Basic Problem, How overcame, His own discovery (Istituto Superiore di Sanita). Then Garrett's discovery, but he makes it his own so Garrett can't top him, only weakly repeat information. . . . Asked if worked together? Farelli: No, this was like 1950 award to Kendall and Reichstein. . . . Future of transplants—Garrett equivocates, speaks of only few cases. Farelli quickly promises immortality, the 'improved' man of future. . . . Garrett speaks of other heart surgeons. Farelli plays up Dr. Öhman, Garrett's Swedish friend. Garrett tries to prove Öhman is *his* friend and not Farelli's. . . . Most-overlooked medical men? Garrett can think of none. Farelli suggests an American and Freud —Garrett jealous, furious, because Italian thought of not only his countryman but someone in his preserve of Dr. Keller and his group therapy."

In the next few days I had written the actual scene in first draft. In this confrontation between the two Nobel Prize winners in medicine, I tried to heighten the conflict, at least from Garrett's paranoidal point of view, by showing the American overwhelmed by Farelli. At the end of the scene, I had a Swedish reporter ask Garrett whether he could think of any great medical names of the past overlooked by the Nobel Committee. In what follows, as it appeared in the published version, I carefully used researched facts not merely to parade information but as a realistic means by which Farelli could prove himself a formidable foe for Garrett, and as a bludgeon to hurt Garrett in order to build his resentment and thus motivate a bigger showdown later in the narrative. Could Garrett think of any medical names that had been overlooked? I wrote:

"Garrett could think of several such names, but his natural timidity prevented him from putting them forward. The Nobel Foundation had been generous to him. He did not want to insult its judges. 'No,' he said, at last, 'I can't think of one great name your committee has ever overlooked. I concur with their decisions completely. Since 1901, they have honored all who deserved to be honored.'

"He relaxed, satisfied with himself. He had accomplished what Farelli had tried to accomplish—he had given the Swedes pride in their judgment—and he had done a better job of it.

" 'Dr. Farelli.' It was the *Expressen* reporter again. 'Are you in agreement with your fellow laureate?'

"The Italian smiled at Garrett, and then at the press. 'I believe Dr. Garrett and I are in accord on most matters, but I am afraid we are not so on this one. You wish to know if your Nobel Committee has overlooked any great doctors, deserving of the prize in the past? Yes, indeed they have. Two unfortunate omissions come to mind. One was an American. I think Dr. Harvey Cushing, of Boston, deserved a Nobel Prize for techniques he introduced in brain surgery. The Caroline Institute had thirty-eight opportunities to reward him, and failed to do so. The other omission, that of an Austrian, was even more serious. I refer to Dr. Sigmund Freud, founder of psychoanalysis. I find his neglect by the Nobel Committee, between 1901 and 1939, incomprehensible. I cannot imagine why he was not honored. Because he had once dabbled in hypnotism? Because organized medicine in Austria fought him? Because psychoanalysis was not an exact science? All mere quibbling. He remains the colossus of our century. His original discoveries in the field of psychology and mental disturbance have enriched our medicine. Those are the only black marks against the Caroline Institute in an otherwise brilliant record of judgment. I am proud to belong to their honor roll.'

"Garrett had listened to all of this with an increasing sense of shame at his own dishonesty and lack of candor. With envy, he watched the scribbling pencils among the press corps. He glanced at Farelli's profile, and hated its Latin smugness more than ever before. He hated Farelli for his own weakness and the other's unerring showmanship. He hated Farelli, an Italian, for extolling the virtues of an American, Dr. Cushing, and thus marking Garrett's own lack of patriotism. He hated Farelli, an extrovert, for robbing him of Dr. Freud, an introvert's property, a property that was justly his own every time he paid ten dollars to Dr. Keller for another group therapy session.

"He hated Farelli, but it seemed useless, like abominating an overwhelming force of nature."

In Chapter V, I planned a scene at the King's Banquet in the Royal Palace, where Craig would first meet Emily Stratman, niece of the prize winner in physics:

Character Notes, October 6, 1960: "Cocktail party. Craig meets other winners—French couple, American and Englishman physicians [a week later, I made latter an Italian], German and niece."

Final Outline, October 18, 1960: "Go to Royal Banquet; action at cocktail hour. Craig has been drinking heavily. Sees Emily, dimly, alone. Attracted by her. Makes advances. She withdraws, after rebuffing him."

Notes Before Writing Scene: "Craig goes to Royal Palace. Describe Palace on tour. . . . Craig introduced to Norwegian peace rep and industrialist Hammarlund—by Ingrid Påhl—they argue Peace Prizes. . . . Craig sees Emily—follows her—scene between them, he rebuffed. Leah breaks it up."

Further Notes Before Writing Scene: "1. Craig had been watching Emily—saw her leave, heading for waiter and last drink. He goes, orders one, too. . . . 2. Introduces self. Yes, she says, he was pointed out. Is she Stratman's daughter? No, niece. . . . 3. She seems upset. He doesn't want say wrong thing. She repeats what happened to upset. Tells about herself. . . . 4. Drink comes to him. Studies her. Feels uncomfortable, against entire room. Explains Leah. Emily knows, has read about him. Also read his books, rereading one now. . . . 5. Discuss his books. . . . 6. He questions how she lives, if ever married. She pulls back. . . . 7. She questions him. He wants to impress her, makes it up, lies. . . . 8. He gets her in next room, says she is beautiful, acts extravagantly, crazy, wants to kiss her. . . . 9. She tightens up, tries to leave. He stops her. Apologizes, senses her inner damage, like his own. Apologizes for drinking, he is not ordinarily like this. She not interested. He pleads. . . . 10. Leah comes in—watches—breaks into scene—King coming—Emily goes—Leah and Craig go in to meet King."

Based on these notes, I wrote a first draft of the scene. My purpose was to bring the hero and heroine of the novel together, to show that Craig could be seriously interested in a woman again, to suggest that there is something strange about Emily, to end their first beginning in disagreement, and to establish Leah's antagonism toward Emily. In the published version, Craig notices the girl across the room, and when he sees her approach a waiter for a drink, he quickly heads for the same waiter. Then Craig introduces himself:

" 'Well, if we haven't met—we might as well. I'm Andrew Craig. I'm—'

" 'I know,' she said. 'You were pointed out to me when you came in. Congratulations.'

" 'Thank you. Are you Professor Stratman's daughter?'

" 'I'm his niece.'

" 'I see. He's a bachelor, isn't he?'

" 'Very.'

" 'And you take care of him?'

" 'Probably the other way around.' She hesitated, and then added, 'My uncle is self-sufficient. I'm not.'

"He regarded her closely. She was taller than he had expected. The short black hair shone as it caught the lights. The curls along her cheeks enclosed her maiden's face and gave it piquancy. The words 'vestal virgin' crossed his mind, yet the slanting eyes, Oriental emerald in color, made 'vestal virgin' impossible. Her serenity enchanted him. Here was the picture of self-possession, yet she had just remarked that she was not self-sufficient.

" 'I was watching you, a few minutes ago, in that group with your uncle,' he said. 'I was impressed by your poise—the gift of *sang-froid,* which the French so admire—until you suddenly seemed upset and broke away. Are you still upset?'

"She considered him, for the first time, with wonder. 'Yes, quite

upset. Don't let the façade deceive you. It took years to build, to
have a place to hide.' She paused, as if astonished with herself. 'I
don't know why I'm telling you this. I must be drunk. This is my
fourth champagne.'

" 'I'm the one who must be drunk, to have even brought it up.'
He was compelled to go further. 'I only asked about your being
upset because I didn't want to say the wrong thing to you. I can't
explain. It suddenly seemed important, that's all.'

" 'I don't mind. It's all right.'

" 'You know my name. I don't know yours.'

" 'Emily Stratman. Birthplace Germany. Naturalized American
citizen. Raised in New York City since fifteen—or was it sixteen?
Now resident of Atlanta, Georgia. Have I left anything out?'

" 'Yes. Marital status.'

" 'Aggressively single.'

" 'The result of a broken marriage?'

" 'Is this how writers get their material? No marriage. Not past,
present, or future.' "

As I wrote scene after scene, I particularly looked forward to
undertaking Chapter VII. I had never forgotten the material that a
director of *Collier's* had censored, in the article I had written thirteen years earlier, and constantly, in the back of my mind, there
was the idea of using some of this censored material to help advance Andrew Craig's personal story in the novel.

For the novel I had created the character of Gunnar Gottling, an
eccentric, scandalous, bombastic, bitter man, one of Sweden's best
writers who had been denied the Nobel award because of his background, behavior, and belligerence. Gottling was based one part on
what I knew of Strindberg, one part on a writer friend of mine now
dead, and one part on what was conjured up in my imagination
(stimulated by my feelings about the material that had been censored by *Collier's* so long ago). I knew that Gottling must meet
Craig—an obligatory scene—and out of his profane bitterness toward, and knowledge of, the Nobel committees, he must give Craig
some secret information about how Craig had won the award. This
information would, in turn, cast Craig into deeper despair, compel

him to perform a certain way, and prepare him for the showdown
confrontation with the politically involved Nobel judge, Carl Adolf
Krantz, in the climax of the book.

Where to set this scene? I remembered an evening outside of
Stockholm on my last visit, and immediately I consulted my Journal. My Swedish publisher had taken me for a drive in his Merce-
des, and under "July 19, 1960," I had recorded:

"Drove to a tavern—Djurgårdsbrunns Wärdshus—Royal Deer
Park Inn—reception room—to left, restaurant—to right a bar—in
bar as you entered, to left a bar with stools and some people
seated, to its right, set high, a TV with children being interviewed
on the single gov't channel, and below it a pock-marked old dart
board—tables and chairs, many covered with plaid or checkered
horse-blanket material, although leather seats along wall. Cognacs
and liqueurs served by bartender who spoke crisp and perfect English."

I had the characters and setting and story point to be made, and
at last I had the proper place in the book to integrate with my
fiction those facts that I had been unable to publish thirteen years
ago. I began to write the scene. Craig and Gottling had been introduced to one another in the Grand Hotel. They had driven to the
Wärdshus for some drinks and writer talk. But soon Gottling was
telling why he himself had not won the Nobel Prize, and elaborating on the nepotism, prejudices, politics that infested the award-
giving. Here is the manner in which I went on to develop the scene,
or a portion of it, in my first draft:

" 'I don't think that's a secret,' said Craig. 'Jacobsson took me
up to the Academy yesterday, and he was damn honest about the
literary voting. He said there was good and bad.'

" 'Jacobsson,' Gottling muttered, rolling his glass on the table.
'Count Bertil Jacobsson? That old stuffed parrot, he should have
been put in a time capsule years ago. He lives in the past. He has
nothing to do with breathing people. Why do you think the Foundation supports him? Because he's a front—he's got blue blood, he
knew Nobel, he makes with the erudition and history—and part of
his gambit is to anticipate criticism. I wager you ten to one, he gave
you the old routine—why Tolstoi and Ibsen and Hardy didn't get

it—but reminding you of all the big names that did. It's all technique to disarm visitors and send them off beaming. Studied frankness to strip you of your objectivity. And another wager. I'll bet you he wasn't frank enough to confess how the Nobel committees have always sucked around the Germans—like that turd, Krantz—and looked down their noses at the Americans, at least until the Second World War, and how they got a permanent boycott going on the Russians.'

"The whiskey had gone to Craig's head, and the room reeled. 'I like Jacobsson,' he said.

" 'You Americans love everybody,' growled Gottling, 'just to be sure somebody loves you. What crap. So you like Jacobsson. But did he tell you how his Nobel crew ass-licked the Germans and put the knife in the Russians?'

" 'No, he didn't. I better have another drink.'

" 'Me, too. . . . Hey, Lars, refills!' He turned his bloodshot eyes back to Craig. 'You like this old Wärdshus?'

" 'Greatest place on earth,' said Craig thickly.

" 'You're damn right.'

" 'What about the hun?' asked Craig.

" 'Germans? Forty-nine prizes in sixty years. Russians? Seven prizes in sixty years, and lucky at that.'

" 'I'd say that shows courage,' said Craig, 'thumbing your nose at Russia, when they're looking down your throat.'

" 'Courage, ha!' exploded Gottling. 'Every Swede is scared stiff of Russia, and when it counts, Sweden crawls. Why do you think we didn't join NATO? Because we're afraid of Russia, that's why. I wish we had half the guts that Norway has. They defied the Nazis, when we didn't, and now they defy the Communists, when we won't. . . . So we're yellow, a yard wide, and we know it, and we don't like it. So how do we salve our national conscience? We make believe we're men by childish crap—by sticking our tongues out and keeping the Nobel Prize from Russia. So where does that put the holy Nobel Prize? It puts it in local politics. It makes the prize a political instrument that you dumbheads in America—except the Polacks—consider an honest honor. Christ, what crap.'

"The new drinks came, and Craig spilled part of his before he brought it to his mouth. 'You said something about the prize being anti-American and pro-German—'

" 'That's what I said. Cold figures. I may be looped, but I got it all in my head. Take chemistry. Only one American, Richards of Harvard, won it in thirty-one years. Take physics. Only one American, Michelson of good old Chicago, took it in twenty-two years. Take literature. Only one American, Red Lewis, in thirty-five years. Take medicine. Only two Americans, Carrel and Landsteiner, in thirty-two years. But the Germans—oh, our Nobel boys worshiped them. Fifteen winners in the first ten years, not counting the peace prize, which isn't worth spitting on. In Sweden, if you could show a degree from Frankfort on the Main or Heidelberg, you were practically nominated. For forty-some years, those krauts were the superior race over here, Nordics just like us. But when you kicked the hell out of them in the Second War, and when you came up with the atom bomb, there was a fast shuffle in all the Nobel committees—and now they pour prizes at you and Great Britain like it was confetti. Don't ever talk to me about impartiality, when you talk to me about that lousy prize you won.'

" 'What's wrong with the prize I won?' Craig peered at Gottling with owl eyes and spilled his drink again.

" 'What's wrong? Haven't you been listening to me? You plastered or something? I told you about Russia—'

" 'I forgot.'

" 'Seven Russians in sixty years in five categories, and not one of them a clean-cut award. It's not just anti-Communism. It's plain anti-Russianism. We been shaking in our boots since the time of the Czar. What happened in physiology and medicine in the first sixty awards? Old Pavlov should have carted off that first award hands down. But no, the Committee kept snubbing him for four years, until there was so much pressure they gave in. And they had to give half of Ehrlich's prize to a Russian in 1908, because it was on the record he deserved half the credit for advances in immunity. Two stinking medicine awards to Russia in sixty years and none in a half century of that sixty years. Take a look at chemistry. One-half of the 1956 prize, and that's it, brother, that's all in sixty years. What about physics? One prize, divided among three Russians, in sixty years. There's your science awards. I'm not a Russky lover. I told you before, they stink. But what's that got to do with accomplishment? That's a country where they've done the best work in longevity and genetics and stuck a Sputnik and a guy named Gagarin in the sky. That's a country where they invented artificial penises for soldiers wounded in the war. That's a country where Popov demonstrated radio transmission before Marconi, and where Tsiolkovsky had multistage rockets in 1911. But not according to our Swedish Academy of Science—no. According to our Nobel idiots, Russia is the land without scientists. And those idiots in Oslo are just as bad. Russia didn't get a single Peace Prize in sixty years, but Germany—Germany!—got three and France eight and you Americans twelve. And now, my son, we're home again—literature.'

" 'Bunin and Pasternak,' mumbled Craig.

" 'Ivan Bunin and Boris Pasternak—two Russians in sixty years. Ever think who lived and wrote in Russia in those sixty years? We all know about Tolstoi being turned down nine times. But what about Chekhov and Andreyev and Artsybashev and Maxim Gorky —Gorky was around until 1936. Nothing.'

" 'Bunin and Pasternak,' repeated Craig.

" 'Phony!' bellowed Gottling, but no one in the Wärdshus bar so much as looked up. 'Bunin was a White Russian refugee, an anti-Communist, who lived in Paris and translated Longfellow's "Hiawatha." He hadn't been in Russia in fifteen years, when you Americans pitched for him and put him across in 1933. And old Boris Pasternak, the matinée idol with good guts, out there in his *dacha*—who gave a damn about him when he was writing solid poetry? Who honored him then? Not the spineless Nobel judges, I assure you. But the minute he put out that novel that criticized communism, the minute he had the nerve to say what every Swede was afraid to say, they crowned him with the prize he couldn't accept. Someday, I got to write advice to writers all over the world. I got to tell them, "Writers, Arise! If you're Russian, if you're American, no matter what, grind out an anti-Russian potboiler and get it translated into Swedish, and you're in. You get the Nobel Prize and the big boodle. Just like Andrew Craig." ' '

"Craig squinted at Gottling through bleary eyes. 'What in the hell does that mean?'

" 'The facts of life, kid,' said Gottling, belching, and swallowing his gin, 'the facts of life. Why do you think you got the Nobel Prize? Because you're a hotshot author? Because you're the best this year? Because you're the leading idealistic literary creator on earth? That what you think? That what Jacobsson and that bag, Ingrid Påhl, told you? Because you're somebody, in the league with Kipling and Undset and Galsworthy and O'Neill? Crap! You're nothing, and the Nobel boys know it, and everyone in Scandinavia on the inside knows it. You're here on a phony pass, because they wanted to use you, and that's all. And, brother, that's the truth. Have another drink?'

" 'What are you talking about?' said Craig. His brain and mouth were fuzzy, but a distant alarm registered. 'Is this some more of your sour grapes?'

" 'I'm the only guy in Sweden with guts enough to level with you, Craig. I got enough pity for that. I don't want to see you making a horse's ass of yourself. The Nobel Prize for literature to Andrew Craig? Ha! Crap. The Nobel Prize for anti-Russian propaganda, that's what it should be. You won because the Swedes have been having a diplomatic squabble with the Russians over two islands in the Baltic Sea—you never read about that, did you?—and the Swedes are going to lose, and crawl, and eat crow. But they got to keep face—that's our one Orientalism, keeping face—and so, knowing they got to lose, they unloaded a rabbit punch at the Commies by honoring your little anti-Communist fiction, *The Perfect State*. That's to show we're big boys, not afraid of anybody, even when we crawl.'

" 'You're making it up, Gottling. You're bitter, and you've got to get your jollies some way. If the Swedish Academy wanted to blast Russia through an award, they could find novelists in a dozen countries who'd written stronger anti-Soviet books.'

" 'Oh, no. You're blind, man, you don't see at all. An award to a writer of a work overtly anti-Russian would be too dangerous— they don't want Pasternak all over again. That was too much of a sweat—they don't want to stand up and body-punch. Like I said, they just wanted to sneak in a quick rabbit punch, for face, for conscience. Your novel is anti-Russian, all right, but you got to cut away the sugar coating to know. If Moscow gets sore, and they have—I read *Ny Dag,* that's our Commie sheet here—the Swedish Academy can just look surprised—and they have, too—and shrug and say they were honoring a pure historical novel about Plato and ancient Syracuse. You see? But everybody knows different. Only the way it is, nobody can prove it. It's a scared gesture, like whistling in the dark, just like yours is a scared book.' "

Thus, *The Prize* was being written.

As I built momentum, the story came out, occasionally rolled out beyond my control. At the start I had pushed my people, my story, but at some crossroad they had suddenly started pulling me with them, after them, and it would surprise and confound me, when I went to dinner after my day's work, that only my son David, my daughter Amy, my wife Sylvia were seated there, and that Andrew Craig and Denise Marceau and Max Stratman and John Garrett were not also at the table.

The chart that I had posted on the wall behind me began to have a busy look. Following that first working day, October 19, where I had noted "Pages—5," there was a run of eight consecutive productive days. There was a faltering on my second day of work, October 20, "Pages—1," my chart said. But after that I was writing hard. The chart describes it: October 21, "Pages—7," October 22, "Pages—7," October 23, Sunday, day of rest; October 24, "Pages—6," October 25, "Pages—8," October 26, "Pages—6," October 27, "Pages—10," October 28, "Pages—3; [made research] notes."

Reviewing this work chart now, I see that in November of 1960, there were five out of twenty-six working days when I produced nothing, nary a page, whereas in the last five days of that month I wrote fifty-four first-draft pages. In December, in the week before Christmas, I wrote forty-two pages, then took off two days for the holiday.

And now it was 1961. On January 3, I noted "Pages—6," and I was well into Chapter VI of a twelve-chapter book. On January 10, when I finished Chapter VI, the chapter ran ninety-eight pages

THE PRIZE

1960

	PAGES
October 19	5
October 20	1
21	7
22	7
October 24	6
25	8
26	6
27	10
28	3
29	0
October 31	12
November 1	10
2	9
3	15

20 —

33 —

NOTES

November 28	12
29	12
30	10
December 1	5
2	11
3	0
December 5	14
6	9
7	9
8	10
9	16
10	0
December 12	0
13	9

50

58

NOVEMBER			
7	0	research
8	0	election	29
9	6
10	7
11	8
12	10
NOVEMBER 14	14
15	6
16	9
17	15
18	12
19	4
21	13
22	10
23	15
24	0	holiday	26
25	20
26	0

16	5	research
17	0
DECEMBER 19	6
20	12
21	12
22	4
23	4
24	3
DECEMBER 26	0	holiday
27	8
28	0	research
29	11
30	7
31	0

36
31 — 41
60 — 26
58 — at this pt 461 pages

THE PRIZE - II

1961

	PAGES			PAGES
JANUARY 2	0	HOLIDAY	FEBRUARY 6	19
3	6		7	18
4	11		8	21
5	11		9	14
6	9		10	20
7	8		11	0 RESEARCH
JANUARY 9	16		FEBRUARY 13	15
10	18		14	24
11	5		15	19
12	12		16	20
13	13		17	11
14	6		18	3
JANUARY 16	20		19	8
17	18		20	20

45

70

92

92

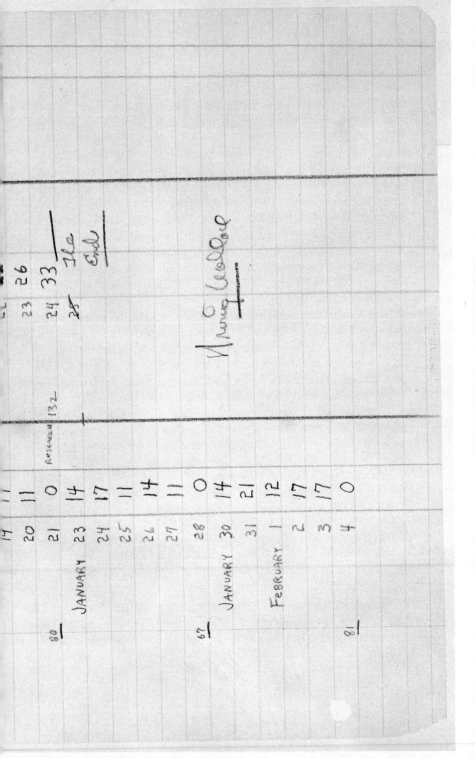

19	11
20	11
21	0
JANUARY 23	14
24	17
25	11
26	14
27	11
28	0
JANUARY 30	14
31	21
FEBRUARY 1	12
2	17
3	17
4	0

80

67

81

Arsenal 132

23 26
24 33
25 The End

Murray Waddell

long, and I had reached page 540 of my manuscript. Ten days later, I had written the 114 pages which composed Chapter VII, and I had arrived at page 654 of my manuscript, which, as it would turn out, meant I was past the midway mark and into the last half of the book.

As I came nearer and nearer to the climax and to the end, I wrote more and more steadily, entirely absorbed, totally pulled, and I started passing up meals, limiting my time with my family, canceling social engagements. On February 18, 1961, I started Chapter XII, the last chapter of *The Prize,* and I wrote with such intensity that I completed 127 pages in six days. Early in the evening of February 24, 1961, I reached page 1,115 of the novel. I wrote the last sentence: "And so, at last, at last, he could go on. . . ." Then I typed in caps THE END, and the first draft of *The Prize* was done.

But a chart can tell only the mathematical history of a book. What had gone on behind the written pages? I've already recounted, from memory, some of the despair and joy of the writing in general terms. Now, to flesh this out, to learn what it was really like behind the number of pages, I must consult my Journal for 1960–61, and my copies of letters written in those years.

In my wretched Journal—in those days I jotted down sum-ups of activity about six times a year (since then I've kept a daily Journal)—I find only two meaningful references to my work in progress:

"December 27, 1960, Tuesday: Today I have 444 pages and it may run to 1,200 pages. Some is very good and some mediocre and I can't tell what it will prove to be yet, except I think it will be true for me and readable for others. . . ."

"May 22, 1961, Monday: Five months since my last entry. Of course, I was busy day and night writing and finishing *The Prize.* What has brought me back to the Journal is to look up how long it took, in 1959, to sell *The Chapman Report* to films. Eight days. Well, today is the sixth day *The Prize* is out to the studios. . . . It has been an excruciating year of hard work. By the end of last December I had 540 pages of *The Prize* done. By the end of January, I had 820. And on February 24, 6:29 in the evening, I had typed page 1,115—in that last five days I wrote 124 pages in a frenzy of determination and inspiration—and the book was done. I lived wonderfully and badly in that long period. Wrote from morning at 10, with short lunches, never saw people in the day, usually wound up around 5:30 or 6 in the evening. I exhausted myself physically—smoking more, drinking whiskey and cognac more, sleeping only four or five hours a night, no leisure, no exercise. Yet, it was worth it to me to do this book into which I poured so much of myself."

Most of my correspondence in those months was devoted to the book I had recently finished, *The Twenty-Seventh Wife,* a biography of Ann Eliza Young, Brigham Young's last wife taken in polygamy. But in many of my letters I made passing reference to the progress of *The Prize.* These letters were written to Paul R. Reynolds, my literary agent, and his partner, Oliver G. Swan; to Peter Schwed of Simon and Schuster, my publisher, and Michael V. Korda, of Simon and Schuster, my editor; to Victor Weybright, my reprint publisher at The New American Library; to Elizebethe Kempthorne, my research assistant. The following extracts from these letters start while I was working on the final outline and before the actual writing began, and they end with remarks on the rewriting after the completed first draft.

To Swan, October 15, 1960: "Now that *The Twenty-Seventh Wife* is done—not that a book is ever, ever done, God help us—I am full time plotting *The Prize.* It can be marvelous. I spent last week tracing each major character's life and his story in the book —tough, but what developed was thrilling. During nights I have been doing further research in depth, adding to all that I started in Sweden fourteen years ago. Monday I resume on *The Prize.* Now I will try to integrate characters and work up a better plot in terms of a book outline for myself—to learn where it is strong and where weak. I should think that in about a month I will begin writing the key first chapter, which is clear in my mind and extremely strong. More on the joys and pains of this later."

To Kempthorne, October 22, 1960: "I am now my third

day into *The Prize* going full steam—did seven pages yesterday—and realize I will require far less detailed scientific research than originally expected."

To Kempthorne, October 29, 1960: "Am fifty pages into the novel already! It is going wonderfully. It will be the longest work I've undertaken to date. Suspect it may run 700 or so mss. pages. Fascinating subject, but requiring much background information. For example, other day I was writing about one character of mine, German refugee physicist with niece saved from concentration camp—and I had to stop to get books on concentration camps and what German physicists did during war, for names of places, feeling, so forth. Same on two chemists in French section preceding this one—had to stop and, though I was just there, pump myself full of France again. Today I am in Pasadena where our doctor will get medical award."

To Swan, October 29, 1960: "I am snowed under with research on *The Prize*—the characters and story are sufficiently worked out by now—and I am fifty pages into the book itself. As I told you earlier, I'm extremely enthusiastic. It seems to be moving well."

To Weybright, October 29, 1960: "I began writing *The Prize* and am well into it and pleased. I know the characters, I know what is going to happen. I have most of my research—which is tremendous at this point—and if the story continues to unfold as it has, we may have something important. We shall see. I hope to have it done in a half year or so."

To Kempthorne, November 5, 1960: "I'm a hundred pages into *The Prize,* and researching nights, so I defer most correspondence for weekends. . . . I'm glad you found the sperm information and are now abstracting most promising. When you have anything good, give me in detail, for easier use and for clarity—remember I'm dim on science, so don't shorthand the stuff too much."

To Kempthorne, November 17, 1960: "I'm moving hard on *The Prize*. Reached 140 pages this afternoon. On my other books that would have been a lot, but whereas *Wife* ran 580 in mss.—this new novel may go to 1,000 pages in mss. So I have a long, long half year or more, I'm sure more, ahead. But it goes smoothly."

To Reynolds, November 19, 1960: "It is going wonderfully—a strong book, I feel—very difficult, with all those characters and that international background and the behind-the-scenes stuff, but it is coming off. The important thing is that the people are developing, I'm fascinated by them, and they're so diverse and distinct they should carry me through without too many major problems. I've been working long, long hours and have nearly 200 manuscript pages, nearly 50,000 words I should guess, and I'm only beginning. I can't even imagine how many pages the novel will be. I sensed quite some time ago that it would be a fat one. This is proving to be so. Perhaps it will run to 1,000 mss. pages, a little less or perhaps a bit more. Certainly it will be over twice the length of *Chapman*. But how can I know exactly at this point? I'm merely giving you a progress report. All that matters, I feel, is whether it is good, whether it is right—and I think it is both. We shall see."

To Reynolds, November 24, 1960: "I thank you for the comments, encouraging, on the length of *The Prize*. The characters are thoroughly laid out—although they take surprising turns as I write—and I have a fairly comprehensive idea of the plot line. Perhaps there is some over-writing—I will comb for that when I am done—but the book is long because it is an enormous story, many, many-peopled, many levels of drama, and a fresh kind of background. I remember when I was in Sweden in July, several press representatives told me there had never been a major novel told against a Swedish background by a foreigner. Graham Greene wrote a mystery once using Stockholm, but, according to the Swedes, my book would be the first one in this century to try to tell a serious story with that background. Of course, as I am beginning to see, the background is finally the lesser thing—for the characters dominate the canvas, and if I am successful, you won't care where they are. If lucky, I should have a quarter of the novel by the end of the year—which would be heartening."

To Korda, December 3, 1960: "Forgive the silence—which you may welcome anyway at the Christmas season—but I have been out of touch all around because I am putting everything I have to say these days into the novel. When you have a new book in the works, or at least this is so in my case, you isolate yourself from the rest of the planet. I have been working night and day on *The Prize*."

To Reynolds, December 10, 1960: "I had been toiling feverishly on *The Prize,* because it has taken hold and I want to get it down while I'm in the mood and before any possible dry spell. But I'm going to slow down for the holidays. I have high hopes for this one. I think it is my best yet. I have it one-third done now and I have 90,000 words."

To Korda, December 26, 1960: "Well, here I am at one o'clock in the afternoon of a holiday. I watched the pro football title game on television with my son, my daughter is wallowing in her Santa toys, Sylvia is dressing for an afternoon open house somewhere—I have the faintest hangover—the weather is mild and the sun out bright—and I want to speak to you of the past year. But what is there to add? We had a best seller and big sales, and what more could we wish for than a bigger best seller, bigger sales, *and* better reviews. And now, looking back, we could wish for a more artful, more expert novel—but these will come, I hope, with time, with experience. . . . *The Prize* goes well. I am over one hundred thousand words into it and nervous but mostly pleased."

To myself, in my Journal, a summary, December 27, 1960: "The busiest and most hectic year of my life is drawing to a close —so busy I have not been able to keep up this Journal. . . . *The Chapman Report* dominated the work year, of course. It was officially published May 24, a Tuesday, in New York. On May 23, Simon and Schuster had 12,000 reorders in a single day. Doubleday Book Shops in New York sold out time and again during the same day. Wouk once had a higher day of reorders on *The Caine Mutiny* but I was told mine was second highest in modern publishing history, although I have since read that Sinclair Lewis also surpassed me in a single day of reorders. . . . The best thing about the year was that it gave me temporary security—and opened the door for my next works of fiction. My publisher now says I have a public, whatever that means. Before, as a screenwriter and author of nonfiction, I had been either a nonentity or curiosity, perhaps both. But so widely was *Chapman* read that now all manner of

people are interested in me. I had made that odd and terrible thing
—an overnight success ('overnight' amuses me, when I read it, remembering all the hours of days of years that came before—as
Guy Trosper [the screenwriter and sports fan] put it—I'm 'the oldest rookie-of-the-year'). Quite honestly, I think I have accomplished a great part of what I've wanted since boyhood: to be independent, to write as I please, to be read, to be an entity on earth. In
high school journalism class it seemed an improbable dream, but
still a hope, to be a Somerset Maugham, to be *read*. As I grew, I
desired it—always writing books, inexpert ones, unpublished ones
—always increasingly sure I would hit, I would make it, and never
making it. Mostly, I avoided fiction, preferring truth and reality
and facts, avoiding it for many reasons, but mostly because I
feared it, feared I was not perceptive enough, and also I was frightened by the standard set by modern classics I had read. *Chapman*
came with little pain, and was to be just one book of many, a brief
expression and a modest livelihood—and then it caught on and
became part of the language and something surprisingly special.
. . . As a result, I have changed and people have changed toward
me. First, it was the people who changed—envied more, grasped
more, showed more malice. Then, imperceptibly and not in major
ways, I changed, from seeing people and seeing what they made of
my work. I became surer because I was more secure, and because
people were interested in what I did. But I am a writer and I know
the way it is out there and I know myself—at the core nothing has
changed, finally, except that along with bewilderment came greater
happiness and the first feelings of fulfillment. . . . We returned
home from France on September 9, a few days before school.
Adjusting to the return was difficult. I did a month of rewriting on
The Twenty-Seventh Wife. On October 19, after completing the
research and plotting, I started *The Prize*. . . . Today I wrote 8
pages of *The Prize* and finished Chapter V. I live rather as a hermit, and except for occasional parties, no lunches out, compul-
sively working every day."

To Weybright, January 6, 1961: "I am half through *The Prize*
and living in a kind of Thoreau-like seclusion."

To Korda, February 18, 1961: "No other news, as it has been

twenty-four hours a day, it seems, on *The Prize.* I'm very close to daylight now and it is a question of no last problems and of a reserve of stamina."

To Korda, March 7, 1961: "You will be interested to know that I—yes—I finished *it.* I refer to *The Prize.* This first draft, it really might be called a second draft, ran to 280,000 words, and now, reading it as a whole, I'm extremely excited. As a work of fiction this is such a great step forward for me over my other novels that— well, let's wait and see. I hope to have you and Peter reading *The Prize* early in June."

I can see now that these excerpts from letters I wrote during the sustained act of creation do not fully reflect the *actual* writing process. That is to say, they do not entirely reflect how I felt as I wrote. They are more optimistic and enthusiastic than I was as I put my thoughts on paper for the novel. They fail to reveal the blocks, the periods of despair, the difficulties. I can think of only two reasons for this not entirely balanced picture at the time: first, I rarely like to parade publicly anything personal that has to do with pain or inadequacy or weakness; second, quite possibly, the feelings I summarized were feelings I had *after* pages had been written, with problems overcome, doubts dissolved; they were reports after the fact of writing, and so they were usually cheerful.

I suspect that the best statement on how I wrote the book, how it went and how I truly felt about it, can be found in Thomas Wolfe's superbly written and highly personal confession, *The Story of a Novel,* in which he tried to explain how he wrote a book.

"I cannot really say the book was written," said Wolfe. "It was something that took hold of me and possessed me, and before I was done with it—that is, before I finally emerged with the first completed part—it seemed to me that it had done for me . . . everything was swept and borne along as by a great river. And I was borne along with it. . . . For one thing, my whole sensory and creative equipment, my powers of feeling and reflection—even the sense of hearing, and above all my powers of memory, had reached the greatest degree of sharpness that they had ever known. At the end of the day of savage labor, my mind was still blazing with its effort, could by no opiate of reading, poetry, music, alcohol, or any other pleasure, be put at rest. I was unable to sleep, unable to subdue the tumult of these creative energies. . . ."

That was it, and at last the work was done, yet it was not done in the absolute sense of the word. Now the result of my labors had to be examined objectively, and improved upon by my own hand wherever possible before it was touched by other eyes and hands. Three weeks after I had completed the first draft, I was writing to my editor:

"I took off only a few days, the lolling kind, no trips, because I wasn't ready to be distracted or rested. My mind is still with it, and I have been daily reading and cutting and adding and rewriting, and will continue same until May, when the novel will be readied for the typist. For better or for worse, this new novel is a mammoth step beyond my last novel—it attempts more and possibly does more—and as a result of its content, I suspect we will have many people on our heads. No matter. Let us just hope that it is good."

I continued to keep the manuscript to myself as I read and reread it and studied it line by line. After the first draft, there were three more drafts. While doing extensive cutting and tightening, I found myself also adding material that seemed necessary and building up scenes that seemed skimpy, so that what I added outnumbered what I subtracted, until the manuscript had grown to 1,213 pages.

During these rewrites, I was concerned with fact as well as fiction, with checking on minor details as well as improving the characters and story. I wrote revision notes to myself, such as the following:

"P. 19, describe Gisèle's Paris apartment more thoroughly. . . . P. 67, how would the analyst actually reply to Mrs. Zane? . . . P. 118, write the Nobel Foundation to find out which winners did not appear in Stockholm in person. . . . P. 297, improve Denise's brown suit. . . . P. 309, did I use Krantz's 'porker features' once earlier? . . . Chapter XII, rewrite opening surgery to describe in more detail. . . . Also, rewrite Emily's confession to get in more authentic concentration camp detail."

Some of the material required for my revisions had to be obtained long-distance. For example, I had a scene that was set against a Balenciaga fashion showing. The memory of my own experience of such an event had dimmed, and I felt that what I had written was too vague. So I rushed off a letter to the wife of a friend of mine who lived in Paris, Mrs. Shirley Katz, and asked her if she would visit a Balenciaga showing and take notes for me. She undertook the assignment, and the results were excellent. In writing to thank her, I explained the use I would make of her material:

"It is for my new novel called *The Prize*. One third of a million words. Forty characters. Now, finally, now that it is done and about to go out, I can speak of it. It concerns one dramatic Nobel award week in Stockholm, the week before the ceremony when all kinds of people are drawn from the ends of the earth to the northern place. . . . The first scene is Paris. A French chemistry couple are about to be notified. The husband is on the town with a—yes —Balenciaga mannequin. They are in the early stages of an affair. At the end of the scene they go to bed, but then a phone call interrupts them—from the wife (who has just found out about the affair) to the husband—telling the son-of-a-bitch to get his pants on and come home, they've just won the Nobel Prize! There is no crudity. It is all done nicely and emotionally and truly. . . . I meant to tell you how I used your Balenciaga material. I did it in retrospect: French husband and wife take English visitors to a Balenciaga show. He sees mannequin for the first time. Later he runs into her on the Champs-Élysées. Gradually the affair begins. Later, when injured wife learns of it through a friend, and confirms it, she wants to set eyes on party of the third part herself. On pretense of buying a gown for Stockholm, wife goes to Balenciaga—and sees the mannequin—and measures her against herself. That was why I desperately needed that good descriptive material you were kind enough to send. Again, again, thanks."

When my rewrite notes were attended to, when I realized I could do no more with the manuscript on my own, I knew that I had reached the point where I had to let it go, had to show it to *someone*. As usual, I chose the two persons close to me whose honesty and creative judgments I respected. I made a Thermofax copy of the entire manuscript and sent it to Elizebethe Kempthorne, my research assistant, and I turned the original manuscript over to Sylvia, my wife.

After several weeks, Kempthorne returned her copy, and almost every page bore a forest of suggested corrections and changes, most of them devoted to spelling, grammar, errors of fact, inconsistencies, omissions, lack of clarity, and so forth. Typical of her notes: "P. 635, Here I start to worry again. First off, how can Walther possibly be both a physicist and bacteriologist? Further, this whole use of bubonic plague seems shaky to me. Also, why an artificial germ when it's easier to cultivate large units of the already available natural cause. . . . P. 976, Damn French verb baffled me. Let me explain. . . . "

Meanwhile, my wife was carefully reading the book and scratching down notes. Her practice on all of my manuscripts is to read her notes to me when she has completed them. The domestic scenes that follow are appalling, and while I fight her as if my life were at stake, I usually find I must concede to at least half of her suggestions. While I pretend to think that she is being hostile, I know that she is as emotionally involved in the manuscript as I am, that she is being completely honest, that she understands me and knows my work, and that she was once an editor (before I rescued her from a life of sin). On *The Prize,* here is a small but representative sampling of her notes:

"P. 12, 'long stride' sounds graceless. . . . P. 21, Wasn't the son-of-a-bitch at any time concerned about hurting her? . . . P. 46, Let's work on this hairdo. . . . P. 127, Only 1 hour 25 min. run from Paris to Stockholm? . . . P. 146, Straighten out this sentence. . . . P. 200, Characters are always retrospecting. Can you get into Sue Wiley's past without having her recollect it herself? . . . P. 257, Too much on the nose. . . . P. 258, Cut. Why is this in—except that it happened to you? . . . P. 384, Wonderful description of Hammarlund. . . . P. 406, A critic will pounce on you for this. . . . P. 457–59, This is of no interest to anyone but ourselves. Cut drastically. . . . P. 463, The Taj Mahal is delicate and beautiful, and anything that looked like it would not be called Thunder Palace. . . . P. 509, The title of the song you want is 'There's a Cowboy Rolling Down Kungsgatan.' . . . P. 523, Is Emily dressed warmly enough for a December night? . . . P. 559, 'friendly,' then 'taciturn'? A contradiction of words. . . . P. 592, How could Stratman get the prize for anything so secret? . . . P. 710, Craig should not talk to Farelli or even to Garrett like this. Too high-handed. . . . P. 755, Denise shouldn't tell him she loves him. Not even a clod would believe that in such a brief meeting. On the other hand, he *could* worship her, since he has known her longer, by reputation. . . . P. 764, Too explicit! . . . P. 873, Cheating? On whom? He's free. . . . P. 1006, You may have to condense this. Dr. Öhman *is* talking to knowledgeable scientists. . . . P. 1086, You're so all-forgiving. Maybe you ought to have Krantz marry Leah Decker. . . . P. 1113, They didn't rise for Dr. Stratman. Why would they rise for him—*a writer?* . . . P. 1086, Re ruminations on Krantz. Craig is overdoing the forgiveness-tolerance-understanding bit. Have him let Krantz go, but skip the pity."

Bloodied, yet secretly grateful, I rewrote once more. But even as I rewrote, I made copies of small sections of the novel to show to experts—portions of *The Prize* went to a Lockheed physicist, a government chemist, three cardiovascular surgeons, and my Swedish publisher in Stockholm.

The response from these specialists was valuable. As I reported to Mrs. Kempthorne:

"I have redone all the Garrett-Farelli sequences so that they are consistent, dealing with one graft, and in redoing it I have worked from the last notes of Dr. Edward J. Berman and Dr. Harry G. Harshbarger. I believe it is close to correct now. I got my Stratman stuff to Lockheed's top physicist, who read the extracts, made notes. I met with him in Burbank for lunch yesterday, and he was exact and excellent. The major thing I had wrong was that I gave Stratman the prize for solar propulsion—too improbable mathematically—and the physicist made suggestions—and I have solidly revised the technical aspects here, too."

The two pages of suggestions from Stockholm were concise and specific. Here is a sampling:

"P. 122, The Count most certainly doesn't use their first names this way, you don't do it in Swedish—'Froken Ingrid, Herr Carl.' He would probably just say 'Good afternoon, good afternoon,' without any names. . . . P. 194, The name of the museum is Rohsska, not Rohass. . . . P. 277, 'Jag roar mig.' You can't say so. She probably said, 'Det var mycket trevligt.' . . . There are no trams on Norrbro, the bridge going from Gustaf Adolfs Torg to the Royal Palace. It should perhaps be Strömbron, the bridge nearest to Grand Hotel? . . . P. 461, There is much more in a 'westkustsallad'—shrimps and crabs and lobster. . . . P. 535, The Orpheus statue is not golden, it is a very dark green. . . . P. 725, 'Schnapps' before dinner? Cocktail, yes, but not schnapps. . . . P. 1126, Never heard of anybody in Sweden using smelling salts."

The last changes were made. The manuscript of *The Prize* went to the typist for copying. Finally, in late May of 1961, I packed the original or ribbon copy of the novel in three ream-sized boxes and similarly packed several sets of carbon copies, and sent them to my literary agent in New York City for distribution to my publishers. Nervously, I waited.

The first response from Simon and Schuster came in the form of a letter written on June 1, 1961, by my editor, Mike Korda:

"I have just received from Paul Reynolds our copies of *The Prize* and I'm looking forward to starting it tonight. Paul says it's wonderful. . . . P.S. I've just read the first two chapters now, before going home. It's absolutely *fascinating* and compelling reading. The characters are just great! Congratulations."

The next day, my publisher, Peter Schwed, wrote:

"The Magnum Opus, and I mean Magnum, is as you know in my hands, and I'm plunging through it at every moment when my time isn't absolutely demanded elsewhere. Since I have only had it for one day, I have only knocked off three hundred pages, but I thought that Book One was absolutely brilliant. If it keeps up this way—and I have every expectation and hope that it will—this one will really be a winner."

Shortly after, Schwed had finished the book, and now he wrote again:

"For the most part, it's a staggeringly impressive and exciting job that you have done, Irving, and I can't congratulate you too heartily."

At once, Simon and Schuster supported their enthusiasm by offering a contract with a dizzy-making $70,000 advance against royalties. Their reaction to and approval of my work was thrilling. I could not forget, on that marvelous day, that not too long before —in January, 1954—I had received an advance of $1,000 from Alfred A. Knopf for my first book, *The Fabulous Originals,* to which I had also devoted years of research and writing.

But the wonder of it was only beginning. While I had already enjoyed my greatest pleasure, which came when I received my publisher's approval, there was still ahead the adventure of learning how my work would be accepted by motion pictures, book clubs, and foreign publishers. The most important of these, financially, was motion pictures. I had written *The Prize* as a book, and with no other thought in mind, least of all the thought of its having value as a possible film. Yet, once my book had achieved its primary goal, through acceptance by a renowned publisher, I began to wonder what more it could achieve in subsidiary markets.

The sale of motion-picture rights is nothing an author can seriously anticipate or count upon. It it simply something additional and exceptional that one can hope for—like owning the right lottery ticket, or hitting the slot-machine jackpot, or holding a wager on a long-shot winner at the racetrack. And so now, as the time approached for a decision on *The Prize* as a possible framework for a future movie, I became anxious and then emotionally involved in a dream about this lottery, jackpot, long shot.

Evarts Ziegler, my West Coast agent in Beverly Hills, who was to handle the motion-picture rights, had received a carbon copy of the manuscript along with a note from me, reading:

"I'm extremely eager for your opinion of the book. Keep in touch.

"I'm not relaxed.

"I'm nervous.
"This
    is
       many
           years
              of
                 my
                    life. . . ."

Ziegler's response came by telephone, and immediately I was reporting his reaction to Paul Reynolds, my New York agent: "Zig read an unproofed copy literally overnight, with little sleep, and was ecstatic. He thinks it surpasses *Chapman* threefold, thinks it a tremendous and moving book as a book. And as a movie—well, one never knows, but he believes it has a good chance."

As a matter of fact, Ziegler felt that, even though great segments of the book could not possibly be transferred to the screen since they were not cinematic, the central idea of the novel and the leading characters might be intriguing enough to make the book an excellent basis for a dramatic vehicle. He determined not to wait for galley proofs or bound books but to present *The Prize* to motion-picture studios in manuscript form. He convinced me that I should have the manuscript mimeographed, and as soon as this had been done, he circulated twenty copies of the novel to motion-picture studios and independent producers.

A week later I was giving Paul Reynolds a progress report:

"Motion picture rights to *The Chapman Report* were sold on the eighth day after its submission. Today is the seventh day since *The Prize* was submitted. What has held back responses, Ziegler learned, is the length of the novel—it demands more time to synopsize (for example, Twentieth Century-Fox and Columbia will have synopses ready only today)—but once a synopsis is out to each executive, decisions will come fast and furious, perhaps in a matter of hours. . . . Movie interest in *The Prize* has advanced to the point where Ziegler now has what might be called three firm buyers —with no response, yet, from the rest."

Two days later, there was sufficient interest from executives and producers for Ziegler to announce the price and terms he expected. The price he expected was $350,000. The next morning I wrote Paul Reynolds the details—and the result:

"On Thursday last, because of mounting interest, Ziegler decided to issue his terms. On *Chapman* he had sent a wire and it took four months of disagreements and wrangling to get a contract. This time he and his lawyers wrote a three-page contract covering all disputable points—and instead of a wire he sent the contract to nine interested buyers at four o'clock Thursday. As you know, two hours later one buyer had met the terms. However, Zig had to wait until the six o'clock Friday deadline he had announced, which was yesterday. He called me to his office at a quarter to six. Three hours before, Metro-Goldwyn-Mayer Studio had met our terms. Of the bidders, we selected M-G-M. Ziegler phoned them, concluded the deal at six, cut off all the phones, we had drinks, and that was that."

That was not quite that. I was utterly exhausted. Nevertheless, I went on a letter-writing spree. First, I wrote my friend Jerome Weidman the news:

"Metro-Goldwyn-Mayer has bought *The Prize*. . . . The purchase price equals Tennessee Williams' sale of his new play to Seven Arts and John Steinbeck's sale of his new novel to Metro. I'm really more pleased than words can convey—words can convey nothing because I had only a few hours' sleep and I am now barely awake in the morning."

Then I wrote my friends Betty and Leonard Slater:

"Sylvia and I are dazed, this occurring only 21 months after *Chapman*. It's all so crazy. I wanted to write novels simply because I had things to say and liked to write them and wanted to be independent—but rewards like this besides—incredible."

Then I wrote my friend Art Buchwald in Paris and concluded my news with:

"So we're mildly hysterical today and determined to celebrate this and our twentieth anniversary next week. What better gift than Europe? We will be in Paris. . . . May we take you to dinner? to the Bois? to outer space? We are bringing our children. Groom yours. . . . Art, that column you did on me was truly a sensation. I congratulate you for my wit. Write without delay. Leave 1,000,- 000 NF, unmarked, behind the entry booth at the Gare St. Lazare, or else. . . . Did you know that Jackie and JFK told the press they read *Chapman?* Like our friend Bill Attwood, I now have the Good White Housekeeping seal."

On June 23, 1961, under a two-column headline, *The New York Times* announced the news in a story filed from "Hollywood, Calif.":

"Today Irving Wallace was very much the man who had returned to the small town after making good in the big city. For Mr. Wallace, who quit movie writing some time ago, was at Metro-Goldwyn-Mayer to sign a contract . . . for the movie rights to his latest novel, 'The Prize.' "

My excursion into Gettyland was brief. My novel required one more major rewrite. My agents believed it was needed. My publisher and editor believed it was needed. And, very soon, I knew that it was necessary.

My literary agent had informed me that my publisher, Peter Schwed, would have some editorial suggestions to make. Immediately, I wrote my agent:

"As to editorial suggestions, I told Schwed I would consider any he makes. I am not bullheaded. I want a good book. I will do what I think is best and what I am creatively capable of doing. As to your idea that I tone down the explicit sex—I already did, because of Sylvia's advice after she had read previous drafts—and may do more. I'll consider it. In any case, this is not a sex book—it is simply that I am a strong believer in writing straightforwardly about sex rather than implying or using asterisks. I thought the sex in Lady Chatterley was beautiful and saved an otherwise tedious book. However, I will seriously think about this—for I know sex scenes, among other things, give me most of my trouble with critics."

Next, I learned that Schwed was troubled most about one specific part of my novel. On June 13, I wrote Schwed:

"Paul tells me the major thing you do not like is something in the last chapter about Craig—I would gather, perhaps, the melo-drama. Well, I won't try to anticipate what you have to say. Simply tell me—"

Schwed responded at once in his usual direct manner. He told me:

"Yes—my major objection to *The Prize* as it stands is the final 150 pages or so. The bad East German scientist and the melodra-matic chase is so out of keeping with the rest of the book that it struck me as violently jarring."

The "melodramatic chase" that my publisher referred to com-prised two sections of my last chapter, and added up to 62 pages out of the 146-page final chapter of the original manuscript. As I had written it, Emily Stratman receives a telephone call that her uncle, Dr. Stratman, has suffered a heart attack. Arriving at the emergency clinic on Ringvägen, Emily is led not to her uncle but to her uncle's former colleague, Dr. Hans Eckart, who is in Stock-holm to woo Dr. Stratman back to Communist East Berlin. Dr. Eckart tells Emily that since her uncle has refused to defect volun-tarily, she will now be used to induce him to change his mind. She will be sent by freighter, this very night, to East Germany, there to resume "the carefree life she lived at Ravensbruck." If Dr. Strat-man, once he has been informed of this, is prepared to follow her behind the Iron Curtain, she will then, and only then, be released.

At the Grand Hotel, Andrew Craig, trying to find Emily, comes upon the tiny tape recorder that announces Dr. Eckart's ransom terms. Realizing that there is no time to seek the help of the law, since Dr. Stratman will be expected to announce his defection at the Nobel Prize award ceremony in a few hours, Craig decides to act on his own. Craig follows a clue that leads him to the spy, Daranyi, who reveals that one member of the conspiracy is none other than the Nobel judge, Carl Adolf Krantz.

Immediately, Craig goes after Krantz, and reaches him just as the judge is leaving his apartment for the Nobel ceremony. Krantz tries to escape in his limousine. Craig, in a car driven by Gottling, gives pursuit, rams into Krantz's limousine, and finally forces the Swedish judge to take him to the motor launch where Emily is being kept. Craig finds Emily alone in the launch, under sedation.

Having no desire to damage the Nobel Prize ceremony with news of a scandal, Craig permits Krantz to go free, to leave for exile in East Berlin. Then Craig rescues Emily, later hears out the terrifying story of her past, professes his love for her, and makes love with her, before going to Concert Hall to receive the Nobel Prize in literature.

This was the segment of the ending to which my publisher and editor objected. Now they were prepared to be more specific about their adverse reactions. On June 26, Korda wrote a key letter in which he elaborated on the major faults that he and Schwed had found with the story and suggested how he and Schwed felt the book might be improved. He wrote:

"Peter and I have three basic suggestions to make, and you might consider these on your way to New York. They concern the plot, which, on the whole, is marvelous. The reader is held on tenterhooks throughout the book, and the opening chapters are enormously suspenseful. In two places, however, it seems to me that the book is weak. One is the scene, at the end, in which Emily and Andrew Craig make love. The other is the melodrama of Dr. Stratman's attempted kidnaping by the East Germans.

"I like the way sex is handled in the book. I don't think any of it should be cut, or needs cutting. But I do feel that the climactic scene between Emily and Andrew is not needed or reasonable. It just isn't in her nature or his.

"As for the spy plot, I think it's by far the weakest spot in the book. The rest of the book is so much more realistic and powerful. Is it absolutely necessary? Couldn't we simply have the East Germans trying to woo Stratman away from the Americans, putting on the emotional pressure, etc., but *not* going to the lengths they do in the present version? Frankly, it's too much like *The Thirty-Nine Steps,* and out of place in *The Prize,* which is on a much, much higher level than this. . . .

"What to do? Obviously we can only make very tentative suggestions, and I hope you will consider them as such.

"1. Eliminate the sex scene between Emily and Andrew. . . . 2. Eliminate the spy story ending. This, obviously, leaves the book without a big scene to end it. In this connection, Peter suggests that Andrew, having won Emily and solved his own problems, should turn down the prize in his speech, saying that he is not worthy of it, that perhaps someday he will be. . . . I think this is an excellent suggestion. It gives the plot a last minute twist. . . . 3. Possibly have Stratman suffer a coronary, and have him operated on by Farelli and Garrett, instead of the King's friend. . . . The cutting is not going to present a problem. The important thing is the plot, or, to be more exact, the resolution of the Craig/Emily story and the Stratman story."

This letter disturbed me. While I recognized that my publisher and editor had put their fingers on certain weaknesses in the novel that would need strengthening, I also felt that most of their suggestions for improvement were wrong. After giving it concentrated thought, I replied with a three-page single-spaced letter to Korda two days later:

"Now and always you must be as frank as you wish. The book—this or any book—must always come before sensitivity. If we can't communicate properly, we will both suffer. All I reserve is the right to discuss, weigh, accept or reject your suggestions. And allow me, now and always, to be as frank with you as you want to be with me.

"You list three points. I appreciate your creative suggestions—invite them—but on these I specifically disagree. I think you and Peter are right that something must be done in the last chapter. I think you are completely wrong as to *what* must be done specifically. Let's review your three points—

"1. Eliminate sex scene near the end. You have convinced me. I will handle it as you suggest.

"2. Eliminate the spy ending. Yes, okay. But we need a big scene. Peter suggests that Craig turn down the prize, and you think that an excellent idea. I think that is anything but an excellent idea. It has absolutely nothing to recommend it, except that it is big, a twist, a surprise—but nothing else, for it rings false. Not only does it smack of Boris Pasternak, where it was logical, but it has nothing to do with the book as it stands or with Craig's past. Of course, Craig thinks he is not worthy, as other true winners have honestly felt, yet he knows, and I make this clear, that writers more inferior than he have been honored. Why should he turn it down, indeed? Because he drinks? Because he's done only four books? Because he suffers guilts and remorse? Nothing in his past would motivate such a shocking action. It would be frivolous for him to turn it down— as GBS was made to see. No one has ever turned it down, except when forced to, i.e., Boris Pasternak and those Germans under Hitler. I say it is out of character. Worse, it somehow destroys Craig, it makes him a phony minor figure who may one day prove himself. No, he's bigger than that—and he deserves the prize.

"3. You suggest 'possibly' having Stratman suffer a coronary and Farelli-Garrett save him. No, impossible. This was the obvious plot point I had a year ago which I immediately rejected. From the time the reader has read the first chapter, he must be saying—aha, one winner has a bad heart—two other winners know how to save people with bad hearts—aha, I know what is coming. I would never let myself walk into such a construction trap. Not only is it coincidental, self-serving, expected—but I don't believe in it.

"On the other hand, once I drop more than half of the last chapter, I *do* need something important to supplant it. I need and want something simple and uninvolved that grows logically out of the people in the story and the condition of the novel at that very point. The last two weeks I racked my brain—made a half dozen notes— but all were wrong. Then I hit on something I have not yet developed but which appeals to me, for it contains the right values, and has drama instead of melodrama. Without prejudice, with love, hear me out—

"Eckart calls Emily to a meeting, invoking her uncle's name. He tries to reason with her to influence her uncle to take the post in East Berlin. She refuses. Under no condition would she help. No condition? Eckart leads her into the next room—and there—there stands her father, Walther Stratman, the beloved father of her teens thought to be dead in a Soviet labor camp. . . . "

And thus, I had come to grips with the last chapter of the book, in an effort to find a better climax.

In the summer of 1961, I went off to Europe once more, to revisit several sites important to the novel, to gather research for a later book, to rest and loaf when I could, but mainly to work on the final rewrite of *The Prize*. I carried voluminous notes and the last chapter in one of my suitcases. I also carried with me three pages of plot changes and broad suggested cuts which Korda had prepared for me under the heading General Observations.

In these observations, my editor once more stated his feelings about the book's ending. "As already suggested, I think the spy plot at the end should go altogether. Krantz and Eckart should try to woo Stratman to East Germany and fail. But no kidnaping. It's too melodramatic and the plot doesn't need it. If this is done, Daranyi, the Hungarian spy, can be eliminated or reduced, and the emotional impact concentrated on Andrew Craig and Emily Stratman, and on the Farelli-Garrett relationship."

From Paris, July 18, 1961, I wrote to my editor:

"Half of your last suggestions are based on 'the spy plot' going out or staying in. Mike, 'the spy plot' as a plot line cannot go at all. We'd have to have a new story top to bottom in its center. I love the spy plot with Krantz and Eckart and Daranyi and all the others involved. What I have agreed to change is the end or outcome of that plot—change it to something less melodramatic and perhaps more in keeping with the entire fabric of the book.

"At the moment I have made one full development of my idea of having Eckart bring Walther Stratman back into the story, and it works in the present structure. I fear I'll be thinking of this damn thing the whole summer—I must—it is too important."

From Venice, July 31, 1961, to my editor:

"As to the last chapter, you simply have no idea how many new ideas I've had and rejected. At one stage I had Emily's beloved mother, Rebecca, alive. At another point I toyed with Emily's having had an illegitimate child by the Nazi commandant and the child is alive. Recently I've played with the notion that when Eckart sees Emily's dossier, he finds a clue in it to something black in Nobelman Max Stratman's past. . . . I could develop this in ten directions, and still keep Max sympathetic. Anyway, anyway, I'm still for the Walther idea, and now it runs roughly like this—

"Eckart summons Emily and begs her to use her influence on Max Stratman so that he will defect. She refuses. Eckart produces

Emily's father, Walther Stratman, whom she had always supposed dead. Emily faints.

"Craig goes to the Stratman bedroom to find Emily. Instead he finds the tape, addressed to Max Stratman, with Eckart's voice indicating that Walther is alive, reunited with Emily, and both will be given freedom in the West in exchange for Max Stratman's defecting to the East.

"Craig knows that once Stratman hears this tape, he will defect to give Emily back her father, his brother. Craig determines to look into this on his own before putting Max Stratman on the spot. He decides Daranyi is his man. Runs into Gottling, who takes him to Lilly who in turn gets him to Daranyi. And Daranyi, whose payment had been an attack on him by hired hoodlums (maybe he is only scratched, but frightened and angered), decides to spill everything and implicates Krantz.

"Craig catches Krantz dressing for the ceremony—makes it clear he knows facts that implicate Krantz—and Krantz, scared, begs off, shows how he was sucked in—says he will do anything not to be involved further or exposed. Craig says: take me to Walther.

"Krantz takes Craig to the launch in the canal where Walther is being kept before being returned to East Germany. Craig and Emily's father, Walther, play a big climactic scene alone. Craig presses Walther, and when he offers Walther a chance to escape to freedom this minute without being traded for Max, Walther backs off—and Craig senses he had become a Communist and never meant to be traded—and Craig makes Walther inadvertently reveal the truth. This victory, admission, saves Max and Emily. After leaving the launch with Emily and Krantz—with Krantz along, no guard would bother to stop them—Craig finally lets Krantz go. Shortly after, Emily explains her horrible past (my problem still is to see that this integrates with the last chapter and is not merely character explanation) and Craig doesn't give a damn about it and takes her in his arms.

"We go to the ceremony as I have it . . . and then Craig and Emily arrive . . . and Craig follows Max Stratman and accepts the award, the prize."

HOTEL ROYAL DANIELI

& NEW DANIELI EXCELSIOR

VENICE

Aug. 11, 1961

Climax scene in 44-foot cabin cruiser tied to berth in Palsundet district — in Stockholm canal —

[sketch of a boat on a canal with handwritten labels: "deck", "main stateroom", "guard", "STAIRS", "canal", and arrows pointing to figures labeled "Andrew Craig", "Krantz", "Walther Stratman seated on cot"]

Opening for new confrontation scene
Chapter XII — final revision

Alberghi di proprietà e gestione della « C.I.G.A. »
VENEZIA: Danieli Royal Excelsior · Gritti Palace Hotel · Grand Hotel Europa & Britannia · Hotel Regina · LIDO:
Excelsior Palace Hotel · Grand Hotel Des Bains · Grand Hotel Lido · Hotel Villa Regina · FIRENZE: Hotel Excelsior
Italie · Grand Hotel · ROMA: Hotel Excelsior · Grand Hotel · NAPOLI: Hotel Excelsior · MILANO: Hotel Principe e Savoia
· Palace Hotel · STRESA: Grand Hotel et des Iles Borromées · GENOVA: Colombia Excelsior Hotel (STAI.)

My editor read my new outline of the last chapter, and on August 4, he wrote me: "I'm sorry that you're having so much heartache with the ending of the Stratman-Craig-Emily story, but of course it's important. I think the Walther Stratman bit that you outlined in your letter is good. It solves a lot of the problems and eliminates the chase scene, which, I think, was everyone's major objection. As far as I can visualize it, it seems to work. That is, it fits into the book organically and is true to the original conception of the characters."

I had gone down to Florence, and when I returned to Venice, I again wrote my editor on August 9:

"We got to the Lido. Adriatic water perfect. Bikinis perfect. Elsa Maxwell perfect. What did Jack Paar say of her? Yes: 'just another pretty face.' Anyway, nights hot, no air conditioning, so we moved back to the cool Hotel Danieli and commute. Last night we went to Harry's Bar, then a concert in S. Marco, and when we returned to the hotel, there was a long-distance call from Hollywood. Dick Zanuck. He said George Cukor had reread *The Chapman Report* novel and wants me to do the polish of the latest script. Promised good money if I'd fly back to Burbank now. As I wrote Ziegler, that's like asking a man to leave Eden for Dachau. But I told Zanuck, honestly, I was really through with films forever and even if I were not I still would be busy on revisions for *The Prize*. . . .

"In Florence I think I licked the missing elements of the Walther last chapter of *The Prize*. It will work now."

Six weeks later I was back at my desk in Los Angeles, and I was writing again. I took time off to report to my editor:

"You can imagine how hard it is to get to work again after all these months. Also, actual rewriting is very hard for me. I don't mean cutting and pruning and small changes. That is routine. But actually creating new scenes for old, as I'm doing in the final chapter. It is hard because a book like *The Prize* is such a prolonged emotional outburst, and when you are done and have rewritten it several times while still in the mood, you seem to have said all you have had to say in the way you hoped or planned. It is *done* in a larger sense. Then you sell it to the publisher and paperback, and to films if you are lucky, and it begins to solidify in your mind as a finished piece of work that has been read by many and is ready for the public. Suddenly, the realization comes that something is wrong and you must or should rewrite something major—and it is wrenching, very much so. Suddenly, you have to get back in the mood of Emily and Craig and Krantz and so on, and you have to summon up the creative energy to build a new person like Walther, and you sweat blood at the pores. Well, after much poking about, you finally get to work. And so I did last Monday. And by today I have a third of the last chapter written. Walther is now in the story —a person."

Two weeks later, the major rewrite was completed. But there was more to be done, still.

There remained endless smaller queries that hovered over me like swarms of bees. Earlier, neatly typed on five sheets of yellow paper, Korda had made fifty-five "suggested cuts and changes." Accompanying these had been a three-page letter from Schwed adding, "Here are my comments about Mike's specific suggestions so that you can evaluate any conflicting opinions, one against the other, and come to your own decision. In the comments below, I am following Mike's memorandum and only making my own comments where I more or less disagree with Mike. If I make no comments at all, the inference is that I agree."

These two suggestion letters, one from my editor, the other from my publisher, pleased me, reinforced my belief in the independence and honesty of the people I was working with at Simon and Schuster. Here there were no company men kowtowing to one another or, indeed, to an author. Here were men speaking their own minds. I had been with other publishers. I had never participated in anything quite like this before.

I weighed Korda's suggestions, and Schwed's comments, and I returned to my typewriter. Two more weeks of work, and I had six pages of notes—in which I agreed to certain changes, refused to make others—to brandish at the bees. Here is a sampling of our three-way exchange:

PAGE 27:

   KORDA: "Suggest cutting out 'you rotten son-of-a-bitch.' This

will come up again. My feeling is that Denise should avoid pro-
fanity. She just isn't the type. Gottling, yes. Märta Norberg, yes.
Denise is an educated Frenchwoman, and unlikely to express herself this way."

SCHWED: "Agree completely with Mike, but do think that Denise
should swear at this point. Not 'you rotten son-of-a-bitch,' however, but 'you rotten pig (cochon?).' "

WALLACE: "There is, as you know, an exact and provocative and
oft-used French phrase meaning son-of-a-bitch. I disagree with you
and Peter that this is out of character. A woman even of this class,
so shatteringly insulted, is capable of saying anything. I could tell
you of a lofty French Ambassador's daughter I knew . . . *but* I
compromise by conceding to Peter's suggestion. It is now 'you rotten pig.' "

PAGE 131:

KORDA: "Cut from 'Because Jacobsson' to end of paragraph."

SCHWED: No comment.

WALLACE: "Okay, made your cut, although kept one line for
smoother transition."

PAGE 220:

KORDA: "Cut from 'There had been a handful of dim years' to
end of paragraph."

SCHWED: "I really don't care. I think Mike has a point, but
would side with you if you felt strongly."

WALLACE: "I simply could not bring myself to cut this out of Sue
Wiley. Yes, I know we will later see what she is like—but here we
learn, in advance, *why*—we understand her and she will be a less
stereotyped bitch."

PAGE 263:

KORDA: "Cut from 'Yes, curiouser and curiouser' to end of paragraph."

SCHWED: No comment.

WALLACE: "Okay, I made entire suggested cut."

PAGE 312:

KORDA: "Can Ingrid Påhl's speech about liquor in Sweden be made a little shorter? It's good, very good, but it goes on for a little too long."

SCHWED: "Another cut suggested by Mike, which eliminates some good atmosphere. Stet in my opinion."

WALLACE: "I could not figure how to cut this. I left it intact. It is sympathetic, I think it is interesting, and as drinking in Sweden relates to Craig's problem in America, I feel it is even pertinent. My instinct says: don't touch."

PAGE 329:

KORDA: "Cut from 'Madame Marceau' to page 330, end of paragraph, '. . . a promising one.' "

SCHWED: "Disagree with Mike."

WALLACE: "Here is an important matter of judgment and feeling that runs the whole way through. I like this kind of intellectual sidelight, which after all is part of the Marceau background. I simply believe it belongs and should not be cut. Concerning the inclusion of factual information or atmosphere, I don't say I am right to keep it in and you are wrong to want it out. I simply say this is a matter of highly individual taste. I like this materal, like to write it, like to read it (in other writers' books), think it belongs in this kind of novel, think it helps the story—and if I took it out, it would be less the novel I had hoped to write. It might be a faster book your way, but, alas, not truly my book."

PAGE 400:

KORDA: "Cut from 'There was a singsong exchange' through second line on page 408. Too much information, which tends to block the reader's attention."

SCHWED: "Another perhaps overlong atmospheric piece of writing, which I'd want to retain although I agree with Mike that it might be a shade too long."

WALLACE: "Now here we are, again, at a question of individual taste. You want eight pages out of the palace walk-through. It would speed the story. But, I tell myself, why speed the story at this point? I want to build slowly to the party scene, I wanted a look at the palace and its former inhabitants myself, I wanted this before meeting the present King. However—I have made some cuts."

PAGE 499:

KORDA: "I think the piece about the artist letting his mother starve is, in fact, from Shaw's *The Doctor's Dilemma*. If Maugham used it, he must have taken it from Shaw."

SCHWED: No comment.

WALLACE: "Just read GBS's *The Doctor's Dilemma*. What you refer to is not in it. Could you have meant another play? Anyway, Maugham did say this once."

PAGE 548:

KORDA: "Cut from 'The spell of the evening' to end of line 9 from bottom, page 549, '. . . perfect day.' "

SCHWED: "Agree with Mike but the transition would be too abrupt if the cut were made exactly as suggested. You have to indicate that Craig has had a fine evening with Emily."

WALLACE: "I disagree with you and with Peter. I want to keep alive the mood of the first romantic meeting between hero and heroine, and also to keep sweetness and light in order to effect a contrast with the terrible scene that will follow moments later with Leah."

PAGE 562:

KORDA: "Cut from 'The questions and now the answers' to page 563, '. . . effects of the alcohol.' "

SCHWED: No comment.

WALLACE: "I was weighing the cutting of this when I saw I had it all wrong—and saw what was the matter—it gave away too much. So I rewrote it almost entirely. I think it is better now."

PAGE 597:

KORDA: "Cut from 'What results?' to page 598, '. . . in the next three years.' "

SCHWED: "Agree with Mike that you don't have to go into a full

explanation of Pavlov's experiment, but would retain the interesting material on page 598."
WALLACE: "I made the entire Pavlov cut."

PAGE 695:
KORDA: "Cut from top of this page to end of line 3 from bottom, page 698."
SCHWED: "Think that if Daranyi keeps his function in the book, this is good stuff. If he doesn't, throw it out."
WALLACE: "No, no, Mike, all necessary to make any dramatic ending plausible. The Enbom case is a plant to show what is possible in the field of espionage in placid Sweden (just as current doings in East-West Berlin make any last chapter I write more acceptable next year)."

Before mailing my reactions to Korda's suggestions and Schwed's alternate comments, I had written my editor a long preliminary letter discussing some of the editorial points with which I was still wrestling. As I wrote him, in part:
"I find one thing fascinating. I find that the points about which you and Peter disagree tend to involve only two items—one, descriptive passages; two, factual information on the Nobel Prizes. You seem to feel these slow the story down and get in the way. Peter seems to feel the background color is helpful and the factual stuff interesting. Who is right? I do not know. There can be no answer now, of course. I suppose it is a problem of striking a delicate balance. Naturally, I put descriptive passages in for many reasons, and factual stuff in to give reality to my fiction, but overall they are in because I felt it was right. Still, your challenges give me pause—I see in places I may have gone too far, obstructed the flow. How much of this I will pare away I cannot yet tell you. Some has been done, of course. I am reading and rereading the rest of it.
"My handling of Denise seems to have bothered you and Peter the most. The swear words. Her two love scenes. Well, that is interesting—I meant to discuss it with you earlier. Surely you have met as many young French ladies and middle-aged French ladies as I have—I don't mean café girls—but women of good family and

marriage. Well, some I have known have talked pretty loosely, to put it mildly. Recently I started reading *The Mandarins* by Simone de Beauvoir and right off one of her French white-collar girls tells a man he has 'a brain at the tip of his prick.' De Beauvoir? In short, your image of the French lady and my own simply differ. However, I am going along with you and Peter for two reasons. First, you feel strongly and I must respect this. Second, I think, right or wrong, the public here may have your image of the French lady and be jolted by my Denise and not accept her or believe in her, since she would not conform to their image. So, the strong language is out. Much more important, I completely rewrote the love scenes. You are absolutely justified here. . . ."

To this, Mike Korda replied two days later:

"Your revisions sound fine. My feeling that some of the background passages slow the story up is, of course, just one person's opinion, and Peter may well be right in thinking that they should stay in. I ought to point out that I find *all* of the background material fascinating! It's just that there seem to be a few places where there is too much of it, and I was afraid the reader might find his attention diverted from the story for too long. I may be wrong, and I'm sure your decision will be right for the book.

"As to Denise, I don't, alas, know Simone de Beauvoir (I wish I did know her!), nor have I ever met any French scientists, male or female. But my experience has been that strong language is rarely used by French women except (a) in moments of crises, and (b) in particular social sets, for example, the literary world, the arts in general, high life and the sporting world. In Denise's case, I just can't see it. She is essentially a bourgeois Frenchwoman (as Mme Curie was), who *believes* in the sanctity of marriage and in morality. That is why her husband's affair is doubly shocking to her, it seems to me, and why her own seduction of Lindblom is such a painful experience for her. If she were really a hard-talking bohemian, she might not have such a strong reaction to her husband's love affair. But she *does* react strongly (and she should), and that's why it seems to me to be more in keeping with her character to have her language toned down. . . ."

On October 14, 1961, I was writing Korda, "Today—selah—I

finished with the revisions of *The Prize*. I delivered the entire new last chapter to the typists several hours ago, and will deliver about a hundred more new insert pages in a few days." Two weeks later I was writing Korda, "I am mailing this airmail at the same time that I am mailing, under separate cover, two revised versions of *The Prize*. I am also enclosing here a six-page memo explaining some of my major cuts and changes, and why I chose to retain other sections."

The rewritten, revised, tightened manuscript of the novel was on its way to New York, and now I suffered a week of anxiety as I awaited the reactions of my editor and my publisher.

On November 6, 1961, my editor gave me his reaction:

"I reread *The Prize* over the weekend, and I enjoyed it as much as I did the first time around. I think that's a good sign. I checked through all the revisions, which seem to me fine. The scenes between Denise and Lindblom are *much, much* better. The Sue Wiley scene is fine, and obviously shouldn't have been cut, now that I read it again. I think toning Garrett down has made him much more real a character. . . . I got the feeling that the book now moves faster, despite the fact that it's about the same length. This is especially true of Chapter XII, which, in its new version, has much more pace and excitement. . . . In the new Chapter XII, by the way, Krantz emerges as a much more interesting person. This seems to me one of the happiest outcomes of the revisions. Anyway, I think we're ready to go, and go we will."

A day later I heard from my publisher:

"My feelings concur with those stated in Mike's letter. Therefore, I'll only say that I think the time and trouble you took with revisions was well worth while, and thank you. I must admit that I still have some reservations about the East German situation being mixed up in this book, and that it still seems to me a little out of place, but we've argued this out long and hard and it's your book and I like what you now have done much better than I did the original version. So let's go. . . ."

But they were not quite ready to go, as it turned out. For now, from two copy editors and stylists, I was inundated with eleventh-hour queries. These arrived the week before Christmas. Accompanying them was an interoffice memorandum from the copy editor assigned to the book, Ann Maulsby, to the chief copy editor, Sophie Sorkin:

"Here is *The Prize,* at last. As you know, I found it a fascinating piece of work, and so full of suspense that it was a struggle for me to keep my mind on my work. I went through it twice, though, and I hope the author will understand that I did so with loving care. In a colossal manuscript like this, containing so many facts in so many fields, and so many words in so many foreign languages, it would have been a miracle if there had been no inadvertent errors. I would like the author to know that all changes in spellings, dates, etc., have been made in accordance with a recognized source: Webster, of course, in the case of many words and proper names. Mr. Lars Malmstrom of the Swedish Information Service was more than courteously helpful, and is my authority on Swedish matters in this ms. I checked French, Norwegian, Danish, and German information with the respective consulates, and the Italian words were checked with an Italian-born teacher of Italian. Mrs. Sienitzsky in the Russian library of Radio Liberation had all the Russian data at her fingertips.

"The attached list of queries to the author will seem very long to you—and to him. But I was careful to make no change in the ms. that he could possibly object to, and where there was even the slightest question, I listed it so that he could make the decision."

A sampling of queries, and my replies:

COPY EDITOR: "Page 33. 'Kurfsdamm.' The Kurfürstendamm is called Ku'damm, not Kurfsdamm, according to my German authority. Change?"

AUTHOR: "I have just phoned my German expert. Ku'damm is correct. Please change."

COPY EDITOR: "Page 170. Note change in re time shown by jewelers' clocks. Time varies between 8:15 and 8:20; many are 8:18. O.K.?"

AUTHOR: "My line is 'she would also remember reading somewhere.' I suspect she read *Nuggets of Knowledge* by George W. Stimpson, NYC, Sully, 1932, who replies in detail to the question,

'Why are dummy clocks set at 8:18?' Legend has it that dummy clocks are usually set at 8:18, because that was supposed to have been the time of Lincoln's death, which it was not. Actually done because it is the most symmetrical arrangement for the hands of a clock. Anyway, leave it as I have it—8:18 is stet."

COPY EDITOR: "Page 222. 'Composed.' This word implies that Key wrote the music for 'The Star-Spangled Banner.' Since he wrote only the words, do you want to change this?"

AUTHOR: "Yes, change 'composed' to 'written.' "

COPY EDITOR: "Page 288. Is this true? Articles in Encyc. Brit. and Collier's Encyc. do not mention Plato's being sold into slavery and being ransomed by Anniceris."

AUTHOR: "My source is Diogenes Laertius. More modern source is *The Story of Philosophy* by Will Durant, 'In the year 387 B.C. Plato received an invitation from Dionysius . . . to come and turn his kingdom into Utopia. . . . Story has it that Plato was sold into slavery, to be rescued by his friend and pupil Anniceris, who, when Plato's Athenian followers wished to reimburse him for the ransom he had paid, refused.' Anyway, as to Plato's being ransomed—truth is not necessary, only legend, for Craig is basing a work of fiction on a possibly true tradition."

COPY EDITOR: "Page 338. Author mentions Knut Hamsun snapping Selma Lagerlöf's girdle. Can author substantiate?"

AUTHOR: "The tale of Knut Hamsun's snapping Selma Lagerlöf's girdle while in a state of insobriety is true and supported by the best authority. I obtained this in a letter dated 1949 from the head of the official —— Office in Stockholm. See enclosed Exhibit A, copy of original."

COPY EDITOR: "Page 480. 'Indent.' Not a Swedish name. There is a title, *Intendent,* and the head of a Swedish publishing house would have this title."

AUTHOR: "Now we come to the case of Mr. Indent Flink—ah, if only Conan Doyle were here. Since 1946 I have always supposed Indent to be Swedish name. See attached Exhibit B, a copy from my 1946 Journal. It says Sylvia had arranged to interview a Lapp expert in Stockholm whose first name is noted as 'Indent.' I loved the Indent for years and now have used it. Could I have got it wrong?

A possibility. But there it is. If there is no Indent in Sweden—can I not create one? Blame it on his mother, a paragrapher. Should we leave it or no? I say leave it. But if you think it is absolutely wrong, then I suppose he will have to become Lennart Flink. What think you?"

COPY EDITOR: "Page 482. 'As baffling as the Rosetta stone.' Is this the simile you want here, when it was the Rosetta stone that helped decipher the Egyptian hieroglyphics?"

AUTHOR: "Ann is absolutely right. Change to, 'And found them as baffling as the inscriptions on the Kensington Stone.' "

COPY EDITOR: "Page 629. Author says *Glogg* is burnt brandy. *Glogg* is a Christmas toddy."

AUTHOR: "My *Svensk-Engelski Ordlista,* published in Stockholm, 1937, supplied by the Grand Hotel, says, '*Glogg* . . . burnt brandy.' William Sansom, in *The Icicle and The Sun,* says, 'a glass of hot Christmas *glogg,* made from *snaps* and steaming spiced wine.' Ma'am, that ain't Christmas toddy to me—that's a falling down drink. Stet."

COPY EDITOR; "Page 844. Author says Märta has 'a concave bosom.' Is that okay? It didn't actually curve *in?*"

AUTHOR: "Well, no, her bosom did not dip inward. There is a type of female figure where, from shoulders down the chest bone, there is a hunched, concave area before the slight rise of the breasts. To be accurate, I should change it to read, 'water sliding down her concave breastbone and slight bosom and sleek flanks and dripping to the poolside.' "

COPY EDITOR: "Page 1038. 'H.M. the King.' O.K.? I don't think 'His Majesty' is abbreviated. H.R.H. would do, but I don't think H.M. will."

AUTHOR: "I know it is curious, but keep it stet. In 1949, Pearl Buck and her late husband were kind enough to send me her original Nobel Prize schedule, entitled 'Memorandum,' handed her in Stockholm. I have followed this official Memorandum, except for altering to suit my fictional characters and their stories, and this Memorandum actually reads, 'H.M. the King.' See enclosed Exhibit C."

COPY EDITOR: "Page 1158. Here you have him 'a hale and boisterous hostage.' But on page 1157 you have him 'this weak old man.' "

AUTHOR: "Thank you. I rewrite here to read now, 'he found himself confronting a hale and boisterous hostage. Craig realized that the façade of weakness he saw was one he had built in his own mind and imposed upon Walther. It had no reality. Craig felt cheated.' "

COPY EDITOR: "General note. In the purely literary department, I made no changes except to correct typos or other outright errors, of which there were few. The chief syntactical error was the dangler. There were several. Where the author had 'Listening, Sue Wiley's eyes glared,' I changed this to 'As she listened, Sue Wiley's eyes glared.' He certainly would want these inadvertent booboos corrected, wouldn't he?"

AUTHOR: "He certainly would. Thanks for catching the danglers. Thanks to all of you for your wonderful help."

I thought that I was through, but the sudden arrival of a legal letter forced me to go to work again. Simon and Schuster had shown the manuscript to their attorney, Ephraim London, and he wanted to be certain that none of the names I had given my individual fictional characters coincided with the names of persons living in the cities in which I had placed these characters. Especially was he concerned about John Garrett and the persons whom I had invented to participate with him in group-therapy sessions. More research and checking, and finally my reply to my editor and the company's attorney, ran in part:

"There is no John Garrett, in fact no Garrett at all, listed under 'Physicians' in Pasadena or in the Los Angeles Central Telephone Directory. Sylvia went to her doctor and leafed through his medical directories. Again, no John Garrett, M.D., in this area. . . . Re Mrs. Perrin. There are 37 Perrins in the Directory. . . . Re Miss Dudzinski. None. The name is common in Kenosha, Wisconsin, where I come from—Polish-Lithuanian—and my high school yearbooks abound with Dudzinskis or variations. That is from where I plucked the name—from memory.

"I assume you will check out the other American names. I usually invent names as follows: for a German physicist I will make up, from five or ten sources (history books, political books, biographies, what not), a long list of common last names—and then, from memory or my set of baby-naming books, assign some different first name. Sometimes I will change spellings slightly. That's how Max Stratman's name was born. . . . My Swedish names I got as follows: I had brought a Stockholm telephone directory back with me. I made list after list of last names, then list after list of given names, scrambled the two lists together, and in this way invented new combinations. Example, Lilly Hedqvist—invented— but both names common in Sweden, common separately. I took great care with Count Bertil Jacobsson. I felt he had a crucial role since I tied him in with the actual Foundation. I deliberately took a name which a Count *could not have* in Sweden—much to the distress of my Swedish experts—but this makes us absolutely safe—and anyway, Jacobsson for this man is so, so right.

"Tell Mr. London I made up Winston Churchill (although there are three Winston Churchills in Stockholm, all sleigh instructors). I also made up Hungarians, since it is obvious they don't exist."

At last, *The Prize* was being set in type.

With the coming of 1962—and with it came two weeks of meticulous and exhausting revisions made in the margins of the galley sheets—the novel was out of my hands, and my involvement with it was less all-consuming and more pleasurable.

At this stage, you have time, at last, to write your friends, and while you speak of your book, you can also speak of other matters. To Jerome Weidman: "Essandess are coming out with *The Prize* in April or May, big plans. . . . I've been avoiding the Hollywood crowd pretty much. The town is having its miseries. Most everyone is in TV, which is often boring, so dinner parties are more boring unless you drink, which I do. . . . What else is there to say? My mother can't find a pill for her nerves. My father's ulcer keeps acting up. Sylvia's father is in the sanitarium and speaks of her old boy friends. My son is in 9th grade and working at French and speaking warmly of the night we took him to the Folies. My daughter is in first grade and watches 'Bonanza' on television. Paul Reynolds will be out here tomorrow and we are dining. . . . And there is always the sun, which is good but which I don't see. (Also, one hamster died.)"

You await mail from your publisher. You see specimens of the paper stock and type face, sent by Helen Barrow, the production manager. You learn what the retail price of the book will be. (To Korda: "$6.95? I cannot believe it. I think it is a grave error. There was a party last night with Kip Fadiman, Irving Stone and Ray Bradbury present, and among other things we talked about publishers' book pricing. . . .") You hear of the crucial reaction of the publisher's salesmen at the semiannual sales conference. (From Korda: "We had our sales conference today, and presented *The Prize* formally to the salesmen. They were enormously excited, and the general feeling was that the subject of the book guaranteed better sales than we had for *The Chapman Report*. Anyway, great, great enthusiasm and conviction on their part. And that counts.")

You learn that your publisher has decided to send out five hundred photocopies of the manuscript version of the first chapter to "our own salesmen, bookstores, and major accounts," and you are ecstatic. You await the first proof of the book jacket (I had objected to the first jacket sketch, and happily another was designed which satisfied everyone). You send off implausible exploitation ideas. You are worried your publisher might use the wrong approach when presenting the book to the public. You are quickly reassured by a letter from your editor: "We agree with you when you say that the Nobel Prize should take a second place to the story and characters, and I think we can devise some way of doing this that will still preserve the excitement inherent in the Prize itself, and yet keep the primary emphasis on the fact that this is a novel about *people.*"

You receive an advance copy of the printed book, fresh from the bindery, and it is difficult to let go of it long enough to acknowledge its receipt. You write your publisher: "May 8, 1962. Dear Peter, IT ARRIVED! It looks marvelous. I love the color and feel of the binding, and the compact bulk of it, and all in all I'm pleased. This is a thrilling day. I've had six before, and this is the seventh, and the pulse still jumps as before. Luck to both of us! . . . ~~Andrew Craig~~ Irving Wallace."

Then other things begin to happen, and you are manic and you are depressive, and you live on the peak of high hopes and you live in the vale of despair, and your wife wishes that she had married that nice accountant after all. The advance orders from bookstores are high, and you sing exultantly if off key. The publisher invests $1,000 in an early three-page advertisement in *Publishers' Weekly*, the book industry's major trade journal, and you vow you will remember him in your will. Although you feel as if you were a castaway on a desert island, three thousand miles from New York (where civilization is concentrated, the publishers say), you are found by representatives of the New York press, and your Crusoe complex disappears.

You know there are two key trade reviews put out six or seven weeks before a book's official publication, and you await them, and they come too soon: the Virginia Kirkus Service, a biweekly newsletter giving advance reviews of forthcoming books, says you have written "a long and popularly prefabricated novel" and that while "this will win no literary prize, it may cop a wide market," and you sulk and morbidly study your razor, because all of your blood, sweat, and backaches, all of your brilliant inventions, perceptions, and researches, all of your dreams of literary glory, have been brought down and down to what the unknowing know as commercialism. Suddenly you have the second judgment; you have *Publishers' Weekly* with its considerably more influential "Fiction Forecast" by Jessie Kitching, and you learn that you have written "a gripping novel . . . tense . . . explosive. . . . The reader will find the personal stories genuinely fascinating . . . expect large sales for this one," and you are off again, in that high place where people walk only on ceilings, and hell is truly become heaven, and where Kirkus is a swearword and Kitching is your other wife.

What is left? Nothing but to sit back, armed with bottle and pills, and wait for publication day.

PART
III

BIRTH

The Prize was published on June 11, 1962.

Publication day, in the novelist's personal world, usually has little meaning. It dawns with much less excitement than does his son's birthday or his daughter's Open House. No rockets go off that day, no gifts arrive, no applause is heard, no feast is held. It is not comparable to a playwright's highly charged opening night or even to a screenwriter's attendance at a sneak preview or the premiere of his latest film. The author was alone before publication day, and usually he is alone, in a sense, all through this day, too. Sometimes a limping telegram of congratulations and good-luck wishes will come in from his agent or editor or an understanding fellow novelist—sometimes, but rarely. His wife, pitying him, may break open a bottle of domestic champagne.

What publication day really represents is an arbitrary date after which bookstores throughout the nation may display the novel (although most stores have received their shipments and put their books on sale weeks before) and a date after which magazines and newspapers may release their reviews of it. Also, this date sets the time at which "advance orders" are replaced by "reorders." The measurement of a book's commercial success is determined by the publisher's weekly count of these reorders. For if a certain bookshop in Cleveland has had ten copies in stock and on display, and then writes or wires in a reorder for ten more, the publisher knows that the store has actually sold its first ten copies.

Publication day for *The Prize* was somewhat different from what it had been for my earlier books. I had gone to New York six days before the official birth of *The Prize* to give interviews. My seventh day in New York, and my last one there, was a Monday and the day of publication. I noted the events of this long-awaited day in my Journal:

"Pub date. Awakened at 9 in our suite at the Plaza. Down to the Edwardian Room for breakfast. Korda called Sylvia, said next Sunday's *New York Times Book Review* carries a big and favorable review. Korda sent a copy over, and I was thrilled. Phoned the publisher. Advance sales till today over 34,000 copies shipped.

"At 12:30, Associated Press Radio's Kay Lawrence interviewed me in Café Louis XIV. Next, long drive downtown to New York *World-Telegram* where feature writer Robert Saffron interviewed me in the city room. Back to Rockefeller Center and up to Simon and Schuster to be interviewed by Martha MacGregor of the New York *Post's* book page.

"Spoke to Korda, Schwed, was shown advance of *Time* magazine review, which ignored discussing book, simply attacked me. Saw John Barkham's review in New York *World-Telegram,* released by Saturday Review Syndicate, and was most pleased.

"Returned to the Plaza. Talked to Amy and David long-distance. Off to have dinner with Peggy and Jerome Weidman at San Marino restaurant. Back to rooms to pack for California tomorrow."

After that, the book began to receive the maximum exposure possible through the appearance of reviews, advertisements, interviews, feature articles, and column paragraphs about it. Upon this exposure—as well as the support of personnel in the nation's bookshops and reader interest in the novel's subject or the author's name—would depend the initial sales of the book. And after that, it would be entirely the public's verdict. The public would either ignore the book or proceed to read it. If read, the book would then be either condemned or praised, and if praised, there might be generated that magical word of mouth that excites more and more people to read a book. This verdict would decide the fate of my book, fifteen years after I had conceived it and two years after I had begun to write it. Curiously, some of the comments and events that followed publication helped underline and highlight, or more clearly define, at least for me, what I had been trying to do during my actual creation of the book.

The reviews came in a deluge. And from the first montage of headlines, I could see that a great play was being made on the words "Nobel" and "noble" and on the word "prize." The headlines were dizzying: the Long Island *Newsday*, NOBLE WORK ON THE NOBEL WORKS; the Oakland *Tribune*, WALLACE NOVEL WILL WIN NO PRIZE, BUT IT'S DELIGHTFUL; the Washington, D. C. *News*, THE BOOBY PRIZE; the Houston *Press*, IG-NOBEL "PRIZE" MAY NOT WIN ONE BUT IT WILL SELL; Charlotte *Observer*, THE PRIZE OFFERS PRIZE CHARACTERS; the Dayton *News*, THE PRIZE IS RIGHT.

The reviews were diverse enough to infect any author, if this were possible, with a lifelong case of schizophrenia. The average reader sees only a few reviews. The author himself, if he wishes, can see them all. Are they instructive? Let us find out.

First, they considered the question: Was the idea of creating a novel around the Nobel Prize awards a sound idea for a book?

According to the Baltimore *Morning Sun*, the Nobel Prize "seems an unlikely subject around which to weave the threads of a novel." Yet the Greensboro, North Carolina, *News*, states that "this is a wonderful ready-made plot."

Next, what were the author's feelings while he was writing the novel?

The author learns from *The New Yorker:* "In a postscript, Mr. Wallace says, 'The gestation period of this novel was fifteen years.' He does not add, because he does not need to, the writing of it was sheer drudgery." But then the author is reassured by the Richmond *News Leader:* "It is clear that this novel has been a labor of love. . . ."

Did the author succeed in his creation and development of lifelike fictional characters?

According to *The National Observer,* the people "are wooden
. . . more caricature than character," and according to the Newark *News,* they are "bloodless, sleepwalking characters." On the
other hand, the Chicago *Sun-Times* announces that the author "succeeded in the difficult task of delineating a number of totally different characters with honesty, depth, and feeling," and the Tampa
Tribune agrees that the "winners are masterfully portrayed in
depth, height, and width."

What were the comments on the plot or story line of the novel?

The Charleston, South Carolina, *Post* states that "the plot con-
trivance shows through at times when the covering wears thin." Yet
the Salt Lake City *Tribune* believes that "the unity of the novel is
perfect," and that the author "has the ability, seldom seen now-
adays, of tying together plot and subplots without leaving any loose
ends."

What were the reactions to the author's writing style?

The author is told by the Washington, D. C., *Star* that the prose
is "inelegant and turgid." But then he is reassured by both the
Hartford *Courant* and the Springfield, Massachusetts, *Republican*
that the book is "well-written."

What were the reactions to the novel's storytelling?

Here there were no dissents. The Associated Press promises that
"There is never a dull moment. This is storytelling for its own sake.
. . . This is popular reading in the good old-fashioned sense.
Wallace has rung the bell of sheer narrative excitement." And this
was echoed in all the city reviews, even the most grudging ones.

What was the response to the climactic final chapter that the
author had revised so often?

The National Observer believes that "the manufactured happy
ending," and other faults, "make *The Prize* a simultaneous literary
failure and a commercial success." Opposing this view, the Salt
Lake City *Tribune* is satisfied that "the climax is unexpected and
completely logical."

How did the reviewers react to the handling of love and sex in
the novel?

There is a deluge of comment, accompanied by violent disagreement.

According to *Time,* "Wallace's intellectual giants have feet of such soft clay that they find it difficult to stay upright for longer than a chapter. They tumble into bed with all the verve of the casual Californians in 'The Chapman Report.' " To which the New York *World-Telegram* added, "What will lift most eyebrows, I imagine, is the emphatically sexual character of the story with which the author fleshes out his facts. . . . What has happened is that some of Mr. Wallace's preoccupation with the boudoir has spilled from 'The Chapman Report' (where it belongs) to 'The Prize' (where it obtrudes). This is not a matter of prudishness but of proportion." And the Detroit *Free Press* announced flatly, "To assure the book's success, Wallace has indiscriminately scattered sex throughout." And the Columbus *Dispatch* lectured, "This author is one who does not need to sensationalize sex to sell books. He has a number of scenes in 'The Prize' all too evidently written for no other purpose but which are unnecessary and serve only to slow down the action. Anyone who writes as well as Wallace does both himself and some of his potential readers a disservice by resorting to a tawdry device that only cheapens and pollutes an otherwise fine novel."

On the other hand, according to *The Book Buyer's Guide,* " 'The Prize' is a staid and restrained narrative." To which the Dayton *News* added, "It makes up in suspense and violence what it lacks in sex." And from Clifton Fadiman in the *Book-of-the-Month Club News* the statement, "Particularly interesting is the candid revelation of the relaxed and wholesome sexual morality of Sweden." And from the Dallas *Times Herald,* "It's a relief from the oversexed 'Chapman Report.' " And from the Springfield, Missouri, *News and Leader,* "Sometimes it is hilarious, particularly in the bedroom scenes."

What about the author's having integrated factual research with fiction in *The Prize?* The degree to which this technique had been employed had caused differences between my wife and myself, and again between my publisher and editor. How had the reviewers reacted to the inclusion of such factual documentation in a fictional work?

Newsweek feels that the book possesses "all the local detail of a

James A. Fitzpatrick Traveltalk." The Chicago *Tribune* decides
that, "The fault of the novel is that Wallace has shoved in every
last word of research." Many other reviews concurred. The Richmond, Virginia, *News Leader* agrees that "the serious defects of
the novel stem from the sheer glut of information such documentation creates; it arrests the narrative pace and even worse, destroys
the plausibility of characterization too often."

On the other hand, an equal number of reviewers feel that the
documentary technique is commendable. According to Clifton Fadiman in the *Book-of-the-Month Club News,* "What gives this . . .
narrative its motive power is the extraordinary vividness of the
Stockholm scene and the seemingly absolute authority with which
Mr. Wallace retails secret after secret involving actual awards of
the immediate and distant past." To this there are many amens.
For the Oakland *Tribune,* "Some of the novel's most absorbing
moments are those having to do with the Nobel Prizes themselves."
For the Newark *News* this research was the novel's "sturdiest virtue," and for the San Francisco *News-Call Bulletin* the use of factual material helped the book rise "to the heights of noble elo-
quence." In fact, to the Spokane *Chronicle* this "prodigious
amount of information" was often "far more interesting than any
of the activities of Irving Wallace's six fictional laureates."

When taking an overall view of my novel, the critics fell into
three distinct categories. A small number hated the book, found no
merit in it whatsoever; the greatest number liked the book, but
found some imperfections in it; and a fair number loved the book,
found it completely wonderful. Here, then, a sampling of the
widely varied reactions:

The out-and-out haters: According to *Newsweek,* "For the con-
noisseur who deliberately seeks out the worst movie of the year or
the most tasteless pop song, this novel is full of rewards." And the
Cleveland *Press,* "For the most part these people are more interested in sex than in scientific or literary achievement. It's not in
good taste, but the movies have it." And the Washington *News,*
" 'The Prize' isn't as nasty a confection as Mr. Wallace's 'The Chapman Report,' but it ought to sell better. There's more of it."

The qualified but favorable ones: According to *The New York*

Times Book Review, "That 'The Prize' is a continuously readable
—and sometimes eloquent—novel there can be no doubt. Mr. Wallace is a cerebral professional with a Balzacian flair, and he is aim-
ing at the widest audience. Whether his novel is equally successful
in form and content is another matter. Now and then the basic
contrivances of plot and character show through, especially in the
closing two hundred pages. . . . For its general information and
style, for its topical interest and historical background, an award of
merit is herewith voted to 'The Prize.' Flaws and all, it's a good buy
for readers." And the Saturday Review Syndicate, "The author has
coped with his cornucopia of research in a manner that must in-
spire respect for his agility, if not his selectivity. 'The Prize' is massive, sometimes discursive, but always hypnotically readable." And
the Phoenix *Arizona Republic,* "In spite of its major faults of plotting and taste, 'The Prize' is nevertheless mesmeric reading. Most
readers will become caught up with the characters, never quite be-
lieving them but compelled to find out how they extricate themselves from their respective dilemmas." And the Washington *Post,*
"The story is marred by several outrageously contrived coincidences and an overdose of sensationalism. Yet, despite its melodramatic aspects, 'The Prize' is an engrossing and fascinating
novel." And the San Francisco *News-Call Bulletin,* "A novel like
Irving Wallace's 'The Prize' embarrasses a book reviewer. He
knows it isn't first-rate, but he had to finish it. He distrusts the
excitement it arouses in him as he reads it, but he is sure it will be a
best seller. He feels that much of it is meretricious and shameless
exploitation of his emotions, but neither was Charles Dickens
above shameless sentimentality."

The ones who loved it: According to the International News
Service, "The word 'remarkable' is applicable to Wallace's opus
because it is (a) a literary work of art; (b) it is thoroughly engrossing reading matter that maintains its quality and interest without a
letdown through 768 pages." And the Boston *Herald,* "The characters are definitely entities in themselves. They have breath and
blood and there are no pauses in the swift movement of the story
and the interest this panoramic novel engenders. A book which I
hope everyone will read not just because it is a fine and honest

achievement; unselfconscious, straightforward, perceptive and true but because of the effect it is bound to have on the heart, mind and outlook of the reader." And the Worcester *Telegram,* "Felicitous in style and insight, it is a literary gem that shines and sparkles in every polished facet." And the Hartford *Courant,* "Most readers will wish the book were twice as long. Well-written, well-plotted, well-researched, this book is certainly one which can be recommended without reservation." And the Boston *Globe,* "Told with excitement and drama that stirs both the heart and the imagination. Each character in the huge canvas stands out as clearly as the unforgettable faces in a Brueghel painting."

Scanning almost two hundred American reviews, I found that while reviewers singled out various scenes in my novel for favorable or unfavorable comment, there was one scene that was quoted, in whole or part, in nine leading reviews. Located on page 25 of the hardcover edition and page 22 of the paperback edition of *The Prize,* this is the tag end of the scene where Denise Marceau telephones her husband Claude in the Paris apartment of his mistress, Gisèle Jordan. Claude and Gisèle are in bed together when the telephone rings, and Gisèle takes the call and learns that the voice on the other end belongs to her lover's wife. The scene goes on as follows:

"Gisèle was dumbfounded, helpless. Her poise was gone. She covered the mouthpiece fully, and looked imploringly at Claude. 'Your wife—she knows—'

" 'No, I cannot. Say anything,' he begged.

"Gisèle would not return to the telephone. 'She says it's important—'

"The length of their exchange had given them away, and Claude knew it. Miserably, he disengaged his body from Gisèle's, took the prosecuting telephone, and sat up, cross-legged, on the bed.

" 'Denise? Listen to me—'

" 'You listen, you rotten pig—you pull your pants on and come home. The press is on its way—we've just won the Nobel Prize!' "

Thus, the end of the introductory Marceau scene, which was used to lead off the reviews of the Washington *News* and Pasadena

Star-News, and was quoted extensively in publications ranging from the St. Paul *Dispatch* to *Time* magazine.

Also, in scanning my reviews, of which perhaps thirty appeared in major newspapers or magazines, I found that fourteen of the reviews devoted much of their allotted space to reporting that Metro-Goldwyn-Mayer had purchased motion-picture rights to the book, and named the six-figure price paid. Most of these reviews that mentioned the film sale also happened to be—possibly by co-incidence—unfavorable reviews, and they included such widely read publications as *Time, Newsweek, The National Observer,* the Cleveland *Press,* and the Austin *American-Statesman.* The lesson, I suppose, is that no novelist should permit premature sale of motion-picture rights to a forthcoming book, or if they are sold, he should not permit the studio or producer to announce the fact until the book itself has been published and the critics have had an unprejudiced look at it.

In the years since, I have frequently found reviewers coupling my books with their motion-picture sales in a way harmful to the novels and detrimental to me as a novelist. Typically, and perhaps more viciously than this sort of thing is usually done, a novelist-lecturer named Herbert Kubly wrote in his article "The Vanishing Novel," published in the *Saturday Review:*

"Ideas are sprung over breakfast Bloody Marys in Hollywood's Beverly Hills Hotel or over Scotch-on-the-rocks in New York's Toots Shor's, or on a long-distance phone between the two. A publisher makes a deal with a film producer who promises an advertising snow job and a seven-star cinematic production. Among such Hollywood-inspired best-sellers are works by . . . Irving Wallace. . . . Such trashy books purveyed as literature with a high price can hardly stimulate long-range buying and reading of fiction."

Literary commentators of this stripe, perhaps because of their own frustrations, are quick to denigrate a novel because it will be adapted into a motion picture. The enormous publicity attending a sale of motion-picture rights inspires countless such falsehoods and calumnies. The Kublys will not bother to investigate in order to find out what is true or what is not true. Nor will the editors of the

Saturday Review. As a consequence, reviewers become prejudiced by misinformation, and through them thousands of readers, librarians, literature professors are equally deceived by untrue or dishonest equations of novels with the motion pictures they spawn.

Speaking as a novelist who has had the good fortune to have sold film rights to six of his eleven books, I have every reason to have affection for motion pictures. But, literary commentators and critics notwithstanding, I cannot conceive that any serious novelist would deliberately slant a novel to effect a possible motion-picture sale.

I would suggest that it is next to impossible to prefabricate a novel successfully with a motion-picture sale as the ultimate goal. I would also suggest it ridiculous to consider receiving motion-picture ideas for novels from film producers over "breakfast Bloody Marys" or to attempt to develop "Hollywood-inspired best-sellers" from these ideas. This kind of malicious backbiting is part of the myth perpetrated by literary commentators who have no knowledge of working novelists or motion-picture executives. For the working novelist to produce a book that would be just right for the screen would require the construction of a book that would be all wrong for the reading public. And without that reading public, the novelist could never sell his book to the screen. As for motion-picture executives, they would hold in disdain any brainchild produced by or written for them through artificial insemination, because they would have no faith in its originality or natural public acceptance.

I adhere to the belief that the novelist, except for his role as a spectator, should have no interest in motion pictures. Every novelist, myself included, hopes and prays that Hollywood will purchase film rights to his novels. Such a subsidiary windfall, as I have stated earlier, just like a book-club sale or a foreign-rights sale, must be regarded in the same way that the writer would regard the lucky possession of a winning lottery ticket. The novelist's only concern must be, as mine has always been, for the book itself, for the novel being written as a book.

Yet it is not always the sale of film rights alone that creates antagonism in the press. There is something else. It is the fact that a motion-picture sale is synonymous with money, just as a best seller is also synonymous with money. And to link a writer's name with money is to bring under suspicion his motives and his literary product, as well as to imply a lack of integrity, a selling out, a pandering to the public.

I have never understood this attitude from the literary press. Any other kind of creative artist, on any level, can allow the amount of his earnings to become publicized, be he Picasso, Olivier, Stravinsky, Nureyev, and his integrity is not impugned and reviews of his work are not prejudiced. Money actually serves to prove his value. He remains pure. But in the literary world, money is equated with corruption. A novelist may perform many abnormal, illegal, or antisocial acts. He may admit to homosexuality, alcoholism, addiction to drugs, a penchant for mistresses; he may beat his wife and kick small animals; and somehow this is acceptable, even colorful, and somehow it enhances the literary image. But money, never money, the root of all evil—including evil reviews.

While discussing this subject, I am reminded of a recent episode which reveals reviewer mentality. The book editor of the Santa Ana, California, *Register,* William Melton, had published a feature story in which authors looked at critics, and in this he had used parallel interviews with Irving Stone and myself. When Melton had asked me what I believed a balanced book review should contain, I had told him what I thought. I had also told him what a balanced review should not contain. "A good book review," I said, "should not contain anything about the author's domestic or social behavior, income tax bracket, or supposed motivations for writing his work. These aspects of the author's life belong to the gossip columnist, the accountant, the psychiatrist. Only the product of the author's pen should be the concern of a good review." In this same feature story I had referred to "newsmagazines" as being among the worst offenders when it came to unbalanced and dishonest reviewing. William Melton passed on copies of his feature story to *Time,* where a lady, authorized to speak "For the Editors," replied, "With all the books that Irvings Stone and Wallace have sold—they should be worrying about what the critics think?"

Yet, despite those who speak "For the Editors," novelists do

worry about what the critics think. They fret over bad reviews because they are, by their very nature, unsure, uncertain, sensitive
human beings whose stock-in-trade consists of fragile ideas and
words. They fret over savage reviews because rejection of their
work before the eyes of the world means rejection of themselves
and of years of their working lives. They fret over unfair reviews
because they fear that such reviews may keep their work from a
large segment of the public.

However, it is clear that no review, no matter how bad or how
unfair, can seriously injure the sale of a book if the public desires
to read it. Most members of the reading public have minds of their
own and somehow determine for themselves what will interest
them. At the same time, there is concrete evidence that a number of
dishonest reviews can turn some segment of the undecided public
away from a specific book or author. I can cite as an example an
experience I had two years after *The Prize,* when I published *The
Man.* Although there was a great demand for this book by library
users, numerous libraries refused to provide the book for these
readers. Not long ago, I was shown a book-review column that had
appeared in the Winchester, Massachusetts, *Star* written by Leila-
Jane Roberts of the Winchester Public Library. In reviewing this
novel, *The Man,* she wrote:

"Irving Wallace is looked down on by librarians and others interested in serious writing as one who sells the movie rights before
he finishes writing a novel, and who creates expressly for the best-
seller market—often building a novel on sensational news headlines rather than on more enduring human values and endeavors.
Therefore, when this book came out, it was prejudged perhaps un-
wisely. Reviews were not encouraging . . . about the place of this
book in a permanent library collection. . . . But alas, reviews are
not any more infallible than the individuals who write them. Here
is one book which the library decided not to buy and which may
well be used in social-studies courses fifty years from now much as
Upton Sinclair's *The Jungle* is used today. . . . We erred in not
adding this book to the collection. . . . It is now a part of the
public library collection and will be in circulation by the time this
review is published."

All the while that I had been receiving clippings of the reviews on *The Prize,* I was in touch with my publisher or my editor, frequently commenting to them upon these reviews. On June 19, I was writing my editor, "The first reviews are starting to come in . . . for the most I am extremely well pleased. The majority I see are good, and even the in-betweens and bads are generally selling ones. Of course, I saw *New Yorker* yesterday. It didn't even upset me. It was simply too ridiculous: this labor of love a 'drudgery.' Of course it was their ass-backward way of making a criticism, but just too silly." On June 27, I was writing my publisher, "Did you see the marvelous International News Service syndicated Kinnaird review? It set me up, along with the other stuff, wonderfully. The reviews are streaming in, and all of them are at least *interesting.*" Then, on July 28, another letter went to my editor, with this added note: "I had a lovely letter from Somerset Maugham today. He just received *The Prize,* which, for sentimental reasons, I had sent him at his villa on the Riviera—and he is about to leave on a long trip and is taking the novel along for reading en route."

Shortly after the reviews appeared, there arose two controversies concerning *The Prize,* both widely aired in the press, and they drew more attention to the book than a novel ordinarily receives.

The first controversy, a lesser and a not unfamiliar one, grew out of the reviews in which critics had speculated on the real-life prototypes of my fictional characters. As the Coffeyville, Kansas, *Journal,* put it:

"A new literary guessing-game will probably be in vogue with the publication of the new novel by Irving Wallace, 'The Prize.' . . . Wallace has chosen as one of his characters a novelist who is a drunkard, which will recall a real novelist who did win The Prize, and who was fond of his cups. He has another in the recipient for the prize for medicine—who shares the prize with another scientist he is convinced stole his own work and glory. This too suggests a real scientist who made just such a charge."

The "guessing-game" had begun. Whom did I have in mind when I created the characters of Denise and Claude Marceau? The Riverside, California, *Press Enterprise* suggested that I had written about "two Pierre and Marie Curie type French chemists on the verge of divorce." The St. Louis *Post-Dispatch* was more certain, although it voted for the Curies' son-in-law and daughter, and spoke of "The Marceaus—pale imitations of the Joliot-Curies."

And who was *really* Mårta Norberg, my Swedish actress in the book? Easy? For *The New York Times,* yes. She was "the Garbo-like movie star with whom Andrew Craig involves himself." For the New York *Herald-Tribune,* also, she was "a Garboesque actress sulking in semiretirement."

And on whom had I based the characters of my Swedish nudist, Lilly Hedqvist, and my brash American newspaperwoman, Sue Wiley? The Montgomery, Alabama, *Advertiser* had the answers. Lilly was the "immoral Swedish girl (shades of Marilyn Monroe)," and Sue was the "nasty newspaperwoman after scandal (shades of Dorothy Kilgallen)."

But most of the speculation revolved around the author-hero of my novel. Of whom had I been thinking when I invented Andrew Craig? Clifton Fadiman, in the *Book-of-the-Month Club News* said, "Andrew Craig is central to the story, and cannot fail to recall the figure of Sinclair Lewis." The Montgomery *Advertiser* disagreed, and offered its own candidate, "shades of Faulkner." The Chicago *Tribune* voted with Fadiman, stating, "Wallace does brilliantly with Craig, who is reminiscent of Sinclair Lewis." The Omaha *World-Herald* also agreed that Craig was "so reminiscent of Sinclair Lewis." However, the New York *Journal-American* could find no literary cannibalism, for it reported that, "Aside from his being a periodic drunk, Andrew Craig doesn't have specific traits of character in common with any actual male U. S. winners of the Nobel laurels." The Norfolk *Virginian-Pilot* concurred in part, when it stated, "The novelist is not identifiable with any novelist I know of, but had characteristics of several recognizable American writers." But then, the Detroit *Free Press* made it a landslide for Sinclair Lewis, with its unequivocal stand that "There are three scientists, two doctors and an American author (Wallace even lacks the imagination to base this character on anyone but Sinclair Lewis)."

The last barb, I felt, was potentially dangerous because it transcended mere sport. Here was no "reminiscent of" or "shades of"

Sinclair Lewis, but Craig-is-Lewis, period. I decided to answer directly, not only this newspaper, but all speculators. On July 12, 1962, I wrote to the Detroit *Free Press* as follows:

"In speaking of the hero-author of 'The Prize,' your reviewer states, 'Wallace even lacks the imagination to base this character on anyone but Sinclair Lewis.'

"If my fictional hero, Andrew Craig, resembles Sinclair Lewis, it would then be proper to conclude that one of my two heroines, Lilly, the young Swedish nudist, is based on Whistler's Mother.

"It is evident to me that your reviewer has absolutely no real knowledge of Sinclair Lewis or any of the other American writers who have won the Nobel Prize. The only habit shared by my fictional author and the late Mr. Lewis is that both drank heavily. On the other hand, my hero shares this habit with several other American Nobel Prize winners in literature—let us name William Faulkner, Ernest Hemingway, Eugene O'Neill—who have had, it is alleged, intimate acquaintance with hangovers.

"I did not draw the hero of 'The Prize' from the character or life of Mr. Lewis or any other actual laureate. I did not find it necessary. I had my own experience as an author, as an author who will take a drink with a Swedish girl. Moreover, all authors, just like people, have problems, and some even have sex lives.

"I leave your reviewer, and his public, with a tidbit about an author now beyond reproach. One day a reporter asked Gustave Flaubert to identify the real-life Madame Emma Bovary. Flaubert snapped at the reporter, 'I am Madame Bovary!' "

In my novel I had two fictional doctors, one John Garrett, an American, the other Carlo Farelli, an Italian, jointly winning the Nobel Prize. The American hated the Italian because he felt the Italian did not deserve to share this honor and the prize money. Immediately after reading about these characters, a number of newspapers, as well as some letter-writing physicians, charged me with having drawn these fictional characters, and their situation, straight out of real life.

It appears that some years before, Dr. Frederick Banting and Dr. John Macleod, both Canadians, actually shared the Nobel Prize in medicine for their discovery of insulin. The award brought their feud into the open. Dr. Banting said that Dr. Macleod had not even been in the laboratory when Banting had made the discovery, and therefore Banting gave half of his money to a third colleague who *had* been present. Dr. Macleod, who had definitely participated in earlier research, responded to the challenge by giving half of *his* money to someone who had worked with *him*.

All well and good, I replied in print, but this kind of professional disagreement is hardly uncommon in medical circles. In my researches I had found that on several occasions feuds had broken out between Nobel winners. I was also aware, from my social contacts with physicians and scientists, that many of these men were normally engaged in professional feuds, just as ordinary men fight over lesser matters. There was simply no necessity for me to base my fiction on the Banting-Macleod disagreement. I had created my fictional feud because I knew such problems were not uncommon, and because this antagonism grew naturally out of my imagined character, John Garrett.

However, the controversy did have one interesting aftermath for me, personally. It stimulated me to enter upon an inner exploration —a search that has not ceased to this day—to attempt to discover the sources of various fictional characters I have invented. The search has provided me with no absolute answer. But it has provided me with clear questions. Does a novelist derive his fictional characters from some remembrance of individual people—actual persons known, observed, heard about, read about—or from general types of persons, or perhaps from mere fragments of actual people? Or does a novelist create his fictional characters out of that unknown inner force, unconscious and mystic, which he calls imagination? Or is it the compounding, the merging, of both the real and the unreal, the known and the unknown?

In more cases than not, I would suggest that fictional characters grow out of a merging process: first, a wisp of fact; then, a cloud of fancy. Add conscious memory. Next, a subconscious development. Followed, last, by controlled embellishment.

Example. This extract from Henry James's notebook:

"Florence, January 12th, 1887. Hamilton (V. L.'s brother) told me a curious thing of Capt. Silsbee—the Boston art-critic and Shel-

ley-worshipper; that is of a curious adventure of his. Miss Claremont, Byron's çi-devant mistress (the mother of Allegra) was living, until lately, here in Florence, at a great age, 80 or thereabouts,
and with her lived her niece, a younger Miss Claremont—of about
50. Silsbee knew they had interesting papers—letters of Shelley's
and Byron's—he had known it for a long time and cherished the
idea of getting hold of them. To this end he laid the plan of going to
lodge with the Misses Claremont—hoping that the old lady in view
of her great age and failing condition would die while he was there,
so that he might put his hands upon the documents, which she
hugged close in life. He carried out this scheme—and things se
passèrent as he had expected. The old woman *did* die—and then
he approached the younger one—the old maid of 50—on the subject of his desires. Her answer was—'I'll give you all the letters if
you will marry me!' H. says that Silsbee court encore. Certainly
there is a little subject there: the picture of the two faded, queer,
poor and discredited old English women—living on into a strange
generation, in their musty corner of a foreign town—with these
illustrious letters their most precious possession. Then the plot of
the Shelley fanatic—his watchings and waitings—the way he covets
the treasure. The denouement needn't be the one related of poor
Silsbee; and at any rate the general situation is in itself a subject
and a picture. It strikes me much."

Six months later, Henry James was writing his novel *The Aspern
Papers*—and a wisp of the real Claire Claremont had, through the
author's imagination and art, become uniquely and individually
transformed into the fictional Juliana Bordereau.

Recently, going through my notes relating to *The Prize,* I tried to
trace the genesis of several minor characters. One of these was
Harriet Decker Craig, the hero's wife, dead long before my book
begins, but alive in the hero's mind and in the minds of several
other characters.

My first description of Harriet Craig, in my published novel, was
the following one:

"Lucius Mack had met Harriet Craig one morning in the first
month of their residence, when she had visited the newspaper to
place a classified advertisement for day help. Memory usually

dimmed with the years, but Mack still retained what had impressed him then: a dark blonde, quiet and self-possessed, with a pleasing, almost gay Slavic face, all features broad but regular—he had guessed that her antecedents were Lithuanian."

Had I dreamed her up? Or was she rooted in reality? If I had forgotten, I would soon be reminded. One morning, from a girl (now a married woman) I had not seen in thirty years, there arrived a letter postmarked with the name of a town in South Dakota, and at the end of it, she signed her name and added, "whose 'antecedents were Lithuanian.' "

It came back to me at once. I had based my description of the fictional character on an adolescent sweetheart. I promptly wrote her as follows:

"As to Harriet whose 'antecedents were Lithuanian'—yes, here and there, I suspect, you will find touches of yourself (that I hold in memory) in my writings. One does not easily, if ever, forget a first or early love. As a matter of fact, these last weeks I have been poring over old papers of mine and I came across many mementos of our time in Kenosha. I still have a battered novel, *Young Man of Manhattan* by Katharine Brush, signed by you—and the silk handkerchief you gave me on my high school graduation—and some photographs. You are forever frozen in my memory as the marvelously attractive blonde of 16 and 17 whom I used to accompany home from school, used to sit with in your parents' living room, used to date. I simply can't imagine you in 1966 instead of 1933 and 1934."

Yet I had remembered her in 1961 when I was writing *The Prize*. But if I thought that I had discovered the entire genesis of my fictional Harriet Craig, I was soon to be surprised. Reading on in my published book, I came upon the scene where the hero first meets his future wife:

"Fortified by two drinks, he arrived in the plush apartment after ten o'clock. The food was, indeed, good, but what was better was Miss Harriet Decker. When Wilson had introduced him to the nearest drunks at hand, Harriet had been stretched supine on the sofa, in stocking feet, her head in someone's lap, as was the fashion for that age that year. She was one of many guests horizontal, but the only guest completely sober. She had acknowledged Craig by shading her eyes, passing her gaze up his lank figure, and saying, 'Hi, up there.' "

Immediately, I realized that this was not my high school sweetheart. This was from another memory. This was my wife Sylvia, stretched out on a sofa, her head in a famous newspaper columnist's lap, the first time I set eyes on her at a party I had attended in 1940.

Reading further, I came on the following:

"Often, he would return to the house, half drunk, half sober, and trudge up to his room, and sit at his desk and stare at the photograph of her face in its leather frame. He would stare at her face and want to share some minute pleasure of the new day, something seen, heard, read, felt, and in his head he would talk to her, and then he would realize with a clutch of inner pain that she understood nothing, heard nothing, that she was only a flat image in black-and-white on glossy paper size 8 by 10."

And then I realized that that had not come from either my high school sweetheart or my wife but from a conversation with an English girl I had taken out to dinner in Paris one evening during 1949. This English girl had not long before been widowed, and now drinking with me, she told me of the first months after her husband's accidental death. "At night I would look at his picture, and want to share with him, as I always had, some of the things that had happened to each of us that day, and I would try, until I realized he wasn't there, he wasn't anywhere, and it was no use. Finally, I buried his picture in a drawer."

There were more moments of my fictional Harriet Craig in the book, and many of those I could not trace to any living source. These, I am sure, had grown entirely from my imagination.

But one conviction had been reinforced by this inner exploration. Just as I owed Harriet Craig to no single source, so did I not owe Andrew Craig to Sinclair Lewis or to any other Nobel Prize laureate, as the Detroit newspaper and other columnists had fallaciously insisted. The controversy was being stirred up by writers who knew little if anything about the creative process.

The second and greater controversy arising after *The Prize* was published was an explosive one that became an international press scandal, and it resulted from the reaction of the Swedish newspapers, the Nobel Prize judges, and the Nobel Foundation directors to the factual concept of the book.

At publication time, there had been many reviewers who felt that the Swedes would not be offended by the book. The Savannah *News* commented, "In the end Wallace manages to . . . not tarnish the glory of The Prize." But most reviewers had thought otherwise, and were less optimistic. "I shudder to think what the Swedes will say about it," said John Barkham in his Saturday Review Syndicate story on the book. "This novel may exasperate a fair number of Swedish citizens," the Houston *Chronicle* predicted. "Considering all the wild doings he has scrambled together with the august proceedings of Nobel Prize awards, I would imagine 'The Prize' will not be too affectionately regarded in Sweden," said the Indianapolis *Times*. While the New York *Post* thought that all readers would be fascinated by the book, the newspaper added, "What the Nobel Foundation will think of the book's melodramatic view of the ceremonies is another matter." United Press International seemed to know what the Nobel Foundation would think and publicly predicted that my book would "blast normally neutral Sweden into a fit of combative outrage."

I regarded this as no more than typical press provocation. The Swedes and Norwegians whom I had met abroad had appeared reasonable persons. And my book had not weighted the scales for or against the Nobel Prize personnel, but had tried to present their human virtues as well as their human faults. I had expected nothing to happen when my book came out, no reaction in Scandinavia whatsoever, simply because I had assumed that the Nobel Foundation, and the Scandinavian press and populace that revered it, would feel the institution too lofty, invincible, holy, to be troubled by the publication of a distant American novel.

I was wrong. And the prediction of United Press International was correct. Not only the Swedes but other Scandinavians, too, were thrown into a wild fit of "combative outrage."

It was the Norwegians, custodians of the Nobel Prize for peace, who reacted with the greatest initial outrage.

On June 19, 1962, the Oslo *Aftenposten,* Norway's most widely read newspaper, ran the headline: SCANDAL NOVEL ABOUT THE NOBEL PRIZES. Their story began: "Protests and excitement have followed the literary enterprises of the young American author, Irving Wallace. He knows how to create a storm around his name, and has done it again with his book, 'The Prize.' "

A little more than a week later, the Oslo *Dagbladet* ran its strongest blast yet. "The attitude of the author is most clearly shown in the story itself. He adds that there is no known proof of blackmail or criminal action or any major scandal in the history of the Nobel Prize. Why does he state this? Because he has provided the Swedish Academy with an atmosphere of hypocrisy, intrigue, cynicism, and blackmail, in other words, criminal activity.

"Wallace has done everything in his power to drag the Prize and the Prize winners down in the mud, *that's* what he has done. He knows that he himself will never be able to win the Prize, therefore, he settled for second best, to try to show the world that the highest honor is not worth anything because the members of the Academy are corrupt, and the Prize winners scoundrels or idiots. He is envious.

"Some of the characters in the novel have a certain life to begin with, but everything ends in emptiness. . . . The reporter, Sue Wiley, is the only one with a sustained characterization because Wallace has created her in his own image. Therefore, she is real."

The most threatening article was one written by Albert Brock-Utne, a Norwegian correspondent assigned to cover the United States, whose story was syndicated throughout Norway. "Irving Wallace's book about the Nobel Prize, 'The Prize,' has created quite a sensation, and raises the question of possible court actions. The named associates of the Nobel Institute in Stockholm are morally duty-bound to insist that their names be removed as sources. The Nobel Institute in Oslo must organize a joint action by all the named sources and demand that the book be withdrawn."

I had seen no reason to enter into this battle, or make any defense of my novel, until it came to my attention that the Swedish press was running front-page attacks on my book. This, in itself, would not have impelled me to act, either. What finally made me enter the battle was word I received of a leading story that had appeared in the Stockholm *Dagens Nyheter* which was headlined: NOBEL PRIZE AND SIN BECOMES BEST SELLER IN USA. In this story, my honesty and integrity were assaulted by the recitation of a series of inaccuracies, and this, I knew, no author could afford to ignore. At once, on July 16, 1962, I wrote a lengthy letter to the managing editor of the Stockholm *Dagens Nyheter*:

"You have interviewed Professor Erik Rudberg, a member of the Nobel Foundation, and he has told you, 'The Nobel Foundation has, as far as we know, had no contact whatever with Irving Wallace during his visit to Stockholm or at any other time.' While I hate to contradict Professor Rudberg, he is uninformed and completely incorrect. I visited the Nobel Foundation in person in 1946. I corresponded with the Nobel Foundation in 1949, 1960, and 1961, and I herewith submit proof. I visited the Nobel Foundation in 1960. I have the following evidence to support this. . . .

"You have also interviewed Uno Willers, Secretary of the Swedish Academy's Nobel committee, who seems to agree with Professor Rudberg. Uno Willers is also wrong. I visited the Academy in the Old Town in 1946 and 1960, was courteously received, and have original interview notes and photographs to prove it.

"You state that 'the private discussions that go on [in the voting meetings] are completely secret, and any account of these proceedings which may be found in the book can be traced to the author's own phantasy.' This is utter nonsense. The various Nobel academies may intend to keep their discussions private and their exact voting secret, but in fact this is not the case at all. In the official volume, *Nobel—The Man and His Prizes,* edited by the Nobel Foundation, and published in America by the University of Oklahoma Press in 1951, innumerable of these so-called private discussions or debates and the votings are brought out into the open for everyone to see. To add to that, during two visits to Stockholm I had long interviews with a number of veteran judges on Nobel committees and they were all cooperative in telling me, quite frankly, what went on in their chambers before and during Nobel voting time. I have the original notes of these interviews. Other material came to me in other ways, from Nobel officials who were not judges, from prize laureates who had heard about the voting, from Swedish information officers and newspapermen. If there be phantasy in what I have written of the 'private discussions,' I assure you that the phantasy is not my own!

"Since I have many friends in Sweden, since I am deeply appreciative of the many Swedish citizens who helped me prepare *The Prize*—since, above all, I have a genuine love for your nation—I feel it imperative that I make a statement here and now about the true intent of my work of fiction.

"My novel, *The Prize,* was not written, in any sense, as an exposé or in an effort to create a scandal. I determined to use the Nobel Prize background in fiction because it appealed to me as having the essence of drama. As stated, I researched the factual aspects with care. If certain elements of my fictional story have been made to seem sensational or indeed are sensational, it is because I am primarily a novelist and the heart of any novel is conflict. It seemed to me that a group of foreigners, visiting your land for the highest prize on earth, would be in a situation that invited character conflict and story drama. And perhaps some of my invention is not so far removed from true life, after all.

"I did not set out to defame the Nobel committees. Anyone who has carefully read my book will see that I have treated all the fictional Nobel judges and officials, save one, with honest respect. The character Bertil Jacobsson is the spokesman of Sweden and the Nobel committees in my book, and I love him and believe him to be an admirable character. For the most, I have given the Nobel committees praise and credit, because I felt this was due them. However, that I have also shown their human weaknesses, I will not deny. Surely, the tradition of the Nobel committees is old enough, strong enough, most often right enough, to stand up under outside criticism. Every human face has two profiles. As a novelist, it is my duty to show not one but both."

While attacks on my "scandal book" continued to appear on front pages throughout Scandinavia, the wide circulation given to my letter had a salutary effect. It forced the Nobel Foundation to confirm that I was right, that some of their people had been wrong, and it left my integrity unimpaired.

It was Nils Ståhle, Executive Director of the Nobel Foundation, who finally came to my defense. He submitted to a telephone interview with the Stockholm *Dagens Nyheter,* and the newspaper featured the story on July 20, 1962:

"The American author, Irving Wallace, is correct in saying that he visited the Nobel Institute and that he received, both orally and by letter, answers to a number of the questions he had asked. . . . This was confirmed by the Institute's Executive Director, Envoy Nils K. Ståhle, by telephone from his summer home in Arild, as a commentary on the author's letter to *Dagens Nyheter.* Envoy Ståhle also agrees with the author on another important point—he believes that Wallace's controversial best seller, *The Prize,* is 'not written in a tone unfriendly to Sweden and the Nobel Prize.'

" 'The book could have profited from a thorough condensation,' says Mr. Ståhle. 'At least for an older reader it is both tiring and unnecessary for the author to have spiced the meal with so many bedroom scenes. Fact and fiction are so interwoven that people not familiar with the milieu could get the most peculiar impression of how things are done in the Nobel circle,' Ståhle fears. 'But on the whole the book is skillfully written.' "

Two weeks later, one of the most prominent of the Nobel judges decided to speak out. In 1946, I had interviewed Dr. Anders Österling, Secretary of the Swedish Academy, which votes the annual Nobel Prize in literature. Now, sixteen years later, Dr. Österling, who had been voting on the literary award for thirty-six years, agreed to receive a reporter from the Stockholm *Expressen.* What was Dr. Österling's opinion of *The Prize?* On August 4, 1962, the newspaper reported Dr. Österling's comments:

"I have been reading my usual summer literature [works by nominees for the next Nobel Prize], but this novel, *The Prize,* I thought I'd better throw in as my responsibility to the Swedish Academy.

"As a thriller, the book isn't bad, but it is almost completely fantasy throughout. Of course, it is in poor taste, but not so vulgar as I expected. Rather amusing, as a matter of fact. . . . Irving Wallace is one of the most successful authors of our time. He has for several years earned millions in Swedish crowns on books about sex, lightly seasoned with scandals. It should be noted that compared to his earlier books, his latest novel, the one about the Nobel Prize winners, is not half as filled with the above ingredients as other best sellers he has written. Lost in all the commotion around Sin with a capital S, Swedish girls and their morals, a little frigidity and alcoholism and extramarital relations is the serious study of how the Nobel Prize winners are chosen."

Now the controversy began to intensify in another direction. I had learned that the Scandinavian countries—Sweden, Norway, Denmark, each of whom had successfully published my previous novel—were refusing to translate *The Prize*. When a reporter from United Press International called upon me, I told him what I thought. I told him there was a "sub rosa boycott" existing in Scandinavia against my novel. According to the wire-service story:

"Book publishers in Sweden, Denmark, Finland and Norway have rejected offers of publishing rights in their countries even though they had an option to buy such rights. They took the options after the success in Scandinavia of an earlier Wallace novel. . . .

" 'The only thing I can think,' said Wallace, 'is that the publishers may be under some kind of pressure because The Prize is against what they feel is the national good. A Copenhagen publisher told me the book was "sacrilegious to a highly important institution in Scandinavia" but the others did not even give me a reason.' "

Once again, there were headlines in Sweden. The front page of the Stockholm *Aftonbladet* carried the head: AMERICAN BEST SELLING AUTHOR ACCUSES SWEDEN OF BOYCOTT ON BOOK ABOUT THE NOBEL PRIZES. The rest of the press carried similar streamers. One newspaper insisted that I was "dead wrong" to think that Scandinavian publishers would ever boycott a book for any reason.

But I was not dead wrong. I was dead right. The Oslo *Aftenposten* decided to interview Norwegian publishers and learn the truth. They pursued Gyldendals, my publisher in Norway, and the director of this firm, Harald Grieg, told them, "The reasons we do not want it are many. . . . It gives a false impression of the Nobel committees' function and depicts the prize winners in a fashion which does not at all correspond with the truth. It would be entirely unnatural for our firm, which has brought out more works by Nobel Prize winners than any other Norwegian firm, to publish it." The *Aftenposten* then spoke to Ragnar Wold, head of E. G. Mortensen's, who had also refused to publish *The Prize.* "We found it would be altogether too dangerous a project to embark upon, what with all the little details and relationships the author describes which we cannot prove. Also, the book is highly uncomplimentary to the Swedes. This is true not only of the prize givers, but of Swedes in general. But I want it understood there has been no pressure put upon us except in the sense that the Swedish people are sticking together on this."

To this day, *The Prize* has not been published in Sweden, Norway, or Denmark, although in the years since, these three countries have brought out editions of either *The Man* or *The Plot,* two of my later novels.

Among the actual Nobel Prize winners who had read the book, at least among those I heard from or about, there were reactions as strong as those I had heard from Scandinavia. However, the reactions of the laureates were more evenly divided for and against.

Dr. Ralph Bunche, who had been voted the Nobel Prize for peace in 1950, disapproved. According to Bent Vanberg, writing for the Oslo *Dagbladet,* "The Undersecretary of the United Nations, Dr. Ralph Bunche, has little good to say about Irving Wallace's book, *The Prize.* 'This is a questionable effort done in bestseller form,' categorically replies the American Nobel Peace Prize winner as an answer to *Dagbladet's* question as to his reaction to the novel. Dr. Bunche is thus the first Nobel Prize winner to publicly comment on the book."

The next laureate heard from was Dr. Linus Pauling, of the California Institute of Technology, who wrote to my publisher objecting to "some errors of fact in the book." Dr. Pauling pointed to a passage where I had a character in the novel speak of Mme Irène Joliot-Curie and her husband as members of the French Communist Party. The passage that offended Dr. Pauling appears in the opening scene of Chapter VII, where Count Jacobsson receives Claude and Denise Marceau, the laureates in chemistry, and senses

that there exists some personal animosity between them which
might develop into trouble before the award ceremonies. The passage in the book reads, in part:
  "Instinctively, Jacobsson wanted this couple to be happier, to be
drawn closer together. He wanted to inform them of how happy
Marie Curie, the first woman to win the prize, had been to share it
with her husband. . . . But somehow, Jacobsson felt that this
might not be the time for such examples. Yet there was his job and
the dignity of the awards, and he must think of something to give
the Marceaus subtle warning. Then he thought of Irène and
Frédéric Joliot-Curie, who had shared the $41,000 prize in 1935,
and with them he thought that he might make his point.
  " 'Indeed, you are in a select circle,' Jacobsson told the Marceaus. 'You are only the fourth husband-and-wife pair in our history to win the prize. We are sentimental about such awards, and
the winners, with one exception, have made us proud.'
  " 'One exception?' said Denise carefully.
  " 'I am thinking of your countrymen, Irène and Frédéric Joliot-
Curie, who won the chemistry award for their discoveries in radioactive elements.'
  " 'What of them?' asked Denise.
  " 'They earned the award for artificial radium, and they received
it here in Stockholm, and we would give it to them again. But their
subsequent history, after the prize, was—in some respects—unfor-
tunate.'
  " 'They were a devoted couple,' said Denise sharply, with an eye
on her husband.
  " 'Oh, yes, yes, nothing like that,' said Jacobsson hastily. 'In-
deed, they were heroes of the Second World War. Frédéric Joliot-
Curie stole the world's greatest supply of heavy water—then important in atomic research—from under the noses of the Nazis in
Norway. He got it safely to England. And in France, despite the
Gestapo, he organized eighteen underground laboratories to make
incendiary bottles for the maquis. I have no doubt you know all of
that.'
  " 'Yes, we do,' said Denise.
  " 'It was their activity after the war that most Swedes deplored,'

said Jacobsson. 'They joined the French Communist Party. And Irène Joliot-Curie told an American visitor that the United States was uncivilized, and that the workingmen should overthrow the government. I remember more that she said, for I have recorded all in my Notes. She told the American, "You are deliberately fomenting war. You are imperialists, and you want war. You will attack the U.S.S.R., but it will conquer you through the power of its idea." I tell you, this caused much headshaking in the Swedish Academy of Science.'

" 'Unfortunate,' said Claude. 'However, surely you judge by the scientific achievement of your laureates, not by their personal activities.'

" 'True,' said Jacobsson. And then, he added slowly, 'Still, our laureates are so much looked up to, so widely respected, that when they commit scandals we are unhappy—extremely unhappy.'

"The shaft, motivated by instinct and not information, hit its targets, Jacobsson was certain. For Denise regarded her husband coldly, and Claude avoided her gaze and lifted his heavy-set frame from the sofa."

Dr. Linus Pauling had not liked that passage at all.

In his letter, Dr. Pauling said that he had met Mme Joliot-Curie in her laboratory in 1952, and that she had personally told him that she was not a member of the Communist Party and had never been one. Furthermore, Dr. Pauling doubted the truth of Jacobsson's statement in the passage that indicated Mme Joliot-Curie had been anti-American. Since the Madame was dead and could not defend herself, said Dr. Pauling, he felt that it was his duty to come to her defense. Also, he felt it his duty to come to the defense of the Nobel Foundation, since I had attributed my quotations to a fictional member of the Foundation. As a whole, the tone of Dr. Pauling's letter was testy.

My publisher forwarded the protest to me, suggesting that I might want to reply to Dr. Pauling. This I did directly. Here, in part, is my reply to Dr. Pauling:

"Let me say at once that I have always had tremendous respect for Madame Joliot-Curie's achievements in chemistry. I make factual mention of these achievements in my novel, just as I salute the

genius and bravery of her husband. At the same time, I have somewhat less respect for the late Madame's politics and her public ut-
terances in fields outside of science.

"I am quite aware that the Madame is dead and cannot defend
herself. I do not feel this is an issue. If one were barred from writing about the dead, there would be no more history. However, in a
manner of speaking, Madame Joliot-Curie is quite alive, for she
has left a published record of her beliefs as well as her accomplish-
ments. As a public figure, her surviving record of speeches and
interviews in France and America also remains to reflect her life.
And, to the end, these speeches and interviews were anti-democ-
racy, anti-United States, pro-Communist, pro-U.S.S.R. . . .

"Do not misunderstand me, Dr. Pauling. I am not saying that
her political judgments were not always justified. I am merely saying that they are what they are, and they exist, and that many lib-
eral democrats in the United States, France, Sweden found them
objectionable.

"In my novel, I was writing a work of fiction, shot through with
factual conversation, almost all of it substantiated by solid sources.
When my fictional character of Count Jacobsson . spoke of the
Joliot-Curies, he spoke as a character in a story. He was not necessarily wearing my cap or thoughts. He was making a story point for
two other fictional characters—and the Joliot-Curies seemed to me
an excellent example of the point he was trying to make. By this, I
am not disavowing my responsibility for what my invented characters say. I merely remind you of my motivation.

"Now let me take up, specifically, your three objections. 1. You
are correct in pointing out that Madame Joliot-Curie was not a
Communist in the card-carrying sense. Technically, I am in error
on page 371 to have a character remark, 'They joined the Communist Party.' The slip is regrettable [I made sure it was corrected in
the third edition], and I can find only one way to explain it: even
though Madame Joliot-Curie did not join the Communist Party, it
always appeared to me, from the evidence on hand, that she was
far more fervent a Communist or fellow traveler than her husband
who held a card. 2. As to the anti-American statements I attribute
to Madame Joliot-Curie, I find no reason to revise them. The Mad-

ame's affection for the U.S.S.R. and its system, and her dislike of 'Fascist' United States, are a matter of printed record in a wide variety of publications. 3. There is no necessity for you to defend the Nobel Foundation against anything I have written. The Foundation, through correspondence I have on hand, through admitting me inside its doors, was entirely cooperative during both my visits to Stockholm. In Count Bertil Jacobsson, fictional spokesman of the Foundation, I tried to create one of the most sympathetic and likeable characters in a long book. . . . Since you have forwarded a copy of your original letter to Professor Arne Tiselius, a scientist I have never met but always admired, I hope you will be kind enough to forward to him a copy of this reply to you."

Dr. Linus Pauling hopped on the last. Two days later he was writing me that he could not resist making a comment on the fact that while I admitted I had never met Professor Tiselius, in my printed acknowledgments I had expressed gratefulness to the professor for research help.

This was nasty, and I was irritated. I replied to Dr. Pauling's letter with the following: "At this rate, we will become pen pals." I added: "At the end of a last letter to me, dated March 21, 1961, a member of the Nobel Foundation replied to my questions and reminded me that the new Chairman of the Foundation was Professor Arne Tiselius. In short, I was being told that the cooperation I was receiving was under the guidance of Professor Tiselius. . . . I had never met the professor. On the other hand, I owed thanks to him for permitting members of his staff to answer my inquiries in detail. Therefore, I thanked him in the book. . . ."

A few days later, I was able to write my publisher, Peter Schwed, of a happier reaction from a Nobel laureate. "A psychiatrist friend just telephoned. She was down in La Jolla yesterday and saw Dr. H. C. Urey, winner of the Nobel Prize in chemistry (1934), lolling on the beach reading *The Prize.* She inquired how he liked it. He said he had just begun, loved it, and both he and his wife were wild about Dr. Garrett's group therapy session and Garrett's obsession with Farelli."

One evening in this hectic period, attending a big-name dinner party, I met the wife of a prominent recent Nobel Prize winner. She told me that she had enjoyed most of the book—"all except that absolute nonsense about Dr. Claude Marceau's having an affair behind his wife's back—it was unbelievable—you simply don't know —I'm married to a Nobel Prize winner, and neither he nor his Nobel winner friends behave like that—they're just not that sort, and they're far too preoccupied with their work." Just three years later, at another dinner party, I met this same Nobel Prize winner's wife again, and she was contrite and apologetic. "My God, what a fool I was," she said. "I was absolutely naïve when I told you that what you'd written was improbable. At that very time—but how could I know?—my husband was having an affair with some younger woman, some slut. Winning the prize had gone to his head. He'd become a public figure. And there were available women everywhere, especially this one, and what happened was just like in your novel. The damn fool. Well, we're getting a divorce. . . ."

Almost every year since the publication of my novel, I learn of some Nobel Prize laureate who is reading *The Prize*. In 1964, the Negro periodical *Jet* wrote, "The two books gracing the hospital bedside table of Dr. Martin Luther King, Jr., in Atlanta, the day he received official notice that he was the 1964 winner of the coveted Nobel Peace Prize: Irving Wallace's *The Prize,* a novel about the behind-the-scenes politicking for the Nobel Prize, and Roger Schutz's *This Day Belongs to God."* A photograph of Dr. King reading *The Prize* in his hospital bed decorates one wall of my study.

In November of 1965, I was invited to a dinner party given by some friends to celebrate the winning of a Nobel Prize by a friend of theirs. The guest of honor was Dr. Richard P. Feynman, of the California Institute of Technology, who had just been notified that he was one of the winners of the 1965 Nobel Prize in physics. At the dinner party I was seated across from Dr. Feynman, a colorful and arresting conversationalist. Dr. Feynman told me that in the week since he'd won the prize, three different people had given him my book as a gift. He suspected that in this way each of them hoped to prepare him for his trip to Sweden. According to my Journal:

"Dr. Feynman said that he has read *The Prize,* and ever since—

all of this spoken with mock seriousness—he had been wondering whether he would undergo adventures similar to those that befell Andrew Craig in Stockholm. In any case, he said, he rather hoped that the Swedish government would assign Count Jacobsson to look after him.

"Since finishing the book, Dr. Feynman went on, he had been wondering about one passage. Did the Nobel committees really investigate the personal lives of winners before giving the award, as I had written in my novel? I said Yes, they certainly did. Dr. Feynman shook his head, pretending to be grave and troubled, and then he said, Well, that finally explained something that had been puzzling him. He had made his prize-winning discovery in 1949, but he had not been honored for it until 1965. And then he added jocularly, Now he could see it was his personal life that had probably kept him from getting the award those many years—until the Nobel people finally saw that he had settled down with his third wife and that now they'd had a child, and that he, himself, was the model of a family man."

Parenthetically, I might add that in 1965 I also had an encounter with Dr. Edward Teller, the renowned nuclear physicist and so-called Father of the H-Bomb, who was often spoken of as being a contender for a Nobel Prize. I had received a wire from Dr. Teller, whom I'd never met, stating he was in the city and asking me to call him. I telephoned, and Dr. Teller, speaking with a heavy Hungarian accent, answered. He said that he admired my work, and invited me to a cocktail party being given for him by a UCLA professor. At the party, I found Dr. Teller overconfident of his own opinion, contentious in all matters, and interesting. According to my Journal: "Dr. Teller said that he had read *The Prize,* which he considered 'too fanciful to constructively criticize,' and later he had read *The Man* and of this he said, 'I have less criticism because you deal with an area I know less about.' " In my Journal I added one final rueful note anent Dr. Teller: "I imagine that he can be a stimulating but not an easy friend."

Meanwhile, through the remaining months of 1962, *The Prize* continued to receive what was for a book an almost unprecedented amount of attention from newspapers, magazines, radio, television. Newspaper and magazine gossip columns carried hundreds and hundreds of items about *The Prize*. Some of these items were true, the great majority were exaggerations of fact, and a few were out-and-out falsehoods. While these one-line items or short paragraphs did nothing to enhance my literary stature, there is little doubt in my mind that they helped increase the public's interest in my book. Here is a random sampling of the type of items that were appearing nationwide:

Sheilah Graham, NANA Syndicate: "I wonder who will play the nasty newshen in the movie version of Irving Wallace's book, 'The Prize.' This female of the fourth estate debunks Mother's Day, the Red Cross, the Boy Scouts and refers to the great Dr. Albert Schweitzer as 'an egotistical Teutonic tyrant.' Is there such a real-life counterpart?"

Hedda Hopper, Chicago *Tribune*-New York *News* Syndicate: "I heard 'The Prize' is worse than 'Chapman Report' and by the same guy who made so much money from 'Chapman' he bought a villa in Europe. Hope he stays there. 'Prize' smears American winners of Nobel Prize; it's unbelievable."

Leonard Lyons, New York *Post:* "All foreign-language rights to Irving Wallace's 'The Prize' have been sold, except in Scandinavia, where the novel is set."

Robert Sylvester, New York *Daily News*: "How to write a best seller: Irving Wallace lived in a nudist camp for several weeks to get authentic background for sequences in 'The Prize.' "

Dorothy Manners, INS Syndicate: "It isn't set—but Ingrid Bergman will get the first chance at the role of the Swedish movie actress in Irving Wallace's 'The Prize,' all about the Nobel Prize awards. I'm half-way through reading the book, and it's a spellbinder."

Louis Sobol, INS Syndicate: "During his research for his new novel, 'The Prize,' Irving Wallace discovered that back in 1921 the Swedish Academy voted the prize in literature to its secretary, Erik Axel Karlfeldt. Karlfeldt spurned the award, insisting, 'Gentlemen, I must categorically refuse. This vote must be buried with us in this

room. The newspapers must never know.' So the judges voted again
—the first and last time any such incident occurred. The prize went
to Anatole France."

References to *The Prize* took many different forms. *The Reporter* devoted its weekly full-page puzzle, The Acrostickler, to my
book. Jerome Beatty, Jr., in the *Saturday Review,* used the success
of *The Prize* to reveal that "in the trunk" I had five full manuscripts "that never saw the light of day," among them a true adventure story of an expedition I had accompanied into the Honduran
jungles and a biography of Daniel Defoe that I had written in my
adolescence. Walter Winchell gave over his entire nationally syndicated column to telling "things I never knew" about the Nobel
Prize, which he had taken from my novel or from additional information obtained from me. "The major fiasco in Nobel history, as
Irving Wallace has a character point out in 'The Prize,'" wrote
Winchell, "was the 1905 Nobel award to Dr. Robert Koch of Berlin for discovering a serum to cure tuberculosis—tuberculin. Six
months after he became a winner, Koch's miracle serum began to
kill instead of save people!"

In the November 1962 issue of *Holiday,* Clifton Fadiman pub-
lished a long article entitled "Awarding the Nobel Prize: A Do-It-
Yourself Kit." Here he nominated ten writers: Robert Frost, Will
Durant, Thornton Wilder, Aldous Huxley, E. M. Forster, Arnold
Toynbee, Robert Graves, André Malraux, Jean-Paul Sartre, Mar-
tin Buber. These men, he personally felt, should receive a Nobel
Prize in literature but up to that time they had been overlooked.
Fadiman added:

"At the moment there is among us perhaps a livelier interest in
the Nobel Prizes than at any time in the past. . . . American interest has also been stimulated by Irving Wallace's best-selling *The
Prize.* This highly readable novel is filled with fascinating Nobel
Prize gossip, local color and inside dope. Many of the questions
commonly asked about the awards are answered in the course of
Mr. Wallace's narrative."

Clifton Fadiman made other references to my book. Among
them, the following:

"Do geographical considerations influence choice? We-e-ll . . .

Alfred Nobel's will is explicit on the point of excluding nationality. However, read Mr. Wallace's book, particularly the volcanic remarks uttered by his character Gunnar Gottling, and decide for yourself."

Then, when the dates approached for Stockholm and Oslo to make their annual announcements of the new Nobel Prize winners, members of the press began calling upon me for statements relating to the forthcoming awards. In the eyes of the press, I had recently been elevated to the status of "expert" on this subject. I was, of course, anything but an expert. I was simply a writer who had done a vast amount of background research for a novel that was in the public eye. But because I enjoyed discussing the Nobel Prizes, whose history was still fresh in my mind, and because I was eager to have my book read as widely as possible, I cooperated with the press and performed as an amateur expert.

A number of periodicals and newspapers were eager for me to predict the winners of the 1962 Nobel Prizes. Since I could not handle these requests on an individual basis, I prepared a detailed statement for Dan Green, head of publicity at Simon and Schuster. He released this to the national press, and it was widely reprinted. Here are two examples of how my statement was used:

Publishers' Weekly, October 15, 1962: "Irving Wallace, author of the best-selling novel 'The Prize,' has given high places to Robert Frost, Sir Charles P. Snow, André Malraux and Leopold Sedar Senghor of Senegal, in his recent predictions for the winner of the Nobel Prize in literature. He adds: 'Had the literary prize been given two months ago, it could have been predicted with considerable certainty that it would have gone to 77-year-old Isak Dinesen of Denmark. . . . Unfortunately her death may deprive her of the 1962 honor.' "

And the *Los Angeles Times,* October 21, 1962: "Novelist Irving Wallace, whose works include a current best-seller about the Nobel Prize, has ventured to draw on his knowledge of the Nobel selection process to predict the top contenders for this year's awards. The author of 'The Prize' conceded that 'the business of prophecy is hazardous' and then listed some of his favorites in the five categories to be announced within a few weeks. . . . Peace—If awarded to an organization, the Cooperative for American Remittances to Everywhere (CARE) . . . Physics—Prof. Charles H. Townes of Columbia University for his discovery of the maser and Sir H. S. W. Massey of Great Britain for his work in upper atmosphere physics . . . Chemistry—Prof. Heinz Fraenkel-Conrat of the University of California at Berkeley for his work in protein synthesis . . . Medicine—Jointly, Dr. Hans Ussing, professor of biochemistry at the University of Copenhagen, and Dr. Arthur K. Solomon, head of biophysics at Harvard, for their independent discoveries involving the transport mechanism across biological membranes.

"Wallace maintains the judges' selections are 'the result of a complex process in which prejudices and outside pressures play a major role.' "

I was awakened one morning five days later by a telephone call from a student-reporter on the *California Sun,* the UCLA graduate students' newspaper, and he told me that John Steinbeck, rather than one of my predicted candidates, had just won the Nobel Prize in literature. I confessed that I was surprised that neither Robert Frost, who had the sponsorship of President Kennedy, nor Jean-Paul Sartre, whom I had mentioned in several personal interviews because his gloomy outlook had such appeal to Swedes, had been the winner. I gave the reporter an interview about Steinbeck, which concluded on the following note:

"When asked if he considered Steinbeck the type of author he described in 'The Prize,' Wallace said that the two men were entirely different.

" 'Andrew Craig, hero of "The Prize," ' he said, 'was not as prolific or as stable as Steinbeck. However, the procedures I described are probably the same as those that gave the prize to Steinbeck.' "

Nor did any of my other predictions for 1962 come to pass that year. However, if I deserved no "A" in Prophecy, I deserved at least a passing grade, because two of the persons I considered likely winners in 1962—Townes in physics and Sartre in literature —were both named Nobel Prize winners in 1964, even though Sartre declined the honor.

The most widely published of the interviews I gave on the Nobel

Prizes was one written by Howard C. Heyn of the Associated
Press. It appeared coast to coast, bearing such headlines as the one
in Florida, ARE THE NOBEL PRIZES BIASED? and the one in Pennsylvania, IS NOBEL PRIZE OUTDATED HONOR? The Associated Press
interview read in part:

"Wallace says Alfred Nobel, who was the inventor of dynamite,
originally planned only three awards—in medicine, physics and
chemistry—but later Baroness Bertha Kinsky von Suttner, a confirmed pacifist, persuaded him to include a peace prize. She got it
herself, in 1905.

"The literature prize was added last in the course of the planning, Wallace said, after Nobel himself wrote a horror play, *Neme-
sis*. It was so bad that his relatives burned every copy they could
find after his death in 1896, according to Wallace.

" 'I suggest the peace prize be eliminated,' said Wallace. 'We live
in a world of non-war, not peace. Furthermore, if the Nobel judges
give a peace prize to an American, the Russians are irritated, and if
they give one to a German, the French are annoyed. It has become
too ridiculous. There was no peace prize this year and, in fact, it
has been skipped 14 times.'

"Wallace proposes as substitutes: A prize honoring the social
sciences, to a sociologist or anthropologist; one encompassing advances in botany and biology; one for the arts outside literature. . . .

"Plenty of money is available for new awards, at the going rate
of about $48,000 each, said Wallace.

" 'Nobel left the fund $9 million. This has now grown to $12
million through investments in Swedish real estate and $250,000 in
Wall Street. If Nobel were alive today I think he would have been
interested in some of the new fields I suggest.

" 'I believe he also would recognize—as his heirs and judges do
not—that the medical award should be revised to recognize mental
therapy and psychoanalysis. Imagine those judges voting down Sigmund Freud every time he was nominated! But they did.'

"He also feels a spot should be reserved for inventors, especially
since Nobel made his money through his patents.

" 'It is incredible that Thomas Edison and the Wright Brothers were never honored, although they were alive during the early awards.' "

There were almost weekly requests, during this period, for me to appear on national as well as local television shows, and on radio programs, to discuss the forthcoming Nobel Prize awards or my novel or my life as a writer. While I had been cooperating with newspaper and magazine interviewers, I found myself refusing television and radio interviews. These were difficult for me to decline, because I was told that this vast exposure to the viewing and listening public had a great practical value. It had been proved, according to several publishing sources, that such public appearances by an author, promoting a title just beginning to be known, could stimulate the further sales of a book by thousands and thousands of copies. My basic insecurity was constantly increased by these offers to parade myself on the nation's screens and speak on the country's radio stations. Briefly, once or twice, I wavered, said that I would reconsider, but in the end I held firm to my resolve.

Several reporters, hearing of my decision and remembering that I had once been ranked by the National Forensic League (the nationwide high school public speaking organization) as one of the ten leading debaters in the United States, wondered why I would not go on television or radio, and I was forced to discover the reason for myself and for them. Finally I was able to explain my decision. In its essence, it is as follows: While the writing of a novel is one of the last absolutely independent careers that exist in this world, it is also a lonely, arduous, and nerve-racking profession. Always, after having completed a novel, I feel that I have earned an added reward—release and relaxation from inner tension and self-generated pressures. To go then before large audiences as a performer, which I believe to be demanding on the nervous system, would be an abdication of one of the many rewards of novel-writing. And so, despite the gains I might sacrifice, I had decided to forgo public appearances to avoid one more pressure in my life. For me, if I may repeat it, one of the wonders of being a novelist is the complete independence that goes with such a career. The novelist is beholden to no one. He has no debt or responsibility to anyone, except to himself and his art. This freedom to write as I please, think as I please, live as I please (within the boundaries of my society's structure) is a way of life too precious to compromise. I feel that doing something that I do not wish to do, an activity that my entire nervous system rebels against, would destroy much of the pleasure that my chosen career gives me.

This was a highly personal decision. Many well-known novelists of my acquaintance would disagree with it. They believe that public appearances are important. They feel that, in an extremely competitive field, where almost thirty thousand new books are published every year, they owe it to themselves and their work to do what they can to bring their books before the public. And they may be right. But I suspect that many of the authors who appear on television and radio do so not only to help their books achieve greater sales, but, perhaps more importantly, because they derive considerable ego satisfaction from such appearances.

I felt that such group therapy was excellent for those writers who needed it. Certainly, it makes the writers happy, and it makes their readers or potential readers happy. I simply have found that, for myself, I do not require this, nor had I required it when I wrote books that were anything but best sellers. Instead, I have preferred to confine my public activities to discussions with newspaper and magazine writers who wish to interview me. I find that these face-to-face, yet relatively private, confrontations are good fun and stimulating, and sufficiently useful to me and to my books. But I would not (and will not) join the electronic circus. That, for me, would not be fun. My book had been written. It was out to be read. In it, any curious reader might learn a good deal about me. If he sought to know more by looking at my corporeal being, I feared he would only be disenchanted.

And so I refused to pontificate about *The Prize* before television cameras or radio microphones. But I did continue the face-to-face meetings with the press in hotel suites and cocktail bars and small restaurants.

Following the series of interviews I had given on the Nobel Prize awards, the preponderance of other press interviews I participated in were concerned largely with my motivations and methods in writing *The Prize*.

After interviewing me for the New York *Herald-Tribune* book supplement, Joe Hyams wrote:

"Does Mr. Wallace set out, as it would seem, to create controversy with his books?

" 'Nothing gets me more angry than to read I set out to manufacture controversy or a best seller,' he said. 'My interest is in people and the hidden things of their lives. Sometimes I get carried away by this interest when I sit down to write. But if you examine anyone or any institution, there is bound to be a controversy.

" 'My instinct is to take what's never shown on the surface and bring it to the surface. That's what makes a novel. . . .' "

Vernon Scott of United Press International interviewed me and then quoted me as saying:

" 'I did not write the book deliberately to attract a lot of attention and money. Naturally, I hope to make a living. My true motive was to write a worthwhile interesting novel. A man doesn't spend 15 years in research and writing 768 pages just to cause a sensation.' "

In response to questions from Roy Newquist of the Chicago *American,* I said the following:

" 'You know, W. Somerset Maugham once said that a book is incomplete until it has a reader. I agree. A book that is unreadable, does not hold the reader, should not have been written or published. A book, whether fact or fiction, must be honest above all, and after that it must communicate, grip, entrance someone else. Otherwise it has no reason to exist, beyond feeding the author's self-indulgence and vanity. It takes not one but two to make a book: the writer *and* the reader.' "

In reply to an inquiry from *Contemporary Authors,* I wrote the following:

"After I have an idea, the characters I need usually come to me automatically. I hardly have to search for them. Once I have a firm grip on these characters, I try to seek an unusual, fresh, storytelling way of encouraging them to perform. Developing the fictional characters usually leads me into specifics of plot. When I have the people and the plot, I begin intensive research into the backgrounds of these people, the setting, atmosphere and whatnot, and this delving usually spades up more characters and situations."

In an interview for *The Writer* magazine, Martha Manheim asked many penetrating questions and I answered them at length. I will limit myself to two examples of our exchange.

She asked: "In novels such as *The Prize,* do you work from character to plot, or are you more interested in the power of a situation to move characters?"

I replied: "The wise ones who teach writing insist that to create a worthwhile novel the author must work out of characterization, from character into plot or story. I think literary history proves this to be partially right. While Gustave Flaubert conceived his *Madame Bovary* from an actual physician's wife in Ry, France, and while the younger Dumas conceived *Camille* from a Parisian courtesan he had known, there is impressive evidence that other highly regarded books came about more from plot situations than from their characters. I need only cite Defoe's *Robinson Crusoe,* which grew out of a spectacular adventure a real mariner had endured, and Dreiser's *An American Tragedy,* which grew out of the Gillette murder case. Despite the instructors, there are actually no rules. . . . Sometimes I create my books out of an idea or situation that leads me straight into character. If the idea or situation is such that it does not naturally lead me into character, I drop the project. Because, in the end, I doubt that any idea or plot alone can sustain a full-length work of fiction."

Then she asked: "Is there any specific advice you would give the beginning writer?"

And I replied: "Among other things, I would like to say something about research. Many novelists feel that research is an alien word that belongs to writers of fact. These novelists believe that they should confine themselves to what they know, or can imagine, and include little else. I disagree with this notion and I am not alone in doing so. Too many young writers publish an autobiographical first novel about the odyssey of a young writer, and having done that, they write another autobiographical novel about a young writer and his parents or his wife or his friends. Well and good, and in rare instances this cannot be faulted. Thomas Wolfe did very well within the frontiers of himself. And so did James Joyce and Samuel Butler before him. But, to me, the limitations are deadening. The whole let's-contemplate-our-navels-and-nothing-else school of writing easily becomes tiresome, to the author, his publisher, and the public alike. . . . I have actually heard a young author complain that, while he had a wonderful idea for a novel, he could not write it because it would have to be about an attorney and his wife, and the author had never been an attorney or been married to an attorney's wife. I wanted to tell this young man to go and act like an attorney for a half year, seek some out, talk to them, sit in their offices with them, go home with them, live with them and their wives, and then he would know enough to pretend how it would be if he were an attorney himself. . . . Another time, I met a writer who had a good novel he wanted to write that had to be set in Bombay. He had never been to Bombay, and felt that if he had not been there, he could not place his story there. I wanted to tell him, 'Look, da Vinci didn't attend the Last Supper, but he produced an authentic masterpiece about it. Novelists have written great death scenes, without having died.' I remember when, after having read *Lost Horizon* and its story of Shangri-La, I met James Hilton and asked him if he had spent a long time in Tibet to get background for the novel. He told me that he had been no closer to Tibet than the pages of the *National Geographic,* where he did his entire research for that wonderful escapist best seller."

Research material obtained from other books is often quite sufficient for a project, but whenever possible, as when preparing *The Prize,* I have tried to visit the locale chosen for a planned novel, just as I try to get beneath the skin of each new type of character I hope to delineate.

When I was preparing *The Man,* I knew that one of my main characters would be a Negro who accidentally becomes President of the United States. I had read a great number of books about the Presidency, but I had not convinced myself that I knew enough about a President's feelings and activities while in office. What I wanted was firsthand experience of the Presidency.

From Rome I wrote Pierre Salinger, then President John F. Kennedy's press secretary, of my need, and he invited me to the White House. At our first meeting, when Salinger asked me what I wanted to see, I told him that I wanted more than what every tourist saw.

Not only did I want to observe President Kennedy close up, in action, but I desired to know how it felt to be the President. "I want to make believe *I* am the President," I told Salinger. "I want to *be* the President." Salinger laughed, and said he would find out how he could help me. He spoke to President Kennedy on my behalf, and President Kennedy was agreeable. And so, regularly, for ten days—just nine weeks before Dallas—I was given the freedom of the White House, and daily between two-thirty and four-thirty when President Kennedy napped upstairs, I was permitted to sit in the Oval Office or spend time in the rooms surrounding it, seeing what the President saw every day, and trying to feel it as he felt it. And all of this research, later modified and molded to fit my fictional character, went into the making of *The Man* and into giving my novel an authentic ring.

Other interviews I gave on *The Prize* brought out other aspects of my approach to writing a book. A particularly illuminating interview for me was one I gave in Paris to Marc Saporta, a novelist and the editor of *Informations & Documents,* the French cultural magazine. Saporta was discussing certain "conveniences and coincidences" in some of my novels, and as I defended them, I went on to discuss with him another area where *The Prize* had been criticized. Here is an excerpt of what I said:

"I've also been told I have a dangerous tendency toward happy endings, such as in *The Prize*. But I am at heart an extremely optimistic person. I am not childishly so. For it is also true that I have a balancing tendency to be cynical. I've seen so much that goes on behind people, their greed and hypocrisy. I am also dismayed by and curious about man's condition on earth—why he was put here, so uniquely, to have so much learning and passion poured into him, and then to be snuffed out of existence so quickly. Yet the very miracle of man's existence at all in the scheme of things excites me, and makes me believe that for every person's problem there must be a possible solution. I believe man is too complex and gifted a marvel not to be able to resolve his own or another's difficulties. Perhaps this is over-optimism on my part. Perhaps it is an anti-death wish. Perhaps it is my unconscious desire as a literary creator (playing god) to make over men and their lives in the best way possible. I don't know. I only know that this is my nature, and that this is the way I was raised.

"My parents came from Russia and I was born and grew up in the midwestern part of the United States, rather than the tense atmosphere of New York. When I wanted to be a writer my parents encouraged me; my friends who had a similar desire were discouraged by their parents. My parents had grown up on Dostoevski and Tolstoi and thought the art of writing to be a noble vocation. I succeeded at it despite being very poor for years. And I think this comes out in my work. This, too, leads me in my books into a certain amount of optimism in the end about the characters. For, from my own life, I see what is possible in the lives of others.

"As for coincidences, I believe life is filled with them. I feel it is nonsense to say 'we mustn't contrive a meeting, a situation which produces such-and-such because this is a convenience for the writer to make the story go ahead.'

"A story creates its own truth. A novel does not have to represent real life, but one often has to go way beyond life to make it seem real."

This, I might add, was not to be the last word on my leanings toward the relatively happy ending in a novel. In July of 1964, after having spent several days with me in California, Richard Schickel wrote an article called "The Big Money Writers," which was published in *Life*. After a superficial examination of my life and career, he wrote, in part:

"Despite the myth that success corrupts, and absolute success corrupts absolutely, the money-writers form perhaps the most circumspect group of wealthy men in our society. They tend to stay married to the same girls, to keep the same homes and living styles they had before they made it. Wallace continues to live, without swimming pool, in the same pleasant but by no means gaudy home he acquired in his screenwriting days, continues to put in a seven-hour day at the typewriter—but with more hours spent each evening researching and mulling his work. . . .

" 'Irving's so optimistic about people, about life, that I sometimes think he's neurotic,' says his wife, Sylvia. 'He wakes up every morning simply beaming.'

"Perhaps, in the final analysis, it is this quality that is most important in the creation of best sellers . . . that the oldest kind of insurance a novelist can buy—the comfortable ending—is still very much in force. . . .

"So, mothers, if you want to raise your boy to be a wealthy novelist, teach him first the secret of living a happy life. He may never win a Nobel Prize, but he might make a million dollars writing about the gloomy types who *do* win it."

Shortly afterwards, in Chicago, Bob Ellison interviewed me for the *Sun-Times.* He referred to the *Life* article, especially to the point made in the article that most popular American novels "had several ingredients in common," and that among these was "the proverbial happy ending." Then Ellison read me the statement that my wife Sylvia had made to *Life,* in which she had said that I was so optimistic about people that she sometimes thought I was neurotic and that I woke up every morning beaming.

According to Ellison, I laughed bitterly at this and told him, "My wife and I didn't speak for two weeks after that appeared. Because I said to her, 'What kind of an idiotic quote is that? You know that's not perfectly true. How can anybody get up that way every morning? That's sickening!' "

In short, *l'affaire Life* was one experience that had somewhat less than a happy ending.

During this period, when I was continuing to meet with the press on my novel, John Barkham, book critic for the Saturday Review Syndicate, flew out to Los Angeles to give a lecture and to do several interviews. He interviewed me about *The Prize,* and then he wrote, in part:

"In one fundamental respect Wallace sides with novelists from Fielding to Maugham. 'Storytelling is vital to the novel,' he asserts. 'If you can't make the reader anxious to know what happens next, all the other things—style, mood, philosophy—are wasted. Storytelling is central to the novel, and I believe in it.' "

Another self-exploration evolved out of the meeting with Barkham. I had long observed that people who do not write books often ask people who do write books, "What is the theme of your novel?" Most authors, I would guess, do not know what the so-called theme of a novel is before or while they are writing it. They usually try to reason out a satisfactory, sometimes fabricated, answer later, when they are asked the question after their book has been published. However, the thought has frequently occurred to me that if people would simply ask an author, "Above and beyond telling a story, what were you trying to say in your novel?" they might receive a more honest and direct answer.

To his credit, when John Barkham had finished his interview with me, and was about to leave, he asked, "I was just wondering —I would very much like to hear in your own words what you hoped to say in *The Prize.*" I had privately rehearsed answers for questions about the book's theme, but I was not sure they were true, and I felt that Barkham deserved a more thoughtful reply. I told him to let me think about his question, and I would write down a reply and mail it to him. Some time later, too late for the published interview but worthwhile for its having forced me to think about the question, I sent John Barkham the following:

"The central point of *The Prize* is that each of us—because of small or large emotional damages, and this made worse by the perilous times in which we live—becomes fatalistic. We become the cripples of ourselves and our time, dying gradually before we are dead—and the greatest prize we can have is the self-knowledge of the worth of living each full day with the use of all our resources.

"The secondary motif of the novel concerns my desire to humanize and make comment on the awesome things in our lives—oh, the Nobel Prizes, for example—to show these things towering above us are mortally made, an extension of us, in our image, for better or for worse. On this secondary point, I let Count Jacobsson speak for me in one scene:

" 'You know, on many days every November and December, people all over the world pick up their newspapers and read of Nobel Prize winners. They come to believe, without thinking, that the laureates are demigods, and that the award is divinely ordained, but I am the first to admit that the winners, often geniuses and saints, are not demigods but human beings. At the same time, I am also the first to admit that the awards are neither divinely ordained

nor decided by judges endowed with superior wisdom, but rather
they are voted upon by ordinary men, of fine intellect, but of human frailty . . . they are mortals—they have personal prejudices,
likes and dislikes, neuroses, vanities. They can be influenced by
others, and influence one another. They can be bold, and they
can be frightened. They can be cosmopolitan, and they can be pro-
vincial. They can be overspecialized in one area, and completely
ignorant in another. . . . You see, they are wise, and they are
foolish, but no wiser and no more foolish than other men.'

"When people ask the theme of *The Prize*—what does the book
try to say—I believe the preceding gives the answers—the first,
Craig's lesson about living, and the second, Jacobsson's evaluation
of the greatest award on earth."

All of the exposure of *The Prize* in the press, through the reviews, columns, news stories, interview features, helped generate
great public interest in the novel. The week before publication date,
the bookstores throughout the country had ordered 34,500 copies
on consignment. The first indication that readers were purchasing
the book, thereby depleting bookstore stocks, was reflected in reorders of the novel from retail stores and wholesalers alike. My
publisher's IBM machines showed the following figures for orders
processed (which did not necessarily include all of the orders actually received) during the first ten weeks after the book was on display:

Reorders	
June 5 to 12	1,570 copies
June 12 to 19	1,833 copies
June 19 to 26	4,000 copies
June 26 to July 3	2,705 copies
July 3 to 10	1,000 copies
July 10 to 18	1,400 copies
July 18 to 24	1,388 copies
July 24 to 31	1,500 copies
July 31 to August 7	2,200 copies
August 7 to 14	1,390 copies

These reorders continued to come in steadily for fifty-three weeks, although toward the end the weekly totals began to decrease.

Yes, *The Prize* was being bought and it was being read those early weeks. But whether it would eventually be widely read would depend, for the most part, on how the first wave of readers felt about the book after finishing it. If they did not like it, then its life in hardcover would be a brief one. If they did like it enough to talk about it, then that magical word of mouth would come into being, and the future life of the book might be considerable. What *did* the reading public think?

Fortunately, Simon and Schuster happens to be one of the few publishers who make an effort to find out such things. They had a postcard printed with the heading A NOTE TO THE READER ABOUT *The Prize*. On the card was the following: "Did you like this book? Yes. No. Please tell us in a few words why." The card also requested, "Business or Profession" and "Name and Address." This postcard was inserted into every tenth copy of *The Prize* shipped to bookstores.

The public response to this postcard questionnaire was immediate and sizable, and it provided an illuminating inside view of the average reader's reaction to a book he had purchased or received as a gift. When asked, "Did you like this book?" seventy-six percent of the readers marked an unqualified "Yes." Twelve percent marked an unqualified "No." And twelve percent, who had mixed feelings, wrote "Yes and No."

The readers were most articulate in explaining their reasons for liking or not liking the book. Among the minority who had checked "No" or written "Yes and No," I found the following:

A United States Navy officer wrote from Gales Ferry, Connecticut, "The story was too pat and trite. Two faults dominated. Character development was dime thin. Even a good bedroom romp (which The Prize was not) grows tiresome with repetition." An electronics technician wrote from Chicago, "A good story buried in erotic pulp." A housekeeper wrote from Sparrow Bush, New York, "Yes *and* No. Not nearly so interesting in theme as *The Chapman Report,* but impressive re the research done by author."

Among the majority who had checked "Yes," I found the following:

A housewife wrote from Setauket, New York, "Imaginative, well-integrated, interesting, knowledgeable, all told a most readable book about an otherwise stuffy subject. Loved every word and sorry to see it end!" A librarian wrote from Avon, Connecticut, "It is a well-written novel with a different plot. From the first to last word it held my attention. That's my criterion for a best seller!" A manufacturer wrote from Springfield, Massachusetts, "Beautifully written. New theme for a novel." A lawyer wrote from Miami Beach, "The author did a magnificent job in writing this book—its composition, its flashbacks, its tying-up of the many characters and events into a composite whole are all outstanding reading." A housewife wrote from Dallas, "A fascinating, unusual and fast moving plot. A little bit of everything—intrigue, etc. Beautifully written. Have recommended it to all my friends."

Beyond Simon and Schuster's poll, there were two other tests of the reading public's feeling about the book. There were the degree to which readers wrote letters to the author, and the tone of these letters, which were being forwarded to me by my publisher. I cannot adequately excerpt from the enormous amount and variety of mail that I received then, and continue to receive to this day. But I would like to give a sampling of extracts from readers' letters to show their reactions pro and con, to the characters, stories, research, and writing problems that had concerned me and had involved my editors and myself for so long.

For *The Prize,* just as with my other books, at least ninety percent of the letters were favorable, letters of warm congratulations, thanks, praise. Fewer than ten percent were unfavorable. With no false modesty, I would attribute this percentage's being lopsided with love-giving to the fact that the most likely letter-writers are those persons who enjoy a novel, are moved by it, and are thus inspired to communicate with its author. Those who do not like the book feel that they have wasted enough on the price paid for it, and see no point in wasting more money on postage.

The dissenters, as I have said, were few, but they were eloquent. From Fort Lauderdale, Florida, a lady wrote me: "It strikes me as your being a bit contradictory—in one book the woman is an unsatisfied, frustrated, neurotic, sex-seeking beauty. In your new book you state you use a Swedish woman as a nudist to reflect the wholesome attitude they have towards their bodies and sex—your excuse for that is to encourage a similar attitude in this country—evidently intimating the American female is a frigid, overly modest woman with great inhibitions and vulgar attitudes toward the whole sex aspect. Why don't you make up your mind what we are? Why don't you confine your literary efforts to the study of the male sex? Why didn't you make the male nude the symbol of wholesome attitude toward the body in your novel The Prize? Is it because of your own inhibitions—is it because the male body is obscene and vulgar?"

A gentleman in Atlantic City wrote me that he considered *The Prize* one of "the most valuable books in our time," but then he added: "One thing only is hampering its value and this is the very often mentioned sexual episodes and their minute description. I hope you will be able to omit such parts in your next books so that teen-agers as such can read and learn from them."

A married woman in Philadelphia did not mind *The Prize*'s being, in her words, "iconoclastic" for it was not my "sling shot aimed at the Nobel Institute" that disturbed her. What disturbed her, she said, was this: "My objection, Mr. Wallace, is that by clever use of thoroughly documented material, culled from the Institute's records, you infused and confused your fictional laureates with the real thing, thus making them and their foibles a part of an institution that every school child is aware represents the highest recognition of human talent and contribution. Thus you defame, by implication, as the clay feet of your fictional characters drop their mud over the real laureates as you have them intermingle. Because the novel form gives you a certain immunity from redress, this is particularly offensive. I cannot let it go without comment, not because I am protesting a shattered illusion, but because I am wondering how you differ from the sensation-seeking sob sister you drew in 'The Prize.' "

From Westminster, Maryland, a lady gave me a lecture: "In my belief sex is a beautiful and holy thing when used as God meant it to be used in the sacredness of marriage. It degrades this holy thing when it is used as a plaything or a joke outside of marriage or is dragged down to the dirt of unlawful lust. Sex should be kept private, as a holy and loving intimate secret between a man and his wife, not paraded obscenely to satisfy illicit passions. So you see because of my belief I could not finish your book *The Prize*. . . ."

And from The Hague a gentleman wished to congratulate me on "this achievement of real literature," and also to point out some flaws in the novel. He thought it strange "that a developed scientist like Dr. Denise Marceau seduces a young chemist like Dr. Lindblom to an adultery scene. It is beyond doubt that Mrs. Wallace would strongly oppose to such an action and this is the best proof of the objection I have against this development." Several more objections, and then one final point. "Now, speaking man to man: I would not be keen on making love to a girl (Emily) just having told me her Ravensbruck story in full detail, with all the sexual intercourse she had to suffer. One can pity such a girl, but, the idea of going to bed with her is too strong for me to swallow. I would experience an anti-climax to love. Now my age is 64 and Craig's 42, maybe this makes some difference."

What seemed to permeate the reactions of the ninety percent who enjoyed the book was a feeling of involvement with its fictional characters.

Typically, a lady in Leawood, Kansas, wrote, "I actually believed what Andrew Craig said in his speech. I do believe it. He was and I like to think he *is* a marvelous character and I only wish I could meet him personally." A male student at La Grange College in Georgia found himself closely identifying with Craig, and "seeing that someone could overcome the past like he did, gave me a little more hope for my own future." A gentleman in Foster, Oregon, found the characters so real that he wanted "to wring the necks of some of them," but by the end "understanding had replaced impatience and irritation" and "insight moved one toward charity" even for Eckart and Walther Stratman and Märta Norberg.

For an author, letters such as these represent the most gratifying public response of all. Most authors are perfectly aware—to cite but one example—that Sir Arthur Conan Doyle's mystery stories will continue to be read year after year not because of their enigmatic plots but because the central character in each story, Sherlock Holmes, has become so real to the public that the London Post Office still receives personal letters addressed to 221B Baker Street.

Many readers who wrote favorable letters gave one or more specific reasons for enjoying the book.

A married woman in Montebello, California, was grateful for a relatively happy ending: "Thanks a lot for having the book end good—I heaved a big sigh of relief!" A lady in Sarasota, Florida, appreciated what she considered patriotism in one of the characters: "I am not a member in any sense of the word of such groups as the John Birch Society, but if possible, a loyal member, slightly on the conservative side, of this great Republic of ours, and as such I thank you for your objective writing in the pages of the book about Professor Max Stratman and his views on our freedoms." A female author in Riverdale, New York, singled out Emily's past: "Because I am a Jew, I want to thank you for reminding the world 20 years later not to forget and so easily forgive Nazi concentration camps." A married lady in Larwill, Indiana, took time out "in the midst of haying, gardening, picking raspberries," to say that she appreciated a realistic novel: "Do you know, you modern boys have something—I can't read Dickens anymore. Too divorced from the reality of today."

And most entertaining of all, from a Constant Reader and self-appointed poet laureate, an elderly gentleman residing in Herkimer, New York, the following paean:

> Wallace showed us, how Pegs can be Square
> Originals can be Fabulous too, anywhere.
> Chapman the Reporter and Barnum Showman wise
> Hold no candle to the Nobel Prize.
> What fabulous research went to the Marceau pair
> Equally to Stratman—he with no hair.
> Garrett, ate a carrot, like a lamb
> Farelli playing showman like a ham.
> Square peg Craig gentle as a dove

With Lilly and Leah tendering him love.
The Prize is replete with characters galore
It's got everything—ask for no more.
Wallace with his skill, did it again
The Prize belongs in the Top Ten!

While the response of the reading public is often held in disdain by its more learned gurus, the literary critics, the fact remains that the public exists, and reads, and judges. For the novelist, especially the novelist who has not always been well received by the literary establishment, the reaction of the public is of utmost importance. Bloodied by attacks from the critics, the popular novelist can seek refuge and find sanity and reasons for survival only in joining with his readers, and he must echo, however feebly, the words once spoken by Mark Twain: "The public is the only critic whose opinion is worth anything at all."

And so the letters continued to arrive, good ones, only one bad one in every ten, and somehow the long years and lonely travail spent in preparing the book began to appear less wasted and more worthwhile.

To be sure, a certain proportion of the weekly mail had little to do with a reader's liking or disliking *The Prize*. The simple fact of the book, of the publicity accorded it and its author, attracted a totally different kind of correspondence.

First there were the flattering letters, familiar to all novelists, that began, as did this one from Utica, New York: "I am writing to tell you how much I enjoyed reading your novel, and to request your autograph. I have a collection of autographs of authors which includes Booth Tarkington, Willa Cather, Rachel Field, Robert Nathan, Robert Frost, Kenneth Roberts, James Hilton . . ."

And then there were, it sometimes seemed, countless readers who wanted to be writers—without writing, or at least without having to write a book by themselves. All of them, it appeared, had lived dramatic lives that deserved to be immortalized in prose. A gentleman in Flint, Michigan, wanted me to ghostwrite his autobiography, and a married woman in Kermit, Texas, wanted me to collaborate in developing her own experiences into a novel.

There were the letters from a few more enterprising readers who, inspired by some historical reference in my book, had decided to write books of their own and sought my advice on procedure. As I wrote to a lady in San Luis Obispo, California: "I am pleased my reference in *The Prize* to the Emperor Maximinus of Rome sparked your interest in doing a biography of this unusual man. It could be a fascinating book. As a beginning, I suggest you check your subject in the following basic histories. . . ."

There were readers who, having heard that the film rights to my novel had been acquired by a motion-picture studio, wished my assistance in developing a screenplay based on their story outline. There were enthusiastic clubwomen who planned to review my book for one of their organizations and desired added information on how I had written my novel. There were generous invitations to address gatherings in many parts of the country, and these came from such diverse groups as the Detroit Sisterhood of Temple Israel, the Long Beach Writers' Conference, the University of Rochester, the Pasadena City College Library, the University of Wisconsin, the University of California at Los Angeles, the New Providence High School in New Jersey, the Centenary College in Shreveport, Louisiana. As was the case with television and radio invitations, I found these requests difficult to refuse, yet to one and all I wrote in this vein: "I am deeply honored . . . I must decline, with considerable regret because I have a personal policy never to make a public appearance on the lecture platform or in a seminar. I am constantly tempted to break this rule of mine, but . . ."

The greatest number of written requests came from high school and college students who had read my recent book—and perhaps my earlier books as well—and wished to write a term paper or thesis on *The Prize* or on its author.

A high school senior in Rochester, Minnesota, preparing a term paper and an article for her school newspaper, posed three questions.

The first two questions concerned the value of journalism as a profession. "What literary value do you think journalism possesses? Can it be employed as a learning device for writers?"

I wrote her that I thought journalism (which I had taken with great enjoyment in high school) could be of inestimable help to a future novelist. It would teach her to write with economy, to write on a variety of subjects, and to write under every sort of adverse condition. But I felt that journalism was useful only up to a point. At that point, the writer could find journalism too constricting as to style and form, and then he must break through the limitations of journalism and attempt to write more freely. But many renowned authors have used journalism as a stepping stone. "The other evening, chatting with Dr. Allan Nevins, I was surprised to learn that even he had once been a journalist," I reported. "He worked on the New York *World*, and then the *Sun*. After he left journalism for books, he became America's most eminent historian and twice winner of the Pulitzer Prize."

Her third question was more challenging. "Pearl Buck once said, 'I can only advise anyone not to be a writer of novels if he-she can avoid it. Writing novels absorbs the entire life and being. If the sacrifice of life and being is not joyfully made, then it should not be made at all.' Would you give the same advice?"

I replied that, for the most, I was in agreement with Pearl Buck. If a beginner wants to undertake a writing career because he thinks it an easy way to make a livelihood, then he or she will have a difficult time of it, will soon be disillusioned, and most likely fail. Too many beginners seem to wish to be writers rather than to write. But there is no such thing as an Instant Author. A successful writing career usually takes years of hard, solitary apprenticeship. Still, I told her, for one with talent and persistence and love of the word and the story, it can be the most satisfying of careers—since success in this field gives one total independence, freedom of movement, and the never-ending pleasure of discovering fascinating new worlds of one's own creation.

From a Language Arts instructor at New Providence High School in New Jersey came a dozen provocative inquiries. One of the instructor's questions turned my mind back to my own beginnings. "What effect, if any, did high school English have on your development as a writer?"

I told him that my high school English courses in Kenosha, Wisconsin, had been valuable to me. They had stimulated my interest in reading more widely. They had forced me to write. They had given me some understanding of the English language. But I remembered that as an English student my performance had been erratic, and my grades had varied from a towering A to a tottering C, simply because I had worked diligently only when the teachers and term-paper subjects had interested me. Whenever I had had a teacher who was enthusiastic about encouraging creativity in her charges, and who had not restricted us with too many hard and fast rules, I had then been stimulated and I had learned much. But whenever I had drawn a teacher whose devotion was strictly to grammar and who adhered to the textbook, I had performed poorly and learned little. As a result, to this day, my grammar is subject to lapses, my spelling is mediocre, and I still, to my shame, do not know the alphabet.

"I'm not proud of this," I wrote my correspondent, "because it causes my publisher considerable anguish. I regret that I was not more attentive to grammar. I should have liked knowing the rules, as long as they did not hamper my creativity. I remember I had one wonderful high school instructor who felt that the most important aspect of English was to teach students to communicate freely, express themselves clearly, appreciate the wonder of words—and I wrote a theme entirely without punctuation, as an experiment, placing all the punctuation in a box at the end of the paper for the reader to use as he wished, and I was crowned with an A grade. I had another instructor who did not appreciate such freewheeling writing, and when I submitted one offbeat paper to her, she gave it a D and said to me that I could write as I pleased only after I had been published. The next day, I brought her a magazine that had in it one of my early published short stories. She fumed, but was decent enough not to flunk me. Looking back, I'm ashamed to have behaved like such a smart aleck. Because she was right, in a way, too. I was in school to learn the rules of composition, the words, the disciplines, and once I had learned, I could then go off and do as I pleased."

The New Providence instructor's question that interested me most was put briefly: "How long does it take you to write a novel?"

To this there was no easy answer. When does a book begin? When does it end? How can the time given over to a book be computed? When I am gazing out the window—daydreaming, remembering, imagining—am I writing? I told my correspondent that *The Prize* had been fifteen years in the making. Yet those fifteen years had not been devoted exclusively to it. Exactly how many hours of how many months of those years had been occupied thus, before the first-draft writing began, would be difficult to calculate. One of my earlier books, *The Fabulous Showman,* a biography of Phineas T. Barnum, had been written in six weeks. However, possibly months of time, in the years before that biography was written, had gone into preparing me for those six weeks. Robert Louis Stevenson had written *Dr. Jekyll and Mr. Hyde* in three days. Feodor Dostoevski had needed only twenty-six days to write *The Gambler.* But Gustave Flaubert had given up seven years of his life to creating *Madame Bovary.* In recent times, Katherine Anne Porter took thirty years to complete *The Ship of Fools.* Yet she was actually working on that novel for a relatively short and concentrated period of months. Although Ernest Hemingway poured out *The Sun Also Rises* in six weeks, and Lawrence Durrell did *Balthazar* in six weeks and *Clea* in seven weeks, there is little doubt that Hemingway and Durrell had been creating these novels in their heads for extended periods of time preceding the actual writing. How long does it take to write a novel? How deep is the ocean? How high is the sky? And what are the answers to Zeno's nine paradoxes?

From a high school student in Warminister, Pennsylvania, who was preparing a research paper "on a twentieth century author," two questions. "Why do you write in general—for money or do you see a different purpose? Specifically, why did you write *The Prize?*"

Why do I write?

"I began at 13, had my first story published at 15, and through all kinds of adversity I have never ceased writing. I write—have always written—because I love to tell stories, to create people and worlds half real, half imaginary. I write, as other authors do (and always have), as my means of surviving on earth—but if I could not earn a penny from my writing, I would earn my livelihood at something else and continue to write at night."

And *The Prize?*

"I wrote *The Prize* to show how worldly acclaim can affect mere mortals, for better or worse—and, to be more exact, to show how the world's foremost prize-givers are as human as the takers or winners."

From a professor at Columbia College, in South Carolina, a request for "a statement about your personal philosophy of life and of writing, to be used in a course for language teachers."

I reflected. I replied. I said many things. And then I said what I had meant to say from the start, and it was this—that when I am dead, the world without my being will not cease to be, and so I believe that every man, beyond what he owes himself, owes to mankind whatever he can offer in the eternal search for truth and wisdom. One of my favorite lines in all of literature, which extends and expresses my true feeling about life, came to me. This is the comment that Seneca made after hearing of a company of Romans trapped in an ambush. Seneca wrote:

"The three hundred Fabiae were not defeated, they were only killed."

And after mailing my letter, I realized that I had quite forgotten to refer my inquiring professor to the last two pages of *The Prize,* where Andrew Craig accepts his award in Concert Hall, Stockholm, and speaks those words and has those thoughts that represent not only his philosophy toward life and writing, but my very own as well.

The foregoing were some of the typical letters that arrived bearing questions, forcing me to find answers. But there were other letters, easier to answer, which provided me with reassurance about my book, besides offering me amusement or satisfaction or pleasure because of their incredible variety.

There was the man whose father had tried to harness the rays of the sun, and who was delighted to find his father mentioned in *The Prize.* There was the vice-president of a New York wine and spirit importing firm who wrote that he was sending a case of their leading brand of whiskey, each bottle labeled: ESPECIALLY BOTTLED FOR IRVING WALLACE IN RECOGNITION OF HIS CONTINUING CONTRIBUTION TO AMERICAN LETTERS OCTOBER 1962. He was doing

this, he said, because I had had Andrew Craig drink their brand of
Scotch in my novel (and I promptly replied, "If a novelist receives
a whiskey he has mentioned in his book, it opens up all kinds of
possibilities. What about the Swedish girl I mentioned in my
book?"). There was the German refugee who wrote that he appreciated the "memorial you created for Carl von Ossietzky" in the
book. He added that von Ossietzky had been "the conscience of
democracy in the later days of the Weimar Republic, and so I am
really grateful that you so beautifully revived the memory of this
now so widely forgotten hero." (Ossietzky, a German pacifist, had
been a prisoner in a Nazi concentration camp when he was
awarded the Nobel Prize for peace. Despite pressure from Göring
and the Gestapo, he had accepted the honor, and I had revived this
almost forgotten story to show his courage and the courage of the
Norwegian Nobel Prize committee in thus daring to defy the Hitler
regime.)

There was my former junior high school teacher in Kenosha,
Wisconsin, who received a gift copy of *The Prize* and was delighted
to inform me, "It came while I was teaching transitive and intransi-
tive verbs to my ninth-graders. I showed it to them and told them
how you sat right where they were, and now, says I very dramati-
cally, see what he's done. One boy raised his hand and asked in an
awestruck voice, 'Did they have transitive verbs then?' "

There was the man who enjoyed my novel but reminded me that
the Talmud was too large for Dr. Stratman to stuff in his pocket.
There was the woman, made distraught by the sex in the book, who
promised to save me (to which I replied, "I am grateful that you
are praying for me. In Sweden, a highly civilized nation, they would
be praying for you"). There was the lady in Batesville, Missis-
sippi, who had been deeply moved by my novel and who told me
that she had had "the pleasure of knowing one Nobel Prize winner,
the late William Faulkner," and that "one of my father's closest
friends accompanied Mr. Faulkner to Sweden, and I have heard
him tell of the events of Nobel Week." There was the man who
enjoyed my reference to Jules Silber as one of the world's greatest
spies, and who told me Silber was his mother's cousin.

There were several letters from scientists and physicians telling me how they had been cheated out of the Nobel Prize by colleagues, or passing on some inside information that they possessed about the awards. One highly respected physician, who practices in Washington, D. C., wrote me the following inside story:

"It might be of interest to you to know that I spoke with one of the members of the Nobel Prize committee, who was active at the time the name of Harvey Cushing came up for selection as laureate in the field of medicine that particular year. The Swedish doctor, a medical neurologist, told me with some satisfaction, I thought, that after it became apparent that the Prize was awarded to Doctor Alexis Carrel some time in the '20s for a work which was subsequently demonstrated not to be his in origin, the Nobel Prize committee of medicine simply and flatly decided that never again would the Prize be awarded a surgeon. Therefore, my informer told me, to repeat with some envious glee, that the obvious reception of the Prize was denied to Doctor Cushing on this basis alone."

There were a number of letters that forced me to examine attitudes or feelings I had had while I was creating the book. A gentleman wrote me from Brooklyn, praising the novel, but he worried about "two facets of incredibility." He insisted a certain scene of lovemaking had not been written with sufficient detail to be believable, and that I had gone too far in writing that Dr. Stratman's winning of the prize would give him financial security. To this I replied, "As to not describing the use of contraceptives in a scene of love, I simply did not think it was necessary. I suspect that Lilly was experienced enough to have taken care of herself before the scene began. As to the money, Dr. Max Stratman did indeed acquire some degree of security by winning the Nobel Prize. You are concerned that after taxes his Nobel money of $50,300 would have been worth no more than $15,780. It will make you happy to know that all Nobel Prize cash awards are permitted to be accepted absolutely tax free."

A Midwestern physician found almost everything in *The Prize* "beautifully described," but he had "one great question" to pose to me. "Why should one, a most capable writer, in combining the data leading to the winning of a Nobel Prize, have interlarded the material and story with objectionable scenes and language?" The question was an important one, presented with sincerity, and I gave it thought before replying. "This is an age-old question, one posed to authors for centuries," I wrote the physician. "Let me take my turn, and reply to it as briefly and honestly as I can. You have made a value judgment about certain scenes and language. By your standards they are objectionable and get in the way of what you find interesting. However, in writing these scenes, I did not think them objectionable—obviously—but regarded them as part of the fabric of the entire narrative. These scenes were part of my total concept of how the characters should and would behave and how the story must be told. None of these scenes were, as you suggest, 'interlarded.' They seemed as natural and proper to me as the scenes you preferred. I presume you are referring to scenes concerned with sex in France and Sweden, and if you are, I can only remark that this was the way I found sex in France and Sweden (among such people), and my story would not have been imaginatively true or real without them."

And from Nairobi, Kenya, a lady in charge of safaris wrote a letter of praise that included one interesting criticism. I replied to her, "As to your one small criticism that very few people in real life come to a 'happily ever after' conclusion, I can only say this: don't be too sure that my characters live happily ever after. As a matter of fact, when *The Prize* concludes, the characters are left receiving their highest honors, but I am sure that Emily and Craig will go on to have the inevitable difficulties common to any marriage; I am sure that Dr. Stratman will have a serious coronary a year or two later; and I am certain that Dr. Garrett will continue to suffer from his persecution mania, if not because of Farelli, then due to some other cause. In short, in my novel, I tried to represent one exciting segment of each person's life. What happens thereafter might take another book."

Yes, the novel was obviously being read, and being discussed, and now favorable news of it passed from reader to reader by word of mouth, and its audience grew ever larger. The worst reviews had long since been forgotten by everyone but the reviewers themselves, a handful of pedants, and the author. The book was being bought and read and discussed and then bought by still others.

The publisher had prepared a first printing of 40,000 copies for the scheduled publication in June of 1962. But by mid-May, advance orders from bookstores were so heavy that the publisher ordered a second printing of 15,000 copies. By August, the publisher had gone back to the presses for a third printing of 7,500 copies. By September, a fourth printing of an additional 7,500 copies was made. And by November, a fifth printing of 7,000 copies was produced. In five months, 82,000 hardcover copies had been sold. Meanwhile, the Doubleday Book Club had made *The Prize* their January 1963 selection, and they were to sell 284,000 copies.

The national best-seller lists, which do not consider book-club distribution, reflected the sales. *The Prize* was on *The New York Times'* best-seller list—the list regarded by the book trade as the most important one of all—for thirty-three consecutive weeks, on *Time's* list for twenty-seven weeks, and on *Publishers' Weekly's* list for twenty-six weeks. All of this, of course, served to whet the appetite of an even larger audience, many of whom could not afford the hardcover edition but were waiting for the lower-priced paperback reprint. A year later, The New American Library issued this reprint, and it soared to Number One on the national best-seller list compiled by *Bestsellers* magazine, the trade journal for the paperback publishing field. The New American Library sold 1,400,000 copies in the first two years, and they have continued to sell the book steadily ever since.

The success of the novel in the United States, as well as its international setting, had attracted the interest of a host of foreign publishers, and during this period foreign editions of *The Prize* were prepared in ten countries. In Great Britain the novel was called, as it had been in America, *The Prize*. Elsewhere the title became more colorful: For West Germany, Austria, Switzerland, the Kurt Desch edition was *Der Preis;* for France, the Gallimard edition was *L'Envers des Lauriers;* for Portugal and Brazil, the Portugalia Editora edition was *O Premio;* for the Netherlands, the A.J.G. Strengholt edition was *De Prijs;* for Italy, the Longanesi edition was *Il Premio;* for Spain and Mexico, the Ediciones Grijalbo edition was *El Premio Nóbel;* and in Japan there was the Kobundo edition; in Israel, the Ayin edition; in Yugoslavia, there appeared the Bratstro-Jedinstvo edition in Serbo-Croatian, and the Zalozba Obzorja edition in Slovenian. These last four editions had titles that were incomprehensible to me. The edition published on the island of Taiwan, by a vagrant pirate publisher, was merely a theft of the American edition, reproduced by means of copying the printed pages photographically.

The first and most gratifying foreign publication occurred in London, where Cassell and Company, Ltd., produced an edition for their outlets established throughout the British Empire. In England, on the whole, the reviews were far better than they had been in the United States. But it was in England that I also received several of my worst reviews, as well as several of the best in the book's history.

The worst individual English review was in *The Times* of London:

"The sheer mass, which to a sophisticated taste means overwriting, may be a manifestation of that exuberance and largeness of heart which also marked the English novel in its great days. Let no one complain, therefore, that Mr. Irving Wallace's *The Prize* seems better suited for stopping doors than for reading; its subject, the award of one year's Nobel Prizes, is not unworthy of such bulk. It is Mr. Wallace who is unworthy. His approach is not epic, but vulgar."

The best individual English review was in the *Illustrated London News:*

"This week has produced a novel of such outstanding excellence that it deserves high precedence. Irving Wallace, the American author who wrote 'The Chapman Report,' has now produced *The Prize,* a long, enthralling story. . . . This book is quite the most brilliant example of this genre that I have ever read; indeed, I cannot recall any novel published since the war of which I can speak with such undiluted enthusiasm. In all its 754 pages, I could not detect a phrase or even a word—let alone an incident or a development—wrongly placed or ill contrived."

Perhaps the British who were encouraged by the *Illustrated London News* review to read my book far outnumbered those who were turned away from the book by the review in the London

Times. Or perhaps neither review had any widespread influence on the British public. I do not know. I only know that in Great Britain the novel ranked among the nation's three top best sellers for many weeks, and that Cassell sold 47,000 hardcover copies in eight printings, while in the Union of South Africa this same Cassell edition achieved the Number One best-seller position. Later in London, a major book club, the Reprint Society, sold 60,000 copies to its membership, and The New English Library issued a lower-priced reprint that sold 214,000 copies. Also, a Braille edition of the book was published in England by the National Library of the Blind.

Paralleling sales in Great Britain, many of the other foreign editions also had large sales, including the Japanese edition, which was published in three volumes, each one issued on a different date. *The Prize* received further exposure abroad when foreign magazines and newspapers either serialized it or ran extracts from it, and the publications using these reprints ranged from London's *Books and Bookmen* magazine to Tel Aviv's Hungarian newspaper *U J Kelet* to Tokyo's *Sunday Mainichi.*

But all of this international acceptance came later.

Now, a little more than four months after the American publication date of *The Prize,* I was sitting down with my Journal to summarize some of the events of the year. On the early Sunday afternoon of October 14, 1962, I noted the following:

"*The Prize* has been a steady best seller. In many places, Los Angeles, Dallas, Chicago, it has been rated Number One. Today it is 4th on *The New York Times* list. The novels by Katherine Anne Porter and Anne Lindbergh have led me, and my book has competed with the books by the late William Faulkner and Robert Ruark and James Baldwin for the next highest position. Among the major reviews, except for three poor ones, the press has been running fairly good to excellent, and the scandal accorded *Chapman* seems to be put down.

"The majority of literary critics, so called, have not mentioned me and will not. However, my acceptance by the public outweighs this, and I am not too disturbed—but when I see pedestrian, precious, or pretentious novelists praised, people who do not communicate, when I see them spoken of highly, I am annoyed. Also, I am annoyed when my literary motives are considered suspect in articles—few realizing how honestly I try to write good books, how little I am consciously motivated by commercialism. The fact is, I suppose, I have a sensational turn of mind as to ideas and scenes, and while the public likes this, these particular critics feel I manufacture best sellers. I doubt that I will ever convince any one of them how far, how very, very far this is from the truth of me. Few authors today, I believe, love and appreciate and seek, in writing, the true perception, the finely wrought phrase or vivid scene or character, more conscientiously than I do, and few work as hard to achieve quality, few prepare so hard for their novels (with research, with thought, by planning, by examining inner feelings) as I do, although much of my creative work is immediate and instinctive, as well. . . . In brief summary, I have been extremely happy with the reception of my new novel. It is deeply satisfying to have achieved, before old age, some of what one dreamt in one's youth. I recommend it to one and all."

There was also noted in my Journal, during this period, the diversion offered by stimulating evening encounters with new personalities as varied as Dr. Willard Libby, Professor A. H. Rowse, Commodore Walter Schirra, Dorothy Dandridge, Eric Ambler, Princess Saroya, Roald Dahl, John Kenneth Galbraith, Viña Delmar, Dr. Ashley Montagu, to drop only a handful of the names. But while such personages met at social gatherings were stimulating, they were less real to me than another set of people who remained uppermost in my mind. During those intense days, the only names important to me were still those of my old friends, Andrew Craig, Claude and Denise Marceau, Professor Max Stratman, Dr. John Garrett and Dr. Carlo Farelli.

For in the United States, throughout the latter half of 1962, *The Prize* was continuing to be widely read and discussed. As a result, on the second to last day of October of that year, I received a telegram from *The New York Times Book Review:* FOR OUR CHRISTMAS ISSUE WE'RE INVITING THIS YEAR'S BEST SELLING AUTHORS TO CONTRIBUTE TO A LITTLE SYMPOSIUM IN WHICH THEY'LL

TELL WHAT IT IS ABOUT THEIR BOOK OR THE CLIMATE OF THE TIMES OR BOTH THAT HAS MADE THEIR WORK SO POPULAR WITH AMERICANS WE'D BE DELIGHTED IF YOU'D JOIN IN. . . .

It was a difficult assignment, trying to figure out exactly why one's work was being read, but at last I joined with James Baldwin, Patrick Dennis, Allen Drury, Herman Wouk and several others in promising to contribute to the symposium. Each contributor was asked to write the equivalent of two pages. I submitted my two pages. Later, along with the other contributors, I was informed that our efforts would have to be cut by half or more, because of space limitations. As a consequence, *The New York Times* published only forty percent of what I had written. Now, in this biography of one book, I should like to print in its entirety the original and uncut statement that I had prepared for *The New York Times*. For, I can see, in having tried to explain why I thought my book was being widely read, I may have unconsciously explained something of my writing of *The Prize* itself. Here, then, is what I had written:

"When I was struck with the fictional concept of *The Prize* fifteen years ago in Stockholm, I was nearly unhinged by the excitement of having the Idea. Had any novel been available on the subject, I would have rushed out to read it. But there was none, and so I was compelled to create one for myself in my own brain, to enjoy it privately, to learn what would happen, before the inevitable desire to transmit it to others would come. The Idea of the novel was 'popular' with me, you see. That was first. I thought then of no public, no best-seller lists, no royalty checks, no acclaim. I thought of nothing except that here was a provocative story, and I wanted to know its outcome. Only afterwards did I put it to paper, black on white, imposing discipline on the dream. I shared it with others out of pride in it, and because I am by profession a writer.

"In the foregoing there may be some explanation of the popular acceptance of *The Prize*. If I have to write a book because I love it, to satisfy my own curiosity in the characters or its subject, then perhaps thousands of other people, too wise to live by dreams, but with the same interests I have, may want to buy or borrow some of my make-believe.

"Can our common interests be defined? I do not know. I can only offer some guesses based on the reactions to *The Prize* that I hear, or read in my mail. For one thing, most of us, I suspect, are impatient with how uninformed we are, how helpless to understand our society. We are conscious of life's sleight-of-hand, and we want to know how things are in truth and not how they seem to be. Perhaps people read novels like *The Prize* because they are eager to get behind façades, both institutional and human.

"Then there is a second place where my author interest may merge with reader interest. We live in the Age of Anxiety, to coin nothing. Fear and inadequacy, in every area, infect most of us. To follow characters in whom one faintly recognizes facets of oneself —whether they be base, shameful, confused, or complex—or even facets not precisely one's own, is intriguing and provides a sense of relief. By standing aloof from these paper people, unseen by them, the reader may watch a small part of himself, or of someone close to him, and know how it will come out, as he will seldom know how it will come out in real life.

"Also, the climate of the time is the climate of candor. As H. R. Hays remarked, society learned from Freud 'that the innocence of childhood and the purity of women, two of its favorite illusions, were pure myth.' Conditioned by the real world, constantly aware of it, more and more readers refuse to accept a lacquered picture of life. They want the unvarnished truth about life, as they know or suspect it to be, and they prefer responsible, naturalistic narratives. In short, man may have been at one time the only animal that blushed, but man has grown to regard the blush as an infirmity. He now knows the Queen has legs.

"Since you have asked why I believe *The Prize* is popular, I can only speculate that in some measure I am one of many storytellers who accidentally or instinctively voice the muted feelings of a body of American readers. I will never be sure, although some critics claim to be, of my exact point of contact with the public. For me, the mystery remains, and I can only continue upon my dream journeys with the hope that I will often have numerous good companions to accompany me along the way."

My brainchild had been born, had grown, had made its mark,

and I was ready to let go. For, with the coming of the new year, I realized that all that had happened to it was the least of it, important only at the time, but really the least of it. For what was the most of it was this—that a casual idea, big and exciting but actually merely an idea, so frail, so often nearly snuffed out, had finally developed and become a book, a world that had not existed before, populated and alive for me, its private Jehovah, and alive for all True Believers out there. What had begun on a rainy afternoon in Stockholm, in a conversation with an oppressive old Swedish gentleman, in a time when I was young, had been fulfilled at last . . . and one part of me was free, forever.

PART
IV

APPENDIX

1. WORK CHART OF A NOVEL

It was suggested to me that it might be interesting to some of the book's readers, and useful to those readers who are also writers, if I tried to determine the exact number of hours and/or days the various stages of my novel *The Prize* consumed of my working time.

After agreeing to attempt such a breakdown, I found that it was anything but easy to do. Few writers keep records of how much time they spend on the individual stages of a novel. For myself, I had only one exact record, and that was of the number of days I spent in the actual writing of *The Prize*. For all the other steps—the research, the rewriting, the revisions, the proofing, the checking—I had no records, beyond such dates as I could find in my correspondence and Journals, and on some of my notes.

As I have pointed out in the preceding pages, I conceived the idea of a novel about the Nobel Prizes in Stockholm during 1946, and I finished my last work on the novel itself and saw it published in 1962. The novel was a part of my life for sixteen years. Yet, in those sixteen years, how much real working time had I given it? I could only approximate the days and the hours, although I suspect my totals may be fairly accurate.

There was just one continuing phase of the act of creation that I could not even approximate as to time spent. That was the time I had expended, during sixteen years, imagining, daydreaming, thinking about aspects of a book about the Nobel Prizes and finally about the book I came to write. As for this part of it, the Muse proved an uncooperative statistician. Yet it is this exact part, the make-believing, that may be the most important stage of all in developing a novel. For people who are not writers, this is difficult to understand. I am reminded of one motion-picture studio head who complained to his story editor about the writers they had under weekly salary. "Whenever I look up at the Writer's Building," the executive said, "I find half of them staring out of their windows. Why in the hell aren't they *writing?*" Nothing could convince him that staring out the window was more often than not a vital part of creative writing. I cannot begin to calculate the productive time I spent staring out the window.

So the time estimates that follow are those that could be either calculated or safely guessed at. What I have set down is actual working time, omitting Sundays, holidays, sick days, writer's-block days. Here, then, are the working days:

	Working Days and Man Hours	
GENERAL RESEARCH		
This includes work time in Stockholm in 1946; in Los Angeles during 1947 and 1948; on the *Collier's* magazine project (much of which later proved useful for the novel) in 1949; in Los Angeles, London, Paris from 1950 through 1959; in Stockholm again, and also Copenhagen, Paris, Rome, Florence, Venice in 1960 . . .	260	857
FICTIONAL STORY NOTES		
This includes development of characters, scenes, main plot and subplots, preliminary outlines, and continuing research done in Los Angeles in 1960 . . .	36	288

Working
Days and Man Hours

FIRST COMPLETE WRITING OF NOVEL
The writing of the first draft covered a
period of 107 days in 1960 and 1961. Not all
of these were working days. The actual work-
ing days add up to . . .   94   752

REWRITING THE FIRST DRAFT
I did three more drafts in 1961, before I
had the final draft to submit to the publisher.
Gathering together suggestions and comments
from my wife, my research assistant, specialists in various fields, along with my own notes
made after reading and rereading the first
draft, I wrote new scenes; rewrote old ones;
revised, corrected, edited both dialogue and
narration; checked facts . . .   84   672

WRITING THE FINAL DRAFT
Using suggestions from my editor, publisher,
Swedish experts, and medical specialists, and
incorporating new ideas that I had had, I
worked in Los Angeles, Paris, Vienna, Florence, Venice, Zurich in 1961 to produce the
final manuscript version . . .   82   328

CHECKING COPY EDITOR'S QUERIES
These were queries sent to me which brought
up points involving factual accuracy, fictional
consistency, word usage, grammar, foreign
phrases, all submitted late in 1961. My work
consisted of double-checking my research and
making decisions for literary improvements
. . .   6   54

LEGAL REVISIONS
The publisher's attorney submitted comments and questions, and I checked them and
made my last changes before the book went
to the printer . . .   3   14

Working
Days and Man Hours

CORRECTING GALLEYS AND PAGE PROOFS
  Not long after the book had gone to the printer in 1962, I received first galley pages. I read these carefully and caught typographical errors, found mistakes I had committed, and whenever possible I still sought to improve the style. I penciled all of my notes in margins of the first galleys. Later, I received final page proofs, and in these I was permitted to make but few changes, since major revisions would have required costly resetting of the type and disruption of printer's and publisher's schedules . . .   17   136

TOTAL WORKING TIME ON NOVEL	582	3,101
	Days	Man Hours

2. SYNOPSIS OF *The Prize*

CHAPTER I

Count Bertil Jacobsson, Assistant Director of the Nobel Foundation, supervises the sending of cablegrams from the Nobel Foundation in Stockholm to this year's Nobel Prize winners or laureates.

In Paris, later that same evening, a wire arrives at the apartment of Dr. Claude Marceau who has collaborated with his wife, Dr. Denise Marceau, on research into sperm structure and vitrification of the spermatozoon—a process for freezing sperm cells so that they can be thawed out centuries after a donor's death and used to impregnate living women. At the moment the wire arrives Denise Marceau is alone, since Claude Marceau is in bed with his young mistress, Gisèle Jordan, svelte Balenciaga mannequin.

Aware of Claude's infidelity and infuriated by it, stocky, fortyish Denise Marceau knows just where to reach her husband. She telephones Gisèle's apartment, interrupts Claude midway in the act of love, and bluntly tells him to get his pants on and come home—they've just been awarded the Nobel Prize in chemistry and reporters are on the way.

Dr. Max Stratman, German-Jewish physicist, once forced to work for the Nazis, now lives in Atlanta and works for the United States Government. Stratman has been worrying that he is not well enough to accept the more strategic and more remunerative post just offered him by the President of the United States. A physical checkup by Dr. Ilman confirms Stratman's doubts: He is suffering from a heart disease. Returning home, he learns that he's been awarded the Nobel Prize in physics for his work in the storage of solar energy and the development of rocket propellants. Dr. Stratman is relieved of the necessity of making a decision about accepting the new position—the money will provide for his niece Emily, who, emotionally scarred by incarceration in Ravensbruck concentration camp and the deaths of her parents, Rebecca and Walther Stratman, at the hands of the Nazis, is unable to respond to the attentions of any young man. Now Dr. Stratman no longer need worry about what will become of Emily after his death, since the Nobel Prize money will enable him to leave her financially independent.

In Pasadena, California, at Rosenthal Medical Center, Dr. John Garrett has won renown for successfully blocking the immunological rejection of cardiac transplantations, and placing healthy but alien animal hearts in human bodies in place of worn-out or diseased hearts. Dr. Garrett's joy in his success was short-lived. Ten days after the announcement of his discovery, he learned that he must share credit for heart transplantations and his new status in medical circles with Dr. Carlo Farelli. Dr. Farelli had simultaneously made the same discoveries as Garrett and had performed the same heart-transplant surgery on patients in Rome. Feeling paranoidal over this turn of events, Garrett has gone into group therapy in the Los Angeles office of a psychiatrist. Now, leaving a therapy session, Garrett receives word from his wife of the Nobel Prize wire that has arrived from Stockholm. His pleasure is destroyed when he also learns that he and Dr. Farelli are to share jointly this year's Nobel Prize in medicine. Garrett decides he will go to Stockholm to accept his half of the award, but promises himself that he will unmask Farelli as a fraud who has stolen a colleague's discovery.

When the telegram from the Nobel Foundation arrives in Miller's Dam, Wisconsin, to announce that lanky Andrew Craig is to receive the current Nobel Prize in literature for his novels *The Perfect State* and *Armageddon* and his writings in support of humanitarian ideals, the novelist is dead drunk. He's been drunk most of the time since the death of his wife Harriet some years before in an automobile accident for which Craig blames himself, since he was driving.

Harriet's younger sister, Leah Decker, a spinster, who came to nurse Craig after the fatal accident and stayed on to keep house for him, and

Lucius Mack, Craig's friend and editor of the local *Weekly Independent,* try to sober him up before the reporters arrive. Craig's reaction, though he agrees to go to Stockholm to pick up the prize money, which he can use to pay off long-standing debts, is cynical. He has written nothing of consequence since Harriet's death, and he wishes the Swedes had left him alone. The award, in Craig's tired and defeated mind, means only that he will be humiliated by being forced to die in public. With that thought, Craig passes out.

CHAPTER II

Two weeks later, Count Bertil Jacobsson sets out for Stockholm's Arlanda Airport with two other members of the Nobel Committee, to welcome the first of the arriving Nobel laureates. One of the judges is Ingrid Påhl, large, fluttery, and herself a Nobel Prize winner long ago for her gentle, lyrical novels about her native land. The other Nobel Prize judge, Dr. Carl Adolf Krantz, is a small, waspish, embittered man. Krantz is sure that he has always been passed over for a Nobel Prize in chemistry or physics because of his Nazi sympathies during World War II, and that he has been discriminated against for these views by his fellow scientists.

On the plane from Paris to Stockholm, a fuming Dr. Denise Marceau demands from her husband, Claude, an explanation for his infidelity. Since learning of her husband's infidelity from a friend, Denise has undergone days and nights of mortification and agonizing self-appraisal. How has she failed Claude? Now, as they land at Arlanda Airport, Denise is as if in a trance when she meets the reporters gathered with Jacobsson. Her married world is coming to an end; the Nobel Prize seems a shallow mockery. Can she maintain this façade for the coming week without precipitating a scandal? She fights back the urge to weep and scream as they are driven to their hotel.

With the Marceaus deposited at their hotel, Jacobsson, Ingrid Påhl, and Carl Adolf Krantz dine together. Their conversation is about Dr. Max Stratman, who is due to arrive in the morning. Carl Adolf Krantz, ignoring Ingrid Påhl's malicious teasing about his support of a Jew, is concerned that the world's foremost physicist might arrive in Göteborg without any kind of special reception. Krantz obtains Jacobsson's permission to telephone Dr. Stratman after they have greeted Dr. Farelli.

Aboard the Swedish-American vessel which is bringing Dr. Stratman and his niece Emily to Europe, Emily Stratman has forced herself to participate in social activities. She has made a tremendous effort to conquer the feelings which have made it impossible for her to enjoy casual relationships with men. The night before the ship is to dock, Emily Stratman has cocktails with a pleasant young Chicago lawyer, and then agrees to have dinner with him. More than a little under the influence of the cocktails, she forgets to lock her cabin door, steps into her shower, and is still there naked when he comes to call for her. He enters and assumes that the half-opened bathroom door and Emily's clothes scattered about the cabin are an invitation. He undresses and attempts to join Emily in the shower. But Emily fights off his advances like a tigress and threatens to scream for help. He concludes that she is a frightened virgin and leaves. Dr. Stratman comes to find Emily and, sensing her distress, half guesses what has happened, but she makes him promise not to go to the captain and "make a fuss." The incident, however, disturbs Dr. Stratman and he feels a slight heart "pressure." But the discomfort passes.

Just before the boat docks, Carl Adolf Krantz telephones, welcoming the Stratmans to Sweden. At the dock, other Swedish officials are on hand to escort Dr. Stratman and Emily from the boat to the Stockholm train. Once settled on the train, Emily Stratman, remembering her reading of Freud and Adler, realizes that by her actions—the drinking, the unlocked doors, the being naked in the shower—she had invited the ultimate act subconsciously, although her conscious ego had not wanted it and had even feared and despised it.

Once more, Count Bertil Jacobsson, Ingrid Påhl, and Carl Adolf Krantz are on their way to Arlanda Airport, this time to greet Dr. John Garrett and his wife Saralee and Andrew Craig and his sister-in-law, Leah Decker.

In the jet airliner approaching Stockholm, Dr. Garrett recalls having visited his group-therapy session one last time before leaving for the Nobel ceremonies. At the session he had poured out his resentment at having to share the award with an Italian mountebank, and was partially mollified by the group's reassurances that there is honor enough for two and that winning it—whether alone or with another—is the main thing. But Garrett was not completely mollified. The trip with Saralee across the Pole and in Copenhagen has been pleasurable, marred only when Garrett catches sight of Dr. Carlo Farelli's handsome face beaming at him from the front page of the Danish newspapers aboard the plane. Knowing about her husband's hidden problem, Saralee suffers for him, tries to remove the offending papers, and to cajole him out of his bad humor.

When Saralee goes to the ladies' lounge, Garrett hears someone call out his name. Sue Wiley, of Consolidated Newspapers, introduces herself. She is going to Stockholm to do a series of behind-the-scenes articles on the Nobel Prize judges and the award winners, and she wants to interview Garrett. Reluctantly he begs off, saying that he has been told not to give out stories until the press conferences which will be held under the auspices of the Nobel Committee. Sue Wiley's brittle charm is turned off and she says nastily that Dr. Keller and Garrett's fellow group-therapy members would disapprove of his present behavior. Even as he panics, Garrett wonders how she has learned he is in group therapy. He realizes that most people think anyone in group therapy is crazy. Obviously Sue Wiley has thrown her knowledge of his private life at him as polite blackmail, an item she has kept in reserve to use if nothing better came along. What would Carlo Farelli, and thousands of others, think of this? Garrett, deciding to be more cooperative, hints to her that there may be a more sensational story if she takes a closer look at Dr. Farelli instead of himself. Sue Wiley appears to agree as she senses an unseen rift between the two doctors.

When the plane sets down at Arlanda, Count Bertil Jacobsson takes the Garretts in tow. He is puzzled—Andrew Craig should also have been aboard. Later that day, Jacobsson has his answer. A telegram from Copenhagen arrives, saying that Craig is staying over for the day and will take the Nord Express for Stockholm that night.

Jacobsson is uneasy. The program has not yet begun and already it is getting out of line. He feels an ominous loss of control.

CHAPTER III

The telegram from Copenhagen had been dispatched by Leah Decker, who felt Andrew Craig was then too drunk to get on the Stockholm plane. She has left him at the Tre Falke Hotel to sleep off his latest drinking spree while she goes shopping and sightseeing.

Waking and wanting a drink, Craig finds Leah's note: ". . . . We had to cancel the airplane to Stockholm because you were drunk. . . . Taking train to Sweden tonight. . . . I'll be back by five. Do behave. LEAH." He determines to get up, locate a bar, and have at least one drink. The hotel bartender, obeying Leah's orders, refuses to serve him.

Furious, Craig boards a bus outside the hotel and finds that it is bound for Amalienborg Castle as part of a sightseeing tour. As the bus gets farther and farther away from the center of the city, and then makes a tour stop, Craig becomes acquainted with one of the sightseers, an exceptionally pretty blond Scandinavian, Lilly Hedqvist.

Not shocked when he bluntly asks where he can get a drink, she promises to point out a place when they come to it. She not only accepts Craig's invitation to have a drink with him but also lets the bus go off without them. To his surprise, Craig finds himself talking openly to this uncomplicated, charming girl. He is comforted, soothed, and well in his cups again, by the time she steers him back to his hotel.

That night when the Nord Express is put aboard the Malmö ferry, Craig escapes from Leah and goes on the prowl, looking for liquor. He is delighted to find Lilly is also aboard. He buys a bottle of liquor and they hide out in an empty car parked on the ferry deck. Lilly tells him she is Swedish, has been vacationing in Copenhagen, and now is on her way home to Stockholm and her job at a large department store there. She is one of the new breed of Scandinavian youths, frank about her enjoyment of premarital sex, honestly curious about life in America where, she feels, young people are still bound by outdated taboos. Lilly is also proud of her burgeoning good health and she credits it to her twice-monthly participation in the activities of a nudist society. Enchanted with her, Craig drinks steadily in the haven of the empty car and arranges for her to sneak another bottle past Leah to him later.

By the time he returns to his train compartment, Leah has missed him and is frantic. She has pictured his falling overboard. She predicts that if he gets drunk he will do something to embarrass them when they reach Stockholm.

Lying in his berth, Craig is surprised at the eroticism of his thoughts. The girl, Lilly, has reminded him of things he had thought forgotten. His mind goes back to his first meeting with Harriet, their love affair, marriage; their honeymoon in Sweden, France, and Italy; the decision to leave Greenwich Village and put down roots in the Middle West and the purchase of a farm in Miller's Dam, Wisconsin; all the happy years of their marriage. Then finally, Harriet's death the night of his birthday party at the country club when he had had several drinks and had later lost control of their car on the rain-slicked road while driving home. Some of it he has not wanted to think of, has put out of his head with the help of alcohol. But now he is alive again, hurting again. He answers a rap at the door to find a bottle with a note saying, "Welcome to

Sweden. LILLY HEDQVIST." Back under the covers, Craig recalls his last
loving with Harriet. Sleepily he is not surprised to see, as the act prog-
resses, that Harriet's face has become Lilly's, and with that he falls
asleep.

CHAPTER IV

When Craig and Leah arrive in Stockholm, they are met by Count
Bertil Jacobsson and Ingrid Påhl. Driven to the Grand Hotel, they are
delayed in the lobby by a mixup over their rooms: a suite with only one
bedroom has been reserved. Jacobsson arranges to have a second, ad-
joining bedroom prepared for the embarrassed Leah. Craig takes the
opportunity to tell Ingrid Påhl that he needs a drink. She leads him to
the hotel's deserted dining room where she has hot chocolate while
he downs a double Scotch, and they discuss Sweden's unsuccessful experiment with prohibition.

That afternoon there are separate press conferences set up for the
Nobel winners in the four fields. Count Bertil Jacobsson, who moves
anxiously from one interview to another, is relieved with the conduct of
the laureates and, in the main, with both the impression they are making and the moderate questions being put to them by the world press. It
seems to be going well. But is it?

Denise Marceau, listening to her husband Claude's monologue and
choking back a desire to shout, "Oh, *merde!*" is determined to make
him suffer for his infidelity. She neatly monopolizes their press conference, giving the reporters the idea that she really led the way for the
scientific discovery which won them the prize, that she did all of the
important research, though her dear husband had been of invaluable
help. Claude splutters but, trapped, must agree. At the first possible
moment, Claude leans close and, whispering fiercely, asks what the hell
she is trying to do. Denise smiles. "Why, dearest, I am simply trying to
do what your darling Balenciaga mannequin has already done. I, too,
am trying to screw you."

Count Bertil Jacobsson, pleased with Denise's public performance,
slips away and joins Carl Adolf Krantz in the circle of journalists surrounding Dr. Stratman. The physicist is handling the reporters' questions with gentle humor and patience. Gracefully, he threads his way
through them, minimizing the fact that he, Stratman, has been awarded
the prize for his invention although the Swedish Academy of Science
traditionally ignores inventors. To the reporters who have been unable

to learn exactly what it is he has invented, he replies, Yes, it is true that the researches for which he is being honored are, largely, classified information. But the United States Government has seen fit to release a few details and to show the end results as proof—but not the means, the process, the storage system for solar energy—to the Nobel officials and on this evidence they have based their decision. The interview changes its direction, and shifts to Stratman's personal history. Yes, he says, he stayed in Germany, where he and his brother Walther worked for the Nazis during World War II. But, the reporters say, why did so many of you Jewish scientists stay in Germany? Stratman answers: Close relatives were in concentration camps, and by cooperating we hoped to save their lives. No, he replies to a Russian, he was not kidnaped by Americans. He went to America of his own free will, and has never been sorry that he did so. Stratman resents these last questions but controls himself, heart pounding. Think of Emily, he tells himself, and relax.

The third conference Count Bertil Jacobsson attends is not going so well as the others. Dr. Carlo Farelli, a large, dynamic, handsome man, dominates the gathering. Beside him, the slight Dr. Garrett is no more noticeable than a dusty piece of sculpture. Garrett's smoldering resentment was dissolved upon their first meeting, blotted out by the Italian's overpowering charm. Now Garrett feels himself deeply inferior to the expansive Farelli, yet knows, as he listens to Farelli's brilliant explanation of their researches and of their amazingly similar surgical techniques, that he must somehow bestir himself. But even in recounting the details of their first successful heart transplants, he cannot compete: Farelli's patient was an internationally famous playwright, whereas Garrett's was only an obscure truck driver.

When Farelli graciously directs the limelight on Garrett, suggesting he answer some of the reporters' queries, Garrett fumbles his opportunity. Farelli has already flattered the Swedes by praising the heart transplantation work of a Swedish surgeon, Dr. Öhman, whom Garrett has been helping through correspondence. Garrett's timidity takes over. He cannot recall any great names the Nobel Committee has ignored in the past, so he assures the reporters that he concurs completely with the Committee's choices since 1901. Not so Farelli, who points out such omissions as Cushing of the United States, and the famous Austrian, Dr. Freud, before praising the Committee. Garrett realizes he must now seek not justice but survival. He must crush Farelli or be liquidated himself. With this knowledge his determination returns, and at last he feels sorry for Farelli.

At Craig's press conference, Sue Wiley is angered by Craig's curt, offhand answers to her questions. Craig is acquitting himself well in spite of the drinks he has consumed beforehand. Sue Wiley, well aware of Craig's recent background, shifts the conversation from a discussion of other literature winners to a pointed discussion of Craig's personal life, and specifically of his drinking and writing habits. Craig bridles, but Jacobsson steps in. He reprimands her sternly, saying that the reporters have not been invited here to badger Nobel winners with unfounded accusations and innuendoes. Sue Wiley retorts that there is such a thing as freedom of the press. Smoothly, Jacobsson takes her assumption—that Craig could be shown to be a drunkard—and, by using as illustration Swedish drinking habits and examples of well-known famous drunkards, injects laughter into the discussion. And on the upbeat swing caused by this laughter, he deftly terminates the conference before she can recover.

Craig remains behind to thank Jacobsson for his intercession with Sue Wiley and expresses his fear that the Count has gone out on a limb in defending him in this way. Jacobsson tells Craig he could not care less, insisting that witches like Sue Wiley must be dealt with firmly to prevent their type of sensational journalism from besmirching the Nobel Prize ideal. At Craig's request Jacobsson personally directs him to a liquor store where Craig can lay in supplies. The Nobel official contents himself with saying only, "Do not let Sue Wiley see you. And do not forget, tonight you are a guest of the King."

CHAPTER V

The evening's Royal Banquet formally inaugurates Nobel Week. Count Bertil Jacobsson is privately worried that Craig may indeed be an alcoholic and a potential embarrassment to the Nobel festivities. But he will wait and see what evolves.

After a tour of the Royal Palace, Craig and Leah are taken to the reception, where they are introduced to Swedish dignitaries including members of royalty, the Nobel Committee, the Royal Caroline Institute, and the Swedish Academy. Konrad Evang, Norwegian member of the Nobel Peace Prize Committee, is also present, although this year the peace prize will not be awarded. Evang is in deep discussion with Ragnar Hammarlund, Sweden's near-billionaire industrialist, a bizarre and mysterious figure who will host a dinner for the Nobel winners at his Djürgarden villa later in the week.

When Craig meets Hammarlund, he fuzzily wonders what the industrialist's connection with the Nobel festivities could be. Evang gives as the reason for omission of the peace award the fact that his committee was "hopelessly deadlocked." Hammarlund bluntly discounts this excuse and claims they were in reality unable to find a neutral candidate who would be acceptable to both the Soviet Union and the United States. They debate the merits of previous choices but agree on the appropriateness of only one: the award to Carl von Ossietzky. Craig attempts to place the name but fails. As he prepares to ask Hammarlund about this winner, the Swede spots the Marceaus and hastens off to meet them.

Earlier, Denise Marceau has intercepted a newspaper clipping, mailed to Claude by Gisèle, announcing that a group of Balenciaga models, including Gisèle, is traveling to Copenhagen for a fashion show. Claude has not known she would be coming and is honestly surprised. Denise doubts his word, assuming he has arranged to have his mistress follow him to Scandinavia. If he humiliates her here, Denise warns, he can accept the whole damn prize by himself.

The Marceau quarrel is interrupted by Jacobsson's introduction of Hammarlund, who is eager to meet them. Claude hastily excuses himself, leaving Denise to cope with the Swedish industrialist. He tells her he hopes to interest her and her husband in his dream of developing a perfect synthetic food. As a vegetarian, he deplores the fact that animals must be killed and eaten, but, he confesses frankly, the real reason he hopes to develop synthetic foods is to add additional millions to his fortune. Already he has a brilliant young analytical chemist working on the problem, a Dr. Oscar Lindblom, whom he wishes to introduce to them. Hammarlund is giving a dinner, as they know, and Dr. Lindblom will be there, of course. And the internationally famous film star, Märta Norberg, will officiate as she often does as his hostess.

In a group composed of Jacobsson, Krantz, the Farellis, Garrett, and others, a discussion begins about past winners and how they used the prize money. Garrett, seeking a chink in Farelli's armor, asks what the big Italian plans to do with his check. Farelli happily says it will go to his favorite charity, the Carlo Farelli Fund. Pompously, Garrett counters with the statement that he is giving his share to the Rosenthal Medical Center in Pasadena. This grandstand play falls flat as Dr. Stratman sides with Farelli, saying that he, too, will keep the award money for himself.

The young Swedish prince who is in the group says that the important thing to remember is that wise investment of Nobel's estate has provided the large cash prizes the winners will enjoy, a testimony to Sweden's sound economy and its years of neutrality. Jacobsson finds himself compelled to defend Sweden as having been pro-Allied in World War II, and this provokes a reply from Krantz that Sweden was actually pro-German. And Krantz, a Swede, proudly states he is glad he worked actively for Germany. A heavy silence descends. Garrett, in a complete *non sequitur*, mentions his own military service as a United States Marine, then asks pointedly where Farelli was in those years. Quietly, Farelli remarks he was in prison. "Not all Italians were Mussolini's blackshirts, you see."

Garrett stands silent, defeated. Farelli turns to Dr. Stratman. As a Jew, surely Stratman must have suffered more than Farelli. The old man, feeling Emily shiver beside him, replies. No, he says, he did not suffer physically, having spent the entire war working in a laboratory, where he was regarded as a hostage. But his sister-in-law had suffered, first in Ravensbruck concentration camp, then Auschwitz. Garrett, without thinking, blurts the question, "Was she put to death in a crematorium?" Stratman winces. Emily's eyes fill with tears and she precipitately flees toward another part of the room. Yes, Stratman replies, watching Emily's retreat, she was. She was Emily's mother. And Emily also spent the war years in Ravensbruck. Conversation reaches a dead end. The Garretts leave the group first, and the others soon move away.

Craig, standing nearby, observes Emily's sudden retreat. He joins her as she is reaching to take a glass of champagne from a tray held by a liveried servant. While they talk, he realizes she is deeply upset. Emily tells him about Garrett's question and says it has brought back the old ache caused by her mother's death in a Nazi gas chamber, although she has not thought of her having died that way in years.

Emily knows about Craig and has read his books among many others in that quiet house in Atlanta. He finds himself talking to this girl, even about Harriet, and explaining why he writes the kind of books he writes: novels with historical backgrounds where he can write brutally, violently, in outrage, but safely, where his real self cannot be discovered and be forced into the open to fight today's battles. But enough shoptalk, says Craig, again semi-drunk. He's eager to see some of the historic state apartments Jacobsson has mentioned. Craig leads Emily into one of the majestic bedchambers, where he is carried away by her beauty and attempts to kiss her. Emily freezes, as she always does when a man comes close. Craig, sensing the same secret damage that he has known within himself, apologizes for his stupidity. Leah Decker, having followed them, interrupts. Coldly, she ignores Emily as she straightens Craig's rumpled jacket. "I thought I should tell you—you will be missed. The King is making his appearance."

In the salon, the guests have formed themselves into a semicircle as the King of Sweden enters. Count Bertil Jacobsson is at his side to introduce the laureates. During Craig's brief interchange with the King, he drunkenly promises the King that he shall have the first copy of his, Craig's, next book. The King chuckles, but Leah is mortified.

The formal dinner which follows is dull. Seated next to Ingrid Påhl, who does her best to maintain a conversation by offering bits of Swedish history, customs, and anecdotes, Craig withdraws within himself and becomes morose. What has he done to Emily? Hell, the fault was hers, not his. He reappraises. No, he had taken advantage of her shy, virginlike nature. Then again he thinks: the hell with all women, Harriet, Emily, all of them. But an emotion, a long-dormant wish, surfaces. Craig feels a need to be loved. Not pity-loved, or respect-loved, but simply loved. The dinner ends, the King departs, and the guests drift back to the salon. Craig tells Jacobsson he needs fresh air and will walk back to his hotel. Outside, he summons a taxi, calls out Lilly's address from the slip she put on the bottle aboard the Malmö ferry, and rides to her apartment.

Lilly is surprised but delighted to see the chilled, very drunk, and very lonely Craig. She tends him, loosening his collar and putting him to bed. He will sleep and she will take care of him.

In the morning, Craig awakes to find Lilly sleeping quietly beside him. Craig feels guilty at having invaded her privacy as a drunken foreigner. Knowing he owes her much, he decides to leave her undisturbed, to remove himself before she awakens. But when he returns from the bathroom, Lilly is already awake. Why is he leaving, she asks, still alone, making such a complexity of loving and being loved? Then she gives herself to him, happily, completely, and after that, Craig sleeps in peace.

CHAPTER VI

It is early afternoon before Craig returns to the hotel. Leah is furious. She has phoned everywhere: the Nobel Foundation, the Foreign Office, even Dr. Stratman, thinking that possibly Craig had arranged to meet

Stratman and Emily since Leah had seen the Stratmans leave the dinner early. Craig fights back at her: What business is it of hers if he did meet them? Then he regrets his outburst, seeking peace at any price, and invents a story that he slept off his overindulgence in alcohol in a bar. Leah pleads for greater propriety, saying they must not take chances like this before the ceremonies are over. Craig apologizes, and docilely agrees to go along on the sightseeing tour their agenda has listed for that day.

With them in the open car are Jacobsson, Leah, the Stratmans, and Indent Flink, the Swedish publisher who has brought out Craig's books in Sweden. Flink mentions the initial press reports provoked by Sue Wiley, who has sensationalized the clash over discussing his drinking habits which ended his press conference. Jacobsson intercedes to explain why he acted as he did, then shifts to an account of the news clippings which discussed Stratman, his work, and previous life in Germany. Dr. Stratman, ever sensitive to Emily's feelings, calls a halt to this reliving of the past. They continue their tour, stopping briefly to see Hammarlund's castle, home of their future host, and proceed on to explore the famous Skansen park.

Craig remains in the car with Dr. Stratman, who pleads sudden tiredness and wishes to rest while the others are led into the park. Craig feels Stratman out, seeking advice as to how he can get back into Emily's good graces. The old man is gently sorry for Craig, knowing his niece's background. But he has one thing to say: If Craig should succeed where other men have failed, he hopes Craig will not disappoint her.

The sightseeing tour resumes its progress through the Old Town, then stops at the Swedish Academy. Here Jacobsson takes the others inside and explains how the literature winners of the Nobel Prize are chosen, and he discusses former winners as well as some giants of literature who were ignored.

Later they arrive at the Town Hall, where Craig detains Emily as the others enter, and he apologizes for his behavior the night before. Emily accepts his apology, saying that she knew he'd had too much to drink, and she should have handled him with good humor instead of behaving like a swooning nineteenth-century maiden. Craig suggests they abandon the tour to have lunch together. She agrees.

They enjoy a wonderful afternoon, aimlessly sightseeing and talking. When Craig asks her to stay with him for dinner, she hesitates only briefly before allowing him to phone Dr. Stratman for approval. The doctor is having dinner with Jacobsson, the Farellis, the Garretts, and Leah anyway.

As they leisurely dine in the Old Town's renowned, beloved, and ancient restaurant, Den Gyldene Freden, which Craig visited during his honeymoon with Harriet, he speaks of his dead wife and persuades Emily to talk about her parents, Rebecca and Walther, and her childhood with them. Now, in their new intimacy, they admit to each other their lives back home are empty. Craig concedes he has done little writing since Harriet's death. But Emily is young, beautiful, her life before her, he says. Doesn't she want a husband, children, a home of her own? Yes, Emily answers; but Craig realizes that the things she has seen and lived through in the Nazi concentration camp have maimed her inwardly although she bears no outward scars. Today, however, has been a happy day. Emily thanks him for it, and says she will never forget Stockholm. Craig doesn't believe he will, either.

Craig leaves Emily at her hotel room and returns to his own room after eleven. He enters quietly so as not to wake Leah, but when he undresses in the dark and crawls into bed, he is startled to find a slightly intoxicated Leah lying there naked. She says she is willing to give herself to him. Having seen what is happening to him here, she realizes that he needs her in this way, too. Craig feels enormous pity for Leah, knowing how hard this decision must be for her. When he asks if she has come to him through a need of her own, she is indignant; women do not need this sort of thing, she replies. He tells her she must not offer her body to him like a sacrificial lamb, that he would not take her in this way. When the virgin Leah realizes he is refusing her, she orders him out of the room while she puts on a flannel nightgown and robe, and then she faces him. He doesn't need her clean, decent love, she says bitterly, "because you've been getting too much these last couple of days from the little Nazi whore-bitch from Atlanta!"

Shocked and disgusted, Craig reminds himself of her devotion since Harriet's death and of how she has nursed him since the accident. Leah's anger subsides and she regains self-control. She tells him he can depend on her and she will stay with him. After she returns to her own room, Craig starts drinking again. The almost perfect day with Emily has ended in yet one more disaster. Was Leah, with her rigid, naked body, honestly trying to help him? Or only herself? What if he married Leah? There they would be forever, he and Leah . . . and Harriet. Leah would perform dutifully in bed, and he would be enslaved for life.

CHAPTER VII

In an office of the Nobel Foundation, listening as Jacobsson talks on the phone to Craig about his official schedule, Denise Marceau examines the latest development in her own predicament. She has threatened Claude with open scandal if he dares to see Gisèle, and he has promised fervently that he will not. But Denise wants a guarantee and Craig's phone call points the way. Firmly, she requests that Jacobsson add new meetings and appointments to the Marceau schedule, which will keep her—and Claude—busy every free moment. To Claude's annoyance, Jacobsson agrees. This cage of activity is superfluous for Claude since he has decided a rendezvous with Gisèle in Stockholm is too risky.

Jacobsson senses the strained relationship between the Marceaus but decides that, without further evidence, he cannot fully interpret their situation. He guides them about the Nobel Foundation, speaking of previous winners in chemistry. There have been several husband-wife teams, he says, wonderful examples of scientific cooperation. Denise glares, while Claude squirms. The effect is not lost on Jacobsson, and he mentions the younger Curies and the pride the Foundation felt when awarding them the Prize for radioactive discoveries, only to suffer embarrassment later because of their public activities. Denise says sharply that they were a devoted couple. Jacobsson agrees, but points out that Frédéric Curie joined the Communist Party and Irène Joliot-Curie made derogatory comments about the United States. Laureates, he adds slowly, are so publicized, so respected, that when they cause scandals, the Nobel Committee is very unhappy.

The chore of escorting Dr. Garrett to the Caroline Institute has been assigned to Ingrid Påhl. Krantz has begged off because he must meet an important colleague from East Berlin. Ingrid Påhl apologizes to Garrett for her lack of knowledge about both the Institute and medicine in general. She gives him such facts on the Institute as she can remember from research she once did for a magazine article.

Garrett has looked forward to meeting the Institute's director, Dr. Eric Öhman, with whom he has corresponded. Öhman has used the heart-transplant techniques pioneered by Garrett, and the hero worship with which Öhman greets Garrett bolsters Garrett's confidence. He seeks to learn more about Öhman, finds out that the Swedish surgeon has served on the Nobel Committee as an investigator of nominees for the medicine award. To his dismay, Garrett discovers that Öhman's next heart-transplant case, an elderly count who is a relative of the King, has already been visited by Dr. Carlo Farelli. The Italian, with Sue Wiley in tow, visited the ward the previous day, and gave Öhman valuable advice on problems over which the Swede had worried. The Swedish newspapers, Öhman says, are picking up the story today. Garrett loses control. "You fool!" he shouts. "Sit down . . . I'm going to give you an earful about that charlatan Farelli." The outburst dazes Dr. Öhman as his hero, Garrett, begins to lay the case for the prosecution.

At Stockholm's Bromma Air Terminal, Krantz greets his visitor, Dr. Hans Eckart, head of the science department at East Berlin's Humboldt University. Krantz, passed over for the vacant chair in physics at Uppsala University, expects that Eckart will offer him an equivalent position at Humboldt. For Krantz believes he has made a deal: in return for this anticipated reward, he has thrown his voting strength and influence behind the selection of Dr. Max Stratman for the physics award. Through year-long hard work, Krantz has secretly discredited or disparaged three other nominees, all originally rated as more deserving than Stratman, and has arranged that Stratman be the laureate to come to Stockholm, so that Eckart might see him here.

Krantz asks why it is so important that Stratman and Eckart should now meet in Stockholm. Eckart explains that he hopes to convince Stratman, here in the neutral atmosphere of Sweden, to return and work for Germany once more. Dr. Max Stratman, his brother Walther, and Eckart had all worked in Kaiser Wilhelm Institute during the war. "We are friends, old friends," Eckart adds, and then requests Krantz to arrange a luncheon appointment for him with Stratman. Communist Eckart has already cabled Stratman, and the physicist will be expecting to see him.

Fresh from his early morning lecture to would-be writers, Craig arrives at the Stratman suite just as Dr. Stratman is leaving for the luncheon with Eckart. Emily and Craig are now at ease with each other and are looking forward to having lunch together. As soon as Stratman leaves, Emily decides to make sure her absent-minded uncle has not left a lighted pipe on the table in his room, which he has been known to do. She comes back troubled because she has found Eckart's telegram. It says he and Max Stratman will have much to talk about, and that he brings news of Emily's father, Walther. Emily is disturbed. "I ask myself . . . what good can come from East Berlin?" she says.

In Riche's restaurant, Eckart enjoys reminiscing with Stratman about their old days together, a feeling which Emily's uncle does not share. Eckart's cable had hinted at news about Walther. Brusquely, Stratman comes to the point: what is the news? Walther, Eckart relates, did not die in a Siberian labor camp, as Max has believed. Rather, Walther willingly engaged in bacteriological warfare research for the Soviet Union until his death in an accidental explosion near Moscow. Eckart has managed to obtain some of Walther's personal effects: a wristwatch, a Talmud, a family portrait showing Emily at the age of two. Perhaps Emily, who Eckart understands lives with Max in America, would like them as souvenirs? Eckart then asks if Max has ever considered returning to the fatherland, offers him a high position at Humboldt University.

Dr. Stratman is shocked. "You mean I should defect from the West and join the Communists?" Eckart hastens to explain that politics would play no part in this: first and foremost, they are both Germans, both scientists. Dr. Stratman does not waver. He says he is now an American and will remain one. Eckart is frustrated. His plan has backfired. In manipulating the Nobel Prize for Dr. Stratman, Eckart has also given him financial independence, so that Eckart's offer can now be rejected. But, Eckart says, perhaps Dr. Stratman will reconsider his offer. He will wait.

Leah has gone to the opera, and Craig looks forward to a pleasant evening alone. He sees a new Craig beginning to rise from the ruins of the old. The lectures and the lunch with Emily have been benign influences on him. However, when Sue Wiley comes to the hotel, she brings along the Swedish novelist, Gunnar Gottling. Craig meets Gottling, joins him for dinner at Djurgårdsbrunns Wärdshus, a popular tavern on the outskirts of Stockholm. Gottling, crude and bitter but honest, tells Craig he's been given the Nobel Prize only because his book, *The Perfect State,* is anti-Communist, anti-Russian. The Swedes, he says, take pride in standing up to Russia. They favor those who take the anti-Russian view, as was exemplified in their giving Boris Pasternak the award when he wrote an anti-Communist novel. Craig's newfound confidence crumbles, and he begins to drink.

When Gottling drops him, very drunk, back at the Grand Hotel, Craig realizes he wants the comfort of a woman's body. He desires Emily, but he knows any suggestion of sex would frighten her away forever. He considers Leah, but this solution would mean his capitulation to her and a retreat to their old way of life. Then he thinks of Lilly, takes a taxi to her apartment. Lilly is not home; she is attending the monthly meeting of her nudist society; and Craig goes to find her. When she invites him to disrobe and join the group meeting, Craig mentally sees Sue Wiley's story: DRUNKEN NOBEL WINNER GOES NUDIST. But he accepts, discovers he's neither embarrassed nor subject to any physical manifestation of his desire for Lilly. The meeting ends and they again dress. Craig, watching her, is enormously stimulated by this reverse strip-tease. He wonders as they return to her apartment how long it will take her to undress again.

CHAPTER VIII

Craig wakes up in Lilly's bed and is startled to hear a man's voice in the kitchen, where Lilly is preparing breakfast. Unabashed, she introduces Craig to Nicholas Daranyi, a Hungarian doing business as a free-lance spy. Daranyi plays no favorites in choosing his clients, is in the game only for the money. Lilly invites both men to accompany her to a government-run children's nursery, where, to Craig's amazement, she introduces him to her son, a blond two-year-old born out of wedlock. Left alone with Daranyi, Craig learns of the casual Swedish attitude toward illegitimacy, unmarried love, and courtship. Lilly, Daranyi says, feels no guilt. Craig's own guilty feelings, however, return. A vision of Emily occurs, and he feels an invisible barrier between them. What, he wonders, does one owe all others? And when does one belong to oneself alone?

Meanwhile, Dr. Hans Eckart has arranged to meet Krantz on a street corner. They narrowly miss being seen together by Daranyi, who has worked for Krantz in the past. As they sit in Krantz's car, Eckart tells Krantz that Dr. Stratman has turned down their offer. They must find greater "inducements" to sweeten the proposal. He orders Krantz to obtain more personal information about Stratman, anything which could be used to persuade him to defect. Krantz balks, but feels trapped. He must carry out Eckart's new request if he is to receive the appointment to Humboldt University. He thinks of Daranyi; perhaps the Hungarian can be used again.

Shortly before Hammarlund's dinner for the laureates begins, Emily phones, explains that her uncle is not feeling well and cannot attend. Hammarlund arranges for Jacobsson to be her escort. At Hammarlund's villa, Craig tries, unsuccessfully, to speak to Emily alone. Withdrawing to the bar, he notices the penciled seating plan for dinner.

Emily is between Jacobsson and a Russian, while Craig has been placed between Leah and Margherita Farelli. The arrangement, he feels, is unromantic; one change should be made.

Hammarlund orders the glamorous Märta Norberg to divert Claude Marceau while Dr. Oscar Lindblom, head of Hammarlund's private laboratory, is to concentrate on Denise. Lindblom, following his instructions, tries to intrigue her with a discussion of synthetic foods, but Denise covertly watches Claude as he fawns over Märta. Denise half accepts Lindblom's invitation to visit the laboratory at some later date, and then, furious, goes to intercept Claude.

Throughout the cocktail hour, Craig fails in his attempts to see Emily alone. He notices that Märta Norberg is about to corner him. In no mood for light banter, Craig slips outside onto the veranda and soon realizes he is not alone. In the garden below, Dr. Farelli and Dr. Garrett are having a noisy discussion.

Garrett, fortified by alcohol, has dragged Farelli out into the cold night for a private conversation. He is accusing the Italian of stealing his fame and half the Prize money. Farelli is angry, but he struggles for self-control, realizing Garrett is drunk. Garrett goes wild and attempts to hit Farelli. In self-defense, Farelli swings and knocks Garrett down as Andrew Craig hurries to come between them. "Are both of you insane?" Craig demands, separating them. "Nobel winners . . . brawlers." He sends Farelli back inside and tries to help Garrett remove the scars of battle. Garrett glares after Farelli; then he vomits, not so much from physical pain as from humiliation and a gross sense of injustice, inadequacy.

In the drawing room, Denise Marceau misses Claude and learns he has been summoned by a long-distance phone call. She follows, listens outside the door of Hammarlund's library to Claude's side of the conversation. Gisèle has arrived in Copenhagen. Claude wavers, then yields and agrees to meet her for an assignation in Stockholm in three days. Denise, heartsick, feels Gisèle has won. But as she remembers where she is, a plan comes into her mind: Dr. Oscar Lindblom, boy chemist, is both single and handsome. She hastens back, finds him, and arranges to visit his laboratory in the morning.

Craig, who has been unable to talk to Emily alone, quietly changes the official seating chart so that Emily will sit beside him at dinner. Märta Norberg again descends upon Craig, but this time he does not mind. She boldly flirts with him without success, and settles for his promise to visit her backstage after the next day's rehearsal of her new play. As Märta rejoins Hammarlund, Craig finds Emily alone, at last, on the veranda. Mindful of the cold night, he places a sheltering arm about her, then kisses her. Emily breaks free from a rising passion which has suddenly gripped them both, rushes inside. Craig now discovers that a second change has been made in the seating plan: He will be sitting between Leah and Märta Norberg. As dinner is announced, a smiling Märta materializes beside him, ready to be escorted to the table.

CHAPTER IX

Krantz goes to see Nicholas Daranyi and hires him for an investigation into the secret lives of the Nobel winners. At first he orders dossiers on all the current winners, as Eckart has suggested, but then narrows Daranyi's task down: Dr. Garrett, Dr. Farelli, and the two Stratmans. When Daranyi is told that the others—the Marceaus, Andrew Craig—are of lesser importance at the moment, he recognizes the novelist's name. His mind leaps to thoughts of Lilly. Obviously, she does not know what a prime catch her lover Craig would be. Daranyi files the information away for future thought.

The job, Krantz says, must be completed within 48 hours. He gives Daranyi a lead: Sue Wiley, who intends to write an exposé of the Nobel Prize and its winners, might provide the specific facts Krantz needs in return for useful gossip from Daranyi. Krantz evades Daranyi's discreet inquiry about his fee for this new assignment and advances only the expense money with which to buy information. The fee, Krantz says, will be settled later.

Denise Marceau, alone, arrives at Lindblom's laboratory and coyly listens as the young chemist proudly guides her through. They enter Lindblom's private study. In short order, she seduces him. But Denise realizes her performance is wasted if Claude does not learn about it. She arranges for an encore in her hotel suite the following evening, promising Lindblom that Claude will be away and they can be alone together.

Humiliated and aching from his brawl with Farelli, Garrett keeps to his bed the next morning. But when Dr. Öhman comes to see him, Garrett's spirits rise. Because of Garrett's astonishing charges against Farelli, Dr. Öhman has again looked into the Farelli dossier, where he has uncovered some disturbing facts. Creditably, Dr. Farelli did oppose Mussolini's regime during World War II, and for this he was confined to prison. But later, Dr. Öhman says, he must have been released, since he turned up in Nazi Germany, and as a doctor, not a prisoner. Öhman's Nobel Foundation sources had run across a brief reference to Dr. C. Farelli, Rome, a doctor who had taken part in infamous medical experiments on human guinea pigs. With all other evidence favorable, however, the mere mention of Farelli's name in this instance had not been thought sufficient to disqualify him.

Garrett knows a terrible joy. Now he has the means with which he can destroy his hated enemy. He will seek out Sue Wiley and expose Farelli as a war criminal. Once Farelli is unmasked, Garrett will be the only laureate in medicine at the Nobel Ceremony. Dr. Öhman pleads with Garrett to wait until such serious charges can be better documented. Garrett refuses, but concedes that neither Dr. Öhman nor the Nobel Committee need be involved in the exposé. Garrett will merely tip off Sue Wiley and let her take it from there.

When Andrew Craig arrives to watch Märta Norberg's rehearsal at the Royal Dramatic Theater, her director, Nils Cronsten, greets him. The great Norberg has already departed, leaving behind her a note inviting Craig for dinner at seven. Driven to Märta's house by Cronsten, Craig finds the famous star and international sex symbol amid the lush, tropical greenery that surrounds her indoor pool while the cold Stockholm winter wind howls outside.

To his amazement, she knows all about the Marceaus' estrangement, the fight between Garrett and Farelli, and Craig's balcony scene with Emily. It's not black magic, Märta says. Hammarlund's home is electronically bugged, a simple matter of good sense in this age of communications. The technique provides business advantages Hammarlund would not otherwise gain. With this knowledge about the Marceaus, she tells Craig, the industrialist will find his task of convincing them to work for him on synthetic foods—and trebling his vast fortune—much easier.

Märta then comes right to the point. She knows—thanks to Leah's confidences last night—that Craig is in bad straits financially. Craig's sister-in-law has also told Märta the entire plot of his unfinished novel, *Return to Ithaca*, which the actress believes will be the perfect vehicle for her return to the screen. Her studio will buy it for $200,000. There is also a fringe benefit: Märta Norberg goes with the deal. Craig would move in with Märta, rewrite the book to suit her. "When I collaborate, it's all the way," she says, standing beside him clad only in her bikini.

Craig is momentarily tempted but turns her down. He cannot change the book, sacrifice his integrity as a novelist, even for the chance to become Märta Norberg's lover.

Märta is infuriated. To the acting profession, she says, she has brought another talent and it is that which put her on top: she has the ability to make love with a unique and consummate skill. She offers Craig not only a new fortune but also an experience in bed he'll never forget. She rages at his continued refusal. Silently, without anger, Craig departs.

CHAPTER X

Craig, feeling alive once again, begins to think about what he will say during his Nobel Prize acceptance speech. Helpfully, and as subtle guideposts, Jacobsson has sent him copies of speeches by former winners in literature including Eugene O'Neill, Albert Camus, and William Faulkner. As Craig lays down Faulkner's speech, Leah interrupts, telling him that she has been invited to lunch by Märta Norberg. Craig is disturbed; surely after last night, Märta would have no further interest in Leah. But he dismisses the sudden uneasiness which comes over him and makes his way downstairs for his own luncheon appointment with Denise Marceau.

Denise's good humor evaporates as Craig tells her the reason why he has asked her to lunch: Hammarlund's mansion is bugged, completely covered by eavesdropping, recording devices. The industrialist knows now about Claude's affair with Gisèle. Denise's face hardens. "The son of a bitch," she mutters. He would also know then about her seduction of Lindblom since the laboratory at the villa would undoubtedly be wired, too. Denise admits that she knows about Gisèle, and she finds herself confiding in Craig. She asks his advice as a novelist about an intricate little plot of her own, with its impending climax when Claude will be allowed to learn of her affair with Lindblom.

Craig urges her to forget it, not to fight fire with fire. He contends it is psychologically wrong. She will have lowered herself in Claude's eyes, and she will never again be the same. But Denise cannot accept Craig's reasoning; she must go ahead.

Dr. Garrett interrupts them, saying that Denise is being paged in the lobby. Garrett, too, has an appointment. His is with Sue Wiley, but she is late. Invited by Craig to sit down until Wiley arrives, Garrett seeks to reinforce his decision to expose Dr. Farelli by showing Craig a brief newspaper clipping obtained from Dr. Öhman. The implications of what Garrett wishes to do dismay Craig. To pass on this bit of unsubstantiated evidence to Sue Wiley would be like giving a loaded Luger to a five-year-old. Without a fair trial, Farelli will be ruined, innocent or not. Over Garrett's querulous protests, Craig advises that he forget this method of revenge. When Sue Wiley finally shows up, Garrett, unsettled by Craig's refusal to condone the exposé, changes his mind. He tells her he has no news. When the disappointed Sue Wiley leaves, Denise reappears, beaming. The phone call is from the party of the third part, she tells Craig. Everything is arranged.

Sue Wiley hurries on to her own luncheon date, a meeting with Nicholas Daranyi. The Hungarian spy baits his trap with the story that he is a historian writing a book about the Nobel Prize awards, needs racy information to spice up routine facts learned during two years of research. But, he says, some of his own researches may be extremely valuable to her. Sue Wiley agrees to swap, dirt for dirt, what she knows for what he knows. Daranyi, although used to meeting the dregs of society in his work, is repelled by her heartless approach but tosses her a few unsavory anecdotes about previous winners. Wiley counters with knowledge of Garrett's group-therapy sessions, Stratman's visits to see a Stockholm specialist because of his heart condition and his rumored meeting with some as-yet-unknown but prominent East German Communist. They reach a meeting of the minds. But, as Sue Wiley catches sight of Leah, arriving with Märta Norberg for lunch, the room suddenly becomes too crowded. She hurries Daranyi through his food, so they can go to her hotel room and finish their afternoon's collaboration in private.

Emily comes back from a luncheon given by members of the Nobel Committee for Physics, quietly happy over the thought of seeing Craig again. Her joy is short-lived. Inside Emily's hotel room Leah Decker awaits her, sitting like a granite statue. Her twisted lips spill out monstrous accusations about Andrew Craig as she repeats what she has been told by Märta Norberg. Andrew Craig, Leah screams, had been drunk as usual, had seen Märta, tried to seduce her forcibly, and been thrown out. But not before he'd bragged to Märta about how he'd lured Emily onto Hammarlund's terrace and kissed her. The words shock Emily; no one but Craig and herself could have known this. What Leah says must be true. Leah raves on that Craig has boasted to Märta that he is getting plenty of sex in Stockholm, paints a depraved picture of a drunken, penniless fraud who killed his wife. The filth she utters is sufficient to make Emily break down. In response to Leah's shout that Emily will only get Craig over her dead body, Emily chokes out, "I don't want him—or anyone." Leah, her vicious work done, leaves.

When Craig arrives that evening for his date with Emily, Dr. Max Stratman greets him and sadly delivers Emily's refusal to join Craig for dinner. Nor will she see Craig to explain why. Craig persists and, as the old man diplomatically leaves, goes into Emily's room to see her. Leah, he learns, has paid Emily a visit. Flatly, without emotion, Emily repeats the entire Leah-Märta fabrication. Craig denies the lies. But he cannot honestly deny Leah's charge that Craig and Leah have been naked in bed together, or her accusation that Craig has been carrying on an affair with Lilly. What *can* he say? That Leah was the unwanted aggressor that night? That Lilly had offered love and kindness when she discovered his need to be wanted? He tells Emily the entire truth. And one thing more: that he loves her. But Emily turns away, bitter, unable to understand.

Craig, very drunk, arrives at Lilly's apartment and bluntly asks her to marry him. Quickly sensing his desperation, that he is on the rebound, she refuses. She tells him that although she has given him her body it does not mean she wants to spend the rest of her life with him. There is also another reason: through Nicholas Daranyi, Lilly has become aware of Craig's love for Emily, and Emily is the girl Craig really wants to marry. Craig admits Lilly is right, then tells her of the scene in Emily's bedroom. His revelation worries Lilly; perhaps she must marry Craig after all, if only to save him from his alternate fate, marriage to Leah. But she will think of a solution later. Meanwhile, she says, her bed is too big for one alone, and she wants a happy memory of him "because I do not think you will be here again."

CHAPTER XI

Daranyi arrives at Krantz's apartment. Impatiently, Krantz fidgets as the spy first reports on Dr. Garrett, giving details about the doctor's group-therapy sessions and his fight with Dr. Farelli. Krantz is annoyed with this useless knowledge, but asks if there is more. Nothing significant, Daranyi replies, except that the Swedish Foreign Office has just requested that Dr. Garrett be at the Royal Palace this morning. . . .

A self-complacent Dr. Garrett appears at the palace, and a minor court official, Baron Johan Stiernfeldt, greets him in the King's Audience Chamber. His Majesty, the King, knowing that Dr. Öhman will operate soon on his next heart-transplant case—Count Rolf Ramstedt, a favorite relative of the King—is troubled over possible complications. At the same time, Stiernfeldt says, the King feels relieved that a kind fate has brought the world's two renowned authorities on this type of operation to Stockholm. Would Dr. Garrett consent to be present during the impending surgery and permit Dr. Öhman to draw upon his experience if the need should arise?

Garrett is secretly elated. He can now demonstrate to the world why he, and he alone, deserves the Nobel Prize. He agrees, upon one condition: in his own experience, he has learned that two is company while three's a crowd. The presence of a third surgeon, such as Dr. Farelli, would only complicate matters. Bluntly, Stiernfeldt rejects the stipulation. The King himself has already accepted Dr. Farelli's gracious offer to be of assistance.

Meanwhile, Daranyi has continued with his report to Krantz, exposing the infidelities of Claude Marceau with Gisèle, and Denise Marceau with Dr. Lindblom. Daranyi speculates that if Krantz wants a scandal this may provide it because he believes that Denise intends to create one anyway. . . .

Denise Marceau's plan has worked perfectly. Claude learns both of his spouse's infidelity and of the identity of her lover. In a rage, he storms to Lindblom's laboratory to thrash him. He finds not Lindblom but Hammarlund, and the Swedish tycoon launches into an impassioned plea for his new pet project, synthetic foods. At first Claude is irritated and impatient for Lindblom's return. But as he listens, Claude becomes intensely interested. It has been months since he's run into a new area for biochemistry research. Now, suddenly, this idea excites him although, he tells Hammarlund, the approach to the problem is all wrong. His thoughts falter and he realizes an important truth. What is really missing is Denise. He needs her by his side, to catch his ideas, to add to them with ideas of her own, and to help him mold these concepts until they arrive at a joint hypothesis, as a husband-wife team.

Lost in concentration over this new project, Claude belatedly recalls why he came here almost two hours ago. He jumps to his feet, also aware that his mistress Gisèle, arriving from Copenhagen, will be waiting for him at the Hotel Malmen. Hastily he tells Hammarlund he must leave, but there is one more minor matter, a short message for Dr. Lindblom: "If I ever find him making advances to my wife again, I shall break his neck." With that threat delivered, Claude departs. . . .

As Denise nervously awaits Claude's return, Lindblom phones.

Claude *knows,* he says, panic-stricken. Denise's initial delight turns to anger as he tells her of Hammarlund's meeting with Claude and her husband's newfound interest in synthetic-food research. And his final hasty departure to keep an important date. Denise's heart sinks: Gisèle is in Stockholm.

Then, when she hears of Claude's threat to break Lindblom's neck if he's caught again with Denise, a new plan unfolds in her mind. Quickly, she persuades the smitten Lindblom to ignore Claude's empty threat and to come to see her as they have planned. Within minutes after Lindblom's arrival, Denise thinks, she will find out everything else Claude has said, and will know whether there is a future for them together.

Soon after his arrival, Lindblom sheds his clothes, eager for love. Denise slowly retreats, but helplessly finds herself in bed while she demands to know more about Claude's new inspiration. Yes, says Lindblom as he continues to seduce Denise, her husband *has* found a new project. Yes, Lindblom gasps, Claude did say he would discuss it with Denise. Later. *"Voilà!"* Denise tells herself as Lindblom begins to make love to her. She has never been happier than at this moment. She knows now that Claude is coming back to her. "Oscar, only be quick," she says. "I think my husband may be coming back earlier than I thought."

At the Hotel Malmen, Gisèle Jordan realizes at once that Claude's feelings toward her have changed. Quietly, he tells of the new miracle that has come into his life to fill the void left when the Prize-winning spermatazoa project ended, a void which he had attempted to fill with Gisèle. Claude attempts to explain about his new scientific interest: synthetic foods. She gently rejects his perfunctory offer to make love. Their affair, she says, is over. He has taken back his passion and given it once again to his work, as she has always known he would. She sends him away. . . .

Daranyi finishes his report on Leah Decker, moves on to Andrew Craig. Abruptly, Krantz expresses his desire to hear only the essentials and Daranyi gratefully concurs, anxious to avoid mention of Lilly's interest in Craig. He sketches a brief picture of Craig's drinking, his life with Harriet, a suspected affair with Märta Norberg, and his present romance with Emily Stratman. Mr. Craig, he says, is not with Miss Stratman at the moment, having gone to the Nobel Foundation building to see Jacobsson. . . .

Craig keeps his appointment to hear the old man reminisce about former Nobel laureates, although dejected over Emily's refusal to forgive him. Leah, aware of Craig's anger over her meddling, has left Stockholm for the day. As Craig listens to Jacobsson, Sue Wiley arrives, seeking verification of a scandalous fact about George Bernard Shaw. Jacobsson, annoyed, mildly criticizes her distorting half-truths into white lies to suit her own ends. Sue Wiley flushes and snaps back that she doesn't invent material but reports it as it is, regardless of whom the story might hurt once published. If her facts are lies or libelous, she says angrily, the Nobel Foundation can sue her.

Jacobsson, his point made, attempts to soothe her with a harmless bit of old scandal, this time with facts straight from the source. He gives her the complete story about Carl von Ossietzky, a German national who had been an early foe of Hitlerism. An almost-universal nominee for the 1935 Nobel Peace Prize, von Ossietzky—already an enemy of the German state—had been unanimously denied the desired award to avoid offending Hitler. The following year, overwhelming worldwide support again forced von Ossietzky's nomination and this time he won, but he never received the prize money. Hitler, who saw to this, also banned any future Nobel awards to Germans and later arrested the Nobel Committee members during Germany's occupation of Norway.

Jacobsson is obliged to leave the room. Sue Wiley, still somewhat abashed by his brief lecture, defends her fact-finding methods to Craig. It's just a part of the job, she says. To show him how thoroughly her Chicago associates did their homework, she relates how the assigned reporter prowled about Miller's Dam, ferreting out facts about Craig's life. Sue Wiley rehashes the details of Harriet's death in the automobile accident, and suddenly Craig learns something he's never been told before. According to the mechanic's report to the coroner, the tie rod on Craig's car failed that night and this caused the fatal skid. The accident, he now realizes, did *not* occur because of his drinking. While Craig lay unconscious in the hospital, Sue Wiley goes on, Leah Decker had signed the legal papers which absolved him of any blame. Didn't he know this?

At Krantz's apartment, Daranyi reaches the dossiers on Dr. Max Stratman and Emily. Does Krantz know of Dr. Stratman's heart condition? This information obviously excites Krantz. Pleased to have aroused a response, Daranyi continues. He passes over Dr. Stratman's meeting with Eckart and discusses his findings on Emily. Never married. Reportedly a virgin. Shy with men, but interested in Andrew Craig. Daranyi's work has been thorough. He has covered her movements in Stockholm right up to this afternoon, at which time he'd seen her entering Nordiska Kompaniet, Stockholm's big department store. . . .

Listening to Lilly at the department store where she works, Emily Stratman feels more inhibited than ever by the beautiful, straightforward Swedish girl sitting across from her. Lilly has requested this meeting to tell Emily that Craig, after leaving Emily last night, had got very drunk, had come to Lilly's apartment and asked her to marry him. Can't Emily believe, Lilly asks, that a man can ever love one woman while he is in another's bed? Lilly says she would marry Craig if there were anything but sex-love between them, if their affair could ever develop into an affair of the heart. But Craig loves Emily. Why can't Emily return that love? Is she afraid, because she's a virgin? Emily sits there, listening to the death knell in her heart. She cannot explain because she doesn't fully understand it herself. She knows only one thing definite: she cannot change. Her ability to love Craig, or any man, has vanished forever. . . .

Daranyi has saved his most astonishing revelation about Emily until the last. He hands Krantz an S.S. file on Emily Stratman, the Gestapo's dossier on this former inmate of Ravensbruck concentration camp. Krantz haggles briefly over Daranyi's following demand for a fifty-thousand-kronor fee, but agrees to discuss this price with his principals. Appeased, Daranyi departs. Dr. Eckart, hidden all the while in the next room, hurries out. Through a concealed microphone, he has heard everything. He insists on having the S.S. file on Emily Stratman. He must examine its contents at once.

CHAPTER XII

The final day of Nobel Week arrives. That morning Jacobsson holds his last press conference and he gives reporters the official memorandum which describes the procedure for the award ceremony. This year's laureates, he tells them, will presently be running through a half-hour dress rehearsal—except for Drs. Garrett and Farelli, who at this very moment are engaged in a project connected with their specialty.

At the Caroline Hospital, Dr. Öhman operates on his heart-transplant patient, Count Ramstedt. Present as observers, Garrett and Farelli ignore each other completely but discuss surgery problems with Dr. Öhman. When the patient is finally sent to the recovery room after the operation, Garrett and Farelli are left alone in Öhman's office. Cautiously, Garrett refers to the Italian's involvement in Nazi medical experiments during World War II. Farelli calmly admits that it is true; yes, he and four other doctors did indeed participate in such experiments. Then he adds, two of them died and the three survivors, including Farelli, are still under medical treatment for aftereffects. Stunned, Garrett realizes that Farelli actually had been a human "guinea pig," not an experimenting doctor. Garrett is weak at the realization of what might have resulted had he given to Sue Wiley an erroneous, even libelous, story about Farelli.

A crushed Dr. Öhman returns and reports that the operation is a failure: Count Ramstedt is dying. Both laureates are dismayed—such a happening, on the eve of the award presentation, would discredit their work, and would oblige them to refuse the Nobel Prize for medicine. Farelli will not admit defeat. He sends Dr. Öhman back to the patient and confers with Garrett. Garrett, his mind now cleared of his black suspicion of Farelli, reviews the alternatives. The new heart is being attacked by the body's rejection mechanism, but this rejection might be neutralized by Garrett's Antireactive Substance AH, a new but unproven mixture. Should they chance it? Yes, Dr. Farelli exclaims, we have nothing to lose and everything to gain. They agree to collaborate in an effort to save the patient.

Three hours later, a release from the Caroline Hospital announces that the surgery has been successful. The two laureates, assisted by Dr. Öhman, have overcome some early complications and have solved the final problem of organ transplantation: rejection of foreign tissue by the human body's immunity mechanism.

While packing, Craig receives a note from Emily which says she must see him at 12:30 sharp; she has something important to tell him. Craig comes alive with hope. When Leah returns, Craig curtly informs her they are going separate ways as of now; he knows she's deliberately led him to think all these years that he killed Harriet. Leah admits the truth but pleads for forgiveness, and tries to explain her actions—forever eclipsed as the drab, younger sister of the glamorous Harriet, she seized upon the unfortunate accident as a chance to shine on her own. But later, when she realized that pretending she was Harriet wouldn't work, that neither he nor anything else of Harriet's belonged to her, it had been too late to tell him the truth. Craig forgives Leah, saying that they both can now bid farewell to Harriet.

Emily Stratman, realizing that her affection for Andrew Craig is too great for her to allow him to recall only their last bitter meeting, intends to see him once more. As she waits, Emily notices a note left by her uncle, in which he mentions a business lunch. Just then the phone rings, and a thin, high Swedish voice tells her that Dr. Max Stratman has had a mild heart attack. He is in a clinic on Ringvägen, and is asking for her. As she rushes blindly from the room, the phone rings again. This time she knows it is Craig, but she does not stop to answer it.

At the clinic she finds not her uncle but Dr. Eckart, who apologizes for his deception. Max Stratman is quite well physically, Eckart says, but he is morally ill. His research for an irresponsible country threatens world peace, and it must cease. Max Stratman must return to East Germany. Eckart assures Emily that their brief meeting will be mutually beneficial. He wants Dr. Stratman, and she will want someone he has. He steps aside and nods. A shabby, elderly figure enters. The stranger swallows nervously, then asks, "Do you not recognize me, my little goose?"

The endearing phrase spins wildly through Emily's head. Where has she heard it before? It goes back to her childhood, she remembers. Eckart's brisk voice spans the years for her: "You must know him, Miss Stratman . . . Walther Stratman . . . your father." Emily faints.

By two o'clock, Craig is in despair. Emily hasn't called and he assumes she has changed her mind about seeing him. Going to her room, he discovers that Max Stratman, who has returned and found Emily out, is taking a nap. There's a knock at the door. Craig opens it, discovers a note telling Stratman that if he wishes to know where Emily has gone, "listen to a friend." Craig also finds a small tape recorder. He turns it on, and Eckart's voice informs him that Walther Stratman is alive and in Stockholm. Walther, under the alias of Dr. Kurt Lipski, has been working for the Soviet Union. But, Eckart says, he has convinced the Russians that the now-resurrected Walther deserves freedom of choice as to where he will live and work in the future.

As he continues to listen to the tape recorder, Craig hears Emily's voice, thick and drugged, telling of her reunion with her father. She states Eckart's offer: Walther goes free if Max accepts a job at Humboldt University. And the decision must be made by the time the Nobel Ceremony commences. Eckart takes over again and names the terms. In Max Stratman's televised acceptance speech, he is to announce his defection to East Germany. Walther and Emily will then be free to go to America. Otherwise, Walther will be returned to Russia, and Emily will lose her newfound father.

Craig tries to think. His mind leaps to thoughts of Daranyi, the spy. Lilly has said he was investigating the Nobel laureates. Was it actually Emily and Max Stratman he was checking on? As he thinks about Max Stratman, Craig realizes that if Max were now to be taken from Emily, and the stranger Walther substituted, Emily's personal world would crumble, sentencing her to a deeper death before dying.

Craig must persuade Walther to return to East Berlin, for his daughter's sake, and Craig must do this before Max Stratman awakes. For if Max knew about Eckart's demand, he would offer himself in exchange for Emily and Walther. Craig hides the recorder and hurries out to find Lilly, and through her, Nicholas Daranyi. As he rushes through the hotel lobby, Gunnar Gottling intercepts him. The eccentric Swedish writer, told about Craig's desperate problem, volunteers his help. At breakneck speed they drive across the city to the Nordiska Kompaniet, where Lilly works.

At the store, Craig finds Lilly. She joins Craig and Gottling, leading them to Daranyi's apartment building. They arrive to find an ambulance parked outside. Sue Wiley has interrupted two hoodlums who were attacking Daranyi and has scared them off before they could kill him. The spy, suffering only minor stab wounds, vows revenge. It's Carl Adolf Krantz, he tells Craig, that they must find—Krantz will know where Emily is being hidden. Lilly rides with Daranyi to the hospital while Craig and Gottling go in search of Krantz.

Gottling knows where Krantz's apartment is, as it was the only one during the war to have a Nazi flag draped from a window. Craig corners Carl Adolf Krantz as he is about to leave for the Nobel Award Ceremony. Craig demands to know where Emily and Walther are being held. Krantz denies knowledge of any plot until Craig tells him that Daranyi has been stabbed. Krantz blanches. Being an accessory to a liquidation ordered by Eckart is too much to pay for a post at Humboldt University.

Craig presses Carl Adolf Krantz harder, and learns that Emily and Walther are now on a boat. At first Krantz refuses to give Craig its location, fearing a scandal that will ruin him. Craig promises not to call in the security police if Krantz will take him to Emily. Krantz insists that Craig must come with him alone and Craig agrees. Craig returns to Gottling, tells him where he is going, and persuades the Swede not to follow them. In Krantz's limousine, they speed across Stockholm to Pålsundet. At Pålsundet, Krantz points to a large cabin cruiser moored near the canal.

By five o'clock in the afternoon, the vast marketplace before the Concert Hall has been cleared of snow, and is crowded with several thousand spectators who are watching the illustrious guests arrive. The King, too, has arrived.

Backstage, Jacobsson directs the assemblage of those who will take part in the final Ceremony, positioning each according to the rules of protocol. Farelli and Garrett are engaged in an animated colloquy. The Marceaus, reconciled, are in deep discussion of the laboratory collaboration which lies ahead of them. Professor Max Stratman draws Jacobsson aside and says he has not seen Emily since early morning, but a note he found in his hotel room said she was going out with Andrew Craig and they would see him at the Ceremony.

For the first time, Jacobsson counts noses. Laureate Craig is missing. Before Jacobsson can make inquiries, trumpets are sounded, and the King enters the auditorium. The Royal March, with its pomp and pageantry, begins. As Jacobsson nervously takes his place on the stage, two chairs remain empty: the ones for Carl Adolf Krantz and Andrew Craig. The novelist's failure to appear will be an insult to Sweden and create an international scandal. Worried, Jacobsson rises and walks forward to deliver the salutatory oration which begins the long Ceremony. . . .

Meanwhile, Craig, with Carl Adolf Krantz leading the way, has boarded the cruiser. The two Swedish guards recognize Krantz and permit them to go below. Krantz heads for the main stateroom to see Walther Stratman, while Craig enters the bedroom where Emily lies, drugged. She wakes briefly, and he reassures her that she is safe. Krantz comes in and tells Craig that Professor Walther Stratman will see him now.

In Walther Stratman's presence, Craig feels awkward and speechless. Somewhat inebriated, Emily's father tells Craig that he has been celebrating his freedom. This unexpected exuberance dismays Craig. As Craig searches for a way to convince Walther Stratman that he should return to Russia, the German describes his life since the day he and his brother Max were first forced to work for the Nazis. He, a nuclear scientist, had been assigned to bacteriological warfare work, but now he has served his sentence and is ready for his new freedom.

Craig suggests that the choice must be difficult, sending his brother Max into slavery in Russia, or sacrificing his new freedom. Walther bridles. Craig has been deceived by the reactionary press of the Morgans and the Rockefellers. Max Stratman will live well in Russia.

("East Berlin," Carl Adolf Krantz interjects frantically, "in East Berlin." But Walther Stratman ignores him—there no longer is any need for deception.) In Russia, Walther Stratman goes on, German scientists are respected, as they would not be in England or America. Craig defends his country. What of the way the United States has treated Max Stratman, for example? An exception, insists Walther, adding that Max Stratman received wealth and luxury, not respect and honor.

As Craig listens to Walther Stratman, he decides to gamble. He tells Walther of his hope to persuade him to remain in Russia, to allow Max—Emily's real father now—to continue his valuable work in the United States. Walther loses his temper. He charges Craig with ignorance of what he, Walther, has undergone. He doesn't intend to make even greater sacrifices for a brother who has usurped his position as Emily's father.

Carl Adolf Krantz attempts to intercede, but Craig brushes him aside. Walther Stratman need not return to Russia, Craig says quietly. All of them can safely leave the boat right now, with Krantz's help. Contemptuously, Walther objects. In the silence which follows, Craig speaks first. He accuses Walther of not wanting to escape, and of not caring what happens to either Max or Emily Stratman.

The old German, losing control, shouts that he is a member of the Communist Party, with a wife and two children in Russia. He has agreed to Eckart's plot only to get Max Stratman on the right side, and Emily, too, if he can persuade her to come. But once Max Stratman is in East Berlin, Walther Stratman intends to return to Russia.

In the doorway behind the ranting Walther Stratman, Emily appears. She has heard everything. "Dr. Krantz," she says, "should you speak to Dr. Eckart once more, tell him this. Tell him there can be no trade— because there is no one for whom Uncle Max can be traded." Carl Adolf Krantz, waiting at the stateroom door, leaves first, followed by Emily and then Craig. Not one of them looks back at Professor Walther Stratman, left behind.

Slowly recovering in Craig's hotel room from the effects of the sedation, Emily tells Craig she wants him to know the truth: the reason why she cannot either love him or see him again. It begins, she says, in the Nazi concentration camp, Ravensbruck, when she was fifteen. First she was forced to lose her virginity by copulating with a naked Jewish boy who'd been immersed in icy water and nearly frozen to death; this inhuman treatment by the camp's doctors had been to see if coitus would aid a freezing victim. Then, for three months, she had been used by Frau Hencke, the lesbian commandant for women inmates. Eventually she'd served the camp commandant, Colonel Schneider, for seven months. After him, many others, until the Americans liberated her . . .

Craig holds her in his arms. "In love," he says, "you are a virgin still." And Craig adds softly that he loves her and intends to marry her. Emily, finally convinced of his love and free at last, buries her head against his chest. For the first time, she can love him, too. . . .

In the Concert Hall, the majestic Ceremony draws toward its conclusion. Professor Max Stratman finishes his acceptance speech and receives a thundering ovation. Ingrid Påhl, ready to introduce Andrew Craig, is in despair. How can she introduce a Nobel laureate who is not present? Then, at the last possible moment, Craig, resplendent in full dress, marches in to take his seat.

Jacobsson stares at Craig and then at Carl Adolf Krantz, now also seated across the aisle, and wonders what detained them. It occurs to him that, no matter what he has heard and seen and read, his precious Notes could never be complete, for some of the mysteries inside of men are not meant to be known. But, at least, his Notes now need not record a scandal.

As Craig rises to receive his award and medallion from the King, his eyes scan the loge which Lilly, Gunnar Gottling, and a radiant Emily have just entered. Then he delivers his acceptance speech. The Nobel Prize, he says, is the foremost of earthly honors, but Alfred Nobel himself would have understood what he is going to say next: Man's honors to men are small beside the greatest prize of all—knowing that each new day's challenge is meaningful, that it must be taken to the bosom, and it must be used. To know and to understand this is the one prize worthy to be man's goal and all mankind's summit.

Never has Andrew Craig felt more reassured and more content. He knows where he is going. And so, at last, he can go on.

About the Author

IRVING WALLACE *was born in Chicago, Illinois, raised in Kenosha, Wisconsin, and educated at Williams Institute, in Berkeley, California.*

He began to write at the age of thirteen, while still in school, and sold his first published story at fifteen, for five dollars. During the next twenty years, as a free-lance writer in America as well as in the Far East and Europe, he published at least five hundred articles and short stories in such magazines as The Saturday Evening Post, Esquire, Collier's, Reader's Digest, Saturday Review, Cosmopolitan, American Mercury *and* Coronet.

After enlisting in the United States Army, Mr. Wallace spent three and a half years in the Army Air Forces and Signal Corps, writing training and orientation films. After the war, he worked in motion pictures, while publishing his first book in 1955. He quit motion pictures ("forever," he says) in 1958 to devote himself entirely to creating books.

Irving Wallace has published twelve books, of which five have become international best sellers. In the United States, Mr. Wallace's books have been the choices of five book clubs, his reprint editions have sold over ten million copies, and one novel, The Man, *was singled out for four major awards. His books have appeared in foreign editions in twenty-four countries. At present he is completing his sixth novel,* The Seven Minutes, *which will be published in 1969.*

Mr. Wallace and his wife Sylvia, a former magazine editor, have two children, David and Amy, and make their home in Brentwood, a suburb of Los Angeles, California.